digital money

The New Era of Internet Commerce

digital money

The New Era of Internet Commerce

DANIEL C. LYNCH

LESLIE LUNDQUIST

John Wiley & Sons, Inc.

New York ◆ Chichester ◆ Brisbane ◆ Toronto ◆ Singapore

Publisher: Katherine Schowalter
Editor: Philip Sutherland
Assistant Editor: Allison Roarty
Managing Editor: Angela Murphy
Text Design & Composition: North Market Street Graphics, Dave Erb

Library of Congress Cataloging-in-Publication Data:
Lynch, Daniel C.
     Digital money : the new era of Internet commerce /
  Daniel C. Lynch and Leslie Lundquist
         p.   cm.
     Includes index.
     ISBN 0-471-14178-X

Printed in the United States of America

10 9 8 7 6 5 4 3 2 1

contents

Chapter 4 Digital Money: The Cuneiform of a New Age 99

Chapter 5 New Business Concepts 123

Chapter 6   The Evolving Cyber Economy   147

Chapter 7   Electronic Information Exchange   173

Chapter 8   The New Wooden Nickel   191

preface

Dan Lynch

I got interested in money about the same time all of us did—before going to kindergarten. A bit later I remember a guy named Joey in the third grade who would loan anyone a nickel if they would pay him back six cents on Friday afternoon. We all thought Joey was a great guy. How were we to know that he was getting over a 20,000-percent annual rate of return on his investment?

Now I am older and I think I see a new way to get a huge rate of return for doing someone a small favor, just as Joey did long ago for his gradeschool pals. That new way is to facilitate the transfer of small amounts of digital information from the creator of that information to the consumer of that information. The world is going digital and things digital can be very fine-grained and yet worth something. I want to help people pay tiny amounts of money to each other, do it by the billions of events, and get paid an even tinier amount for facilitating that new kind of commerce. Okay, I don't expect to get 20,000 percent like Joey did, but just like Joey's pals, if there is no other way to do it, it is worth a lot just to make the transaction happen.

This book explores the new frontier of online commerce. I think it will be more important than the industrial revolution because it creates a direct path between the consumer and the producer, thus eliminating huge amounts of waste that has developed in the world of hard goods. It also makes the concept of boundaries and nations a bit silly. What is a *digital neighbor*? Whom do you trust in an online world?

Technology changes the social contract. Two well-known examples in the twentieth century are the birth-control pill and the atomic bomb. Another technology that will change the social contract very soon is cryptography for everyone. Besides explaining some of the cryptographic technology that makes this all possible, we want the reader to consider the marvelous frontier we are all traversing as the twenty-first century arrives.

Leslie Lundquist

A Brief and Highly Subjective History of the Internet

Once upon a time, the Internet was the Arpanet. The architecture of the Arpanet was developed in the decade between 1959 and 1969, envisioned by the military and implemented by a host of brilliant engineers and scientists working in concert with universities such as MIT, research institutes such as MITRE and SRI, and major research and development corporations such as BBN. The main goal of the Arpanet was to provide a distributed computer communications system that could survive an attack, so that even if a portion of the system were lost, the rest of the network could still function. It originally had four sites. The first site was installed in September, 1969. What amazes me now is how much it all has grown.

I stumbled into this arena in 1978, when Dan Lynch approved my hire as a weekend graveyard-shift computer operator at SRI International. We had a huge computer room with five mainframe computers: One was a PDP-10 (SRI-KL) with 4.5 megabytes of memory, a state-of-the-art machine. At that time, a megabyte of memory was a little larger than a refrigerator, with all sorts of interesting flashing lights that I eventually learned to interpret. Dan was the director of this remarkable computing facility at SRI International, which had been one of the original four Arpanet sites.

I was 17, a student at Stanford. I was oblivious to the lofty purpose of the Arpanet, and totally unaware that this was a revolutionary technology. At the time, all I knew was how cool it was to be able to telnet to Helsinki in the middle of the night and see who was on the system there, or to check out the status of the Coke machine at Stanford AI Lab by telnetting to SU-AI. (What did they do there, anyway, I wondered?) I think I perfectly held the mindset of most Internet users today: Wow! What fun!

Figure F.1   Portrait of Leslie at SRI, circa 1980.

Since I worked on graveyard shift, I seldom saw my boss (Steve A. Dougherty). Instead, I received my assignments by E-mail. And I could send E-mail to a few friends at Stanford, who had wheedled E-mail accounts from the system administrators there. Wow! What a playground we had! And at the time, in the way of the young, I never stopped to wonder who had created all this, or why—I just accepted it.

As you all now know, E-mail has caught on in a big way. Any number of reasons might account for E-mail's success. First, it gives the receiver time to think before responding. Certainly I liked having that time to respond to my boss's assignments. The informal nature also helps. Dan Lynch says:

> I think it was because it suddenly was there, and it was real
> easy for people to communicate informally. People didn't
> bother to correct their typos and structure their documents
> when they sent them to each other, because they knew it took
> three minutes or less to get the message there; and if there was

any kind of confusion, the guy would send you a message back and say: Hey, what did you mean? There was no predefined length of the message. It is not a piece of paper or a form of a specific size. You can type a one-character message, you can type a million-character message. You're not . . . there's no expectation of how long the message is by the physicalness of the sheet of paper that's in front of you.

By the way, we could all say thanks to Ray Tomlinson and Dan Murphy, the authors of Tenex, who probably wrote the original E-mail program. As Lynch recalls:

Tomlinson and Murphy created E-mail because they had a PDP-10 to themselves to do the development of Tenex. They had one machine—a BIG thing, right? Two guys, one machine, and they worked in shifts, I mean they basically worked twelve hours. Twelve on, twelve off, and sometimes they'd overlap, physically, and sometimes they wouldn't. As soon as they got the file system to the point where it actually would stay together, they started writing notes to each other and leaving them in a place on the disk. You know: I did this. This now works. Just little notes back and forth, and it kept the history. When they reached the point where they had to interface the system to the Arpanet (note: the University of Utah installed a PDP-10 with Tenex), they said: "Oh, well, let's do it so it works from one machine to another." They made that leap because they were writing the network code as well. Larry Roberts later wrote a little program to take these E-mail files, which were just appended, one message after the other, and parsed it into something nice so you could pick the message you wanted.

I also remember the times when the head of the NSF or ARPA or someone like that would be down in the NIC Library in the evening. Dan, who of course was the reason for their presence there, would come down, giving me permission to leave my computer printouts and my backup tapes for a few minutes and have a glass of wine. After a while I thought: Yep, this is the life. So here I am, 17 years later, writing this book. With many, many thanks to all the members of the community that *raised* me, a child of the 'Net. How fortunate can one be?

Dan and I have a running joke as we work on this book: Just wait long enough, and you're not a nerd anymore. Certainly the Internet is one of the most exciting and formative vehicles of our culture at this time. In this book, we intend to discuss and illustrate the central issues that will influence the development of Internet commerce and therefore of the world as it evolves toward the twenty-first century. May we all benefit by such understanding as we gain through this effort.

acknowledgments

The authors wish especially to thank the following individuals and groups, who contributed in many expected and unexpected ways to the development of this book:

Tom Pressburger of Recom Technologies at NASA Ames Research Center

Jeanette Johnston of the Information Sciences Library at NASA Ames Research Center

Debbie Johnson of Exodus Communications

Eric C. Weaver of Sony Corporation

Robert Olson of Virtual Vineyards

David Kaiser and Molly Fucilla at AOL

Steve Shaw at Kaleida Labs

Ken Lim at The CyberMedia Group

Jay Fenton, Doug Crockford, Chip Morningstar, Douglas Barnes, and Randy Farmer at Electric Communities

Adam Au and Auco, Inc.

Women's Wire

Agorics, Inc.

Bill Hogan

Julius Smith

Brad Beitel

Karen Lynch

Katherine Lynch

Michael Lynch

Celeste Tillson

Christopher Lundquist

Mary Reed

Don Reed

Bud Smith

Jon Singer

Irene Freer

Wayne Heeter

Tom Heeter

Shirley Styles

Rev. Stan Hampson

Rev. Melanie Schley

Rev. Alyzsa Van Til

Walter Andrews

Lew Sachs

Phil Sutherland, our editor at John Wiley & Sons

Carole McClendon, our agent at Waterside Productions

about the authors

Daniel C. Lynch

Dan Lynch is a founder of CyberCash, Inc. and serves as Chairman of the Board of Directors. He also is Chairman and founder of Interop Company, which is now a division of Softbank Expos, and formerly was Ziff-Davis Conference and Exhibition Company, in Foster City, California. As a member of ACM, ISOC, and IEEE, Lynch is active in computer networking, with a primary focus in promoting the understanding of network operational behavior. The annual Networld + INTEROP conference and exhibition is the major vehicle for his efforts. Lynch is also a member of the Boards of Trustees of the Santa Fe Institute, the Bionomics Institute, the Internet Society, the ISODE Consortium, and is an investor in a number of private startup companies in the Internet arena.

As the director of Information Processing Division for the Information Sciences Institute in Marina del Rey (USC-ISI), Lynch led the Arpanet team that made the transition from the original NCP protocols to the current TCP/IP-based protocols. He directed this effort from 1980 until 1983.

He was Director of Computing Facilities at SRI International in the mid to late 70s, serving the computing needs of over 3,000 employees. He formerly served as manager of the computing laboratory for the Artificial Intelligence Center at SRI, which conducts research in robotics, vision, speech understanding, automatic theorem proving, and distributed databases. While at SRI, he performed initial debugging of the TCP/IP protocols in conjunction with Bolt, Beranek, and Newman (BBN).

Lynch received undergraduate training in mathematics and philosophy from Loyola Marymount University of Los Angeles, and obtained a Master's Degree in mathematics from UCLA.

Leslie Heeter Lundquist

Leslie Lundquist is a Silicon Valley pioneer. Her presence on the Internet began 17 years ago at SRI International. Ms. Lundquist's career began in mainframe operations and moved into software engineering in the field of Artificial Intelligence at SRI, then expanded into the realms of personal computing and multimedia.

Ms. Lundquist specializes in writing about new technology. As a writer and software engineer, she worked with some of the industry's groundbreaking products, including SRI's Prospector expert system, the Xerox Development Environment, which was used to create the Xerox Star Office Workstation, Apple Computer's MacApp environment, the Taligent operating system, and Kaleida Labs's ScriptX multimedia player. Her research as a Visiting Scientist at MIT was sponsored by professor Marvin Minsky, and she consulted for Dr. Alan Kay at Atari's Sunnyvale Research Center.

Ms. Lundquist formerly managed the publications group at Kaleida Labs, a joint venture of Apple Computer and IBM. She now owns a successful writing and Internet-consulting business, and serves as Director of Communications at Electric Communities, a small start-up firm in Silicon Valley. Ms. Lundquist received her Bachelor of Arts degree in Philosophy from Stanford University.

chapter one

Introduction: The Foundations of a New Commerce

Money is like manure: It doesn't do any good unless you spread it around.

—Horace Vandergelder, *Hello Dolly*

The purpose of this book is to encourage people to enter the world of online business, to stimulate them to create new products and services, and to help them prosper in the new era of Internet commerce. The Internet is a better tool than we've had before for spreading the money around. And it probably will become a tool for making new forms of money, as we will see in later chapters.

Who Should Read This Book?

This book is written primarily for decision makers and technical professionals at businesses that want to set up transactions using digital money on the Internet. It covers the salient issues involved in establishing an Internet business, especially a business that accepts digital money. It gives examples of existing businesses, and offers speculations about future businesses that could be created. It gives some answers, and it encourages you to find your own answers as well.

This is not a *hands-on* book, but it provides a wealth of general guidelines and considerations. The book's goal is to help you make intelligent decisions by giving you a feel for how the world of Internet commerce and digital money is likely to operate, and where it is likely to lead. It includes overviews of several aspects of the technology, and detailed background discussion of relevant issues, just to get every reader up to speed.

Typical readers of this book would include anyone interested in selling products or services on the Internet. Through its examples, it can help you evaluate whether you have the staff and technical resources to support digital money transactions, what additional hardware or software you might need, the costs involved, strategies you might use, and so forth. For example, if you are an expert in a field such as medical records management or claims management, or if you are involved in buying and selling of services, products, or components for large concerns, you may wish to read the book to find inspiration toward the future shape of your work.

If you are a buyer of Internet products and services, particularly secure Internet services, you also should read this book, since it can help you evaluate the quality of services you might receive. Educators may wish to use this book for their courses.

As you will learn by reading here, a new world order is arising in mechanisms for value exchange among human beings. Digital money is the cuneiform of a new age.

There's no more illustrative bottom line on why you should read this book than Figure 1.1.

Over the next ten years, the growth of electronic commerce will outstrip the growth of traditional commerce. If anything, these figures probably are too low. It is the commercialization of the Internet that's leading the way to this remarkable growth in electronic purchases. The Internet serves as a foundation for all of these new opportunities in commerce.

Many businesses are struggling right now to get themselves onto the Internet. One of the biggest selling points for creating an Internet presence has been that it's cheap to get going, and it's easy to reach millions of potential customers on the Internet. Actually, you can spend arbitrarily large amounts of cash to get going if you like. The costs of developing customized server software, billing

Purchases, in Billions of Dollars

	1994	2000 (est.)	2005 (est.)
Traditional (wholesale, retail, service, mail-order)	$5,150	$8,500	$12,000
Electronic	$ 245	$1,650	$ 2,950
TV/Cable	$ 45	$400	$ 650
Business-to-business	$140	$450	$ 650
Internet	Negligible	$600	$1,250
Other online commerce	$ 60	$200	$ 400
Proportion of all purchases	4.5%	16.2%	19.7%

Figure 1.1 The projected growth of electronic purchases 1994–2005.

and accounting software, and home pages on the World Wide Web can add up. On the other hand, by utilizing some of the services available now, such as First Virtual, a business can get started inexpensively. For example, to become a CyberCash merchant, the merchant software is free; and the customer's free software works with virtually any Web browser. We will examine several of the available options in more detail in Chapter 2, *Dramatis Personae*. For smaller companies with limited resources, these options make especially good sense, although larger companies are adopting them as well.

Besides the advantages of creating a presence on the Internet for purposes of marketing, advertising, and sales, companies also can benefit by utilizing the Internet to improve their own corporate *networking.* More employees can work from home or from the field full time, and as a result some companies already are reducing their overhead by renting smaller offices. Companies can begin to work together in closer consumer-supplier relationships, thus reducing costs of maintaining a large procurement staff in some cases. The latter part of Chapter 7, *Electronic Information Exchange,* gives specific examples of advantages businesses are gaining by using these new processes.

Besides the business case for investing in Internet commerce, your personal life is likely to undergo a dramatic transformation over the next decade as well, right down to the way you work, the way you purchase the necessities of life, and the way you play.

Managing Your New Financial Identity

You personally are going to manage your financial identity, using applications much like Quicken is used today in new and powerful ways. You'll sit at your computer and transfer money between various bank accounts, buy or sell shares of stock, pay your bills and your taxes. You'll purchase the necessities of life, from groceries to real estate. Your financial identity, in some sense your entire portfolio, will consist of collections of bits, some of which lie in institutions, some of which lie in your personal computer, some of which lie on your person in such vehicles as smart cards, as cash does now. And your company will manage its identity in much the same way you'll manage yours.

You may choose to manage your online identity anonymously, publicly, or some combination thereof; and the technology will allow for privacy as needed. You'll verify your identity for online transactions using your digital certificate, which will be as valuable to you as your driver's license is today. The first part of Chapter 7 gives details about how this process of certification and online verification of identity probably will work.

How will this new scenario come about? This enlightened style of living will be enabled partly by an advancement of trust due to enhanced Internet security, partly on technological saturation (everyone has a PC and cable TV, right?), partly on social and cultural developments, such as increased telecommuting and flextime at work. Eventually, Internet commerce promises to lead to a global economic community and better global distribution of wealth. Chapter 10, *Technology in Service to Humanity,* looks at the social and humanitarian developments that could result from the shift to Internet commerce.

The Internet: Foundation of a New Commerce

The Internet originally was a Department of Defense project, called the Arpanet, or ARPAnet, since it was funded by the Advanced Research Projects Agency (ARPA). The architecture of the Arpanet was developed in the decade between 1959 and 1969, envisioned by the military and implemented by a host of brilliant engineers and scientists working in concert with universities such as MIT, research institutes such as MITRE and SRI, and major research corporations such as BBN.

The primary goal of the Arpanet was to provide a distributed computer communications system that could survive an attack so that even if a portion of the system were lost, the rest of the network could still function. Other important goals of the Arpanet were:

◆ To enable dissimilar computers to exchange information easily

◆ To reroute information automatically around parts of the network that were not functioning

◆ A somewhat later goal: through the use of Interface Message Processors (IMPs), to act as a network of networks so that only one computer at a site (the IMP) had to be connected directly to the Arpanet. (This quality is commonly known as *internetworking*.)[1]

All of these goals were met by the original Arpanet, which had four sites: SRI International, UCLA, UC Santa Barbara, and University of Utah (Figure 1.2).

In the 1970s, universities and other institutions doing defense-related work were allowed to connect to the Arpanet. By 1975, it had about 100 sites. Researchers who maintained the Arpanet

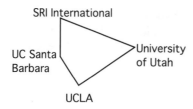

SRI International

UC Santa Barbara

University of Utah

UCLA

Figure 1.2 The four original Internet sites.

studied how growth changed the way people used the network. Early on, the researchers assumed that keeping the speed of the Arpanet high enough would be the biggest problem, but actually the biggest difficulty turned out to be keeping the computers communicating (or interoperating, as we would say today).

In the late 1970s the Arpanet had grown so large that its original packet-switching protocol, called Network Control Protocol (NCP), became inadequate. In a packet-switching system, data to be communicated is broken into small chunks. The chunks are labeled to show where they come from and where they are to go, rather like postcards in the postal system. Like postcards, packets have a maximum length, and they are not necessarily reliable. Packets are forwarded from one computer to another until they arrive at their destination. If any are lost, they can be re-sent by the originator. To eliminate unnecessary retransmissions, the recipient acknowledges packets received.

After some research, the Arpanet was changed from NCP to a new protocol called Transfer Control Protocol/Internet Protocol (TCP/IP). As director of USC-ISI, one of the authors headed this transition effort. The biggest advantage of TCP/IP was that it allowed for (what seemed at the time to be) almost unlimited growth of the network, and it was easy to implement on a variety of different computer hardware platforms.

As the Arpanet became increasingly devoted to academic and research use, the military created a new military-only network, called MILNET, in 1980. Subsequently, the National Science Foundation (NSF) adopted the model of the MILNET to create NSFNET, thereby linking together NSF researchers. By the late 1980s, the Arpanet had faded away, absorbed by the NSFNET. When the NSFNET backbone finally was retired at the end of

April 1995, a system of commercial backbones had been erected in its place (Figure 1.3).

Meanwhile, around 1980, two other networks started up: Usenet and BITNET. These were grassroots networks dedicated to the concepts of free access to information, and ease of use. Connections among the three networks grew as people wanted to exchange E-mail and information. New commercial networks began, such as CompuServe and America Online. All of these networks, collectively, are what is referred to as the Internet today.[2]

The Internet today is a free-for-all, a rough-and-tumble electronic frontier, growing at an exponential rate. It has gone from near-invisibility to near-ubiquity in little more than one year. (Near-ubiquity may be a bit of an overstatement, but Valvoline's promotion of its Internet World Wide Web home page in its Indianapolis 500 television advertisements speaks worlds about the phenomenon that we are witnessing.)

The Internet now encompasses an estimated 50,000 networks worldwide, about half of which are in the United States. As of July 1995 there were over 6 million computers permanently attached to the Internet, plus at least that many portable and desktop systems

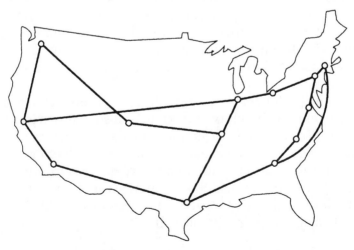

Figure 1.3   The NSFNET, backbone of the Internet until April 1995.

that were only intermittently online.* Traffic rates measured in the recently *retired* NSFNET backbone approached 20 trillion bytes per month and were growing at a 100-percent annual rate.

A Commercial Market Emerges

By the mid-1980s there was sufficient interest in the use of Internet in the research, educational, and defense communities that it was possible to establish businesses to manufacture equipment specifically for Internet implementation. Companies, such as Cisco Systems, Proteon, and later Wellfleet (now Bay Networks) and 3Com, became interested in manufacturing and selling *routers,* the commercial equivalents of the *gateways* that had been built by BBN in the early Arpanet experiments. Cisco alone is already a $1 billion business, and others seem headed toward that level rapidly.

The Internet is experiencing exponential growth in the number of networks, number of hosts, and volume of traffic. NSFNET backbone traffic more than doubled annually from a terabyte per month in March 1991 to 18 terabytes a month in November 1994. (A terabyte is a thousand billion bytes.) The number of host computers increased from 200 to 5,000,000 in the 12 years between 1983 and 1995—a factor of 25,000. It's extraordinary to note that when the NSFNET backbone was retired in April, there were almost no visible effects to the users. Indeed, the key networks that once made the Internet possible are now gone—but the Internet thrives.

Another major force behind the Internet's recent growth is the availability of new directory, indexing, and search services that help users discover the information they need in the vast Internet. Most of these services began as university research efforts and grew into businesses. They include the Wide Area Information Service (WAIS), Archie (which was spawned in Canada), YAHOO from Stanford, and The McKinley Group and INFOSEEK, which are private companies in Silicon Valley.

* [Information obtained from Network Wizards Internet Domain Survey, http://www.nw.com/]

As 1996 unfolds, many Internet service providers have gone public and others have merged or grown by acquisition. Market valuations of these companies are impressive. America Online purchased Advanced Networks and Services for $35 million. Microsoft supplied more than $20 million in capital to UUNET for expansion. UUNET and PSI have gone public. MCI has unveiled a major international Internet service, as well as an information and electronic commerce service called MarketplaceMCI. AT&T is expected to announce a major new service soon. Other major carriers, such as British Telecom, France Telecom, Deutsche Telekom, Swedish Telecom, Norwegian Telecom, and Finnish Telecom, among many others, have announced Internet services. An estimated 300 service providers are in operation, ranging from very small resellers to large telecom carriers.[3]

Mechanics of a Connection to the Internet

In general, any computer that runs the TCP/IP protocol and is connected to a computer that is connected to the Internet is itself (for all practical purposes) connected to the Internet. For instance, many dial-up accounts offer an Internet connection that lasts just for the duration of the session. Dial-up connections are typically made using Serial Line Internet Protocol (SLIP) or Point to Point Protocol (PPP). Several commercial software programs exist that implement these protocols.

The computers in the Internet backbone (Figure 1.4) are constantly connected to one another by a T3 data connection, which passes data at about 45 megabits per second (Mbps). Other computers, such as Internet service provider host computers, connect to the backbone at relatively high data rates using a T1 connection at 1.544Mbps. Leased lines provide some businesses with a full-time Internet connection at 56Kbps per second or better. Modem dial-up connections are most commonly used by individuals. Modems commonly operate at speeds from 2,400bps to 28.8Kbps.

Several types of services and file exchange protocols exist on the Internet. Probably the oldest way to transfer files across the Net is called FTP, or File Transfer Protocol. It is a simple protocol

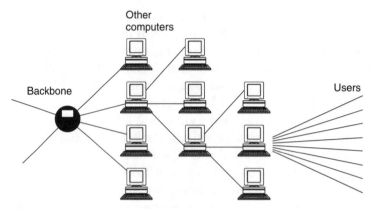

Figure 1.4 Internet backbone and connected computers.

that can be used without even a graphical user interface. The newest and perhaps most glamorous protocol is probably the one used for the World Wide Web, called HTTP, or HyperText Transfer Protocol. HTTP allows for transfer of multimedia data. E-mail could even be thought of as an Internet protocol, although it actually relies on lower-level data exchange protocols, because people use it regularly to exchange files and information. Any of these protocols can be used as a basis for electronic commerce, because they all work to allow the exchange of data across the network.

TIP: A dial-up modem connection is much less expensive to maintain than a leased line, and it is quite effective for transferring electronic mail (E-mail) over the Internet. On the other hand, if a business wishes to operate a file server for FTP (file transfer protocol) or a site on the World Wide Web (WWW), it may be cost-effective to consider a persistent Internet connection, such as a leased line. Any of the numerous Internet service providers can explain in detail the options available for persistent Internet connections.

Want to get your company on the Web right now? Here's what you'll need:

Computer: Any 486 PC is powerful enough to become your Web server. A higher-end Macintosh also makes a good Web server.

Communications: You will need a router that supports TCP/IP and SNMP protocols, and at least two connections to your local area network. You'll need more connections if you anticipate heavy Web traffic.

Connection: To serve as your pipeline to more than 25 million Internet users, you'll want at least a 56Kbps communications line. We recommend a T1 line, which provides 1.544Mbps.

Consulting Services: To create your home page, you'll want the services of a consultant to convert your informational and promotional files into HyperText Markup Language (HTML). For a simple home page, you can expect to pay about $400 for a few hours of consulting services. For a multipage brochure, about $4,000. For a full-length catalog that includes interactive links through which customers can receive more information or order products, you can expect to pay about $40,000.

The World Wide Web

The recent development of the World Wide Web (WWW, or the Web) has made the Internet much easier to use and navigate, from a user's point of view. Groups of Internet users developed the Web as a general-purpose architecture for information retrieval. You can think of the Web as a net *within* the Internet, or as a single gigantic document consisting of thousands of pages of hypertext. More accurately, the WWW consists of discrete files and directories spread throughout the Internet, connected by hypertext links in a client/server architecture (see the next section), but you can think of it as one, giant hypertext document, because the hypertext links let a user connect directly and transparently to any computer that has the needed information.

The key to the growth of the Web has been the development and free distribution of HTML (HyperText Markup Language) browsers, such as NCSA Mosaic and Netscape, that allow any X Windows, Macintosh, or Windows user access to the servers on the WWW.

Many books and articles have been written about the HTML, Mosaic, and the World Wide Web in the last year. It quickly has become nearly an accepted practice in the business community to gain a presence on the Internet by establishing a *home page* on the World Wide Web, either by setting up an in-house corporate Web server or by renting space on a server maintained by an Internet access provider. In the next chapter, you can see several examples of organizational home pages that appear on the World Wide Web.

Client/Server Architecture

Client/server architecture refers to a model for building software, wherein two software modules work together to perform a task: There's a server, which provides a specific function or service such as information storage, searching, and retrieval; and a client, which requests services from the server. File servers are one of the most important concepts about the Internet. You could envision the Internet as a huge collection of file servers, constantly being browsed by a huge number of clients.

Essentially, a server on the Internet is a storehouse of information, which usually is stored in files, thus the term *file server.* The client is another piece of software that communicates with the server to obtain information. If the server doesn't have the information that the client wants, it must respond to the client software gracefully so that neither system suffers a crash or other data loss.

Many companies offer client-side software. Essentially, any Internet browser, such as Mosaic, Netscape, or Lynx, is Internet client software.

Many vendors provide Internet file server software. Essentially, a server program must be powerful enough to handle all the client programs that may be requesting files or services at the same time. Programs, such as MacHTTP, are doing an excellent job of providing reliable servers. Any type of hardware and operating system can be used as the basis for an Internet server, but probably the most commonly used at present is a UNIX system.

Internet Naming Conventions

Internet naming conventions are simple. There is an *address* convention for each type of communication a person might want to use on the Internet: one type of address for E-mail, a different one for the World Wide Web, another one for Gopher, one for FTP, and so forth. For instance, E-mail addresses all have the same basic form:

user@[hostname.][subdomain.] domain.type

The first part, *user*, is the online name of the person to whom the message is directed. The @, or *at*, sign is a separator. *Domain* is the Internet-registered name of the company or group with which the user is affiliated, and *type* refers more or less to the tax status of that organization, whether governmental, commercial, or educational. Outside the United States, many countries use their national two-character country code as a type; for instance, FR for France, IE for Ireland, JP for Japan, and so forth. Often there are one or more optional *hostname* or *subdomain* fields before the *domain* field in the address.

For instance, if my friend Beverly works at NASA's Ames Research Center and has an E-mail account there under her own name, I could send her an E-mail message by addressing it to:

beverly@ptolemy.arc.nasa.gov

Ptolemy is the name of an Internet host machine at Ames Research Center, *arc* is a subdomain of the larger domain, *nasa.gov*. NASA has a *.gov* type extension because it is a governmental agency.

The most common type extensions for Internet addresses are:

.com	Reserved for commercial corporations such as Microsoft (microsoft.com)
.gov	Reserved for government organizations such as NASA (nasa.gov)
.org	Reserved for nonprofit organizations such as the EFF (eff.org)
.net	Reserved for Internet service providers such as Women's Wire (wwire.net)

World Wide Web address conventions, briefly, are as follows: A Web address is called a Universal Resource Locator, or URL. URLs are generally of this form:

http://www.domain.type [/subdirectory/index.html]

The letters *http* stand for *hyper text transfer protocol,* which is the file transfer protocol used on the Web. The letters *www* stand for World Wide Web, and the domain and type you've already seen in the E-mail address convention.

The optional *[/subdirectory/index.html]* provides a directory path to the Web site's home page. A home page is, by default, named *index.html.* The letters *html* stand for HyperText Markup Language, which is the language used to create home page files that are readable on the Web.

Knowing these two forms of address, you can probably figure out any other address you'd be likely to see on the Internet.

Internet Culture and Online Transactions

Actually, one of the most interesting characteristics of the Internet today is its pervasive atmosphere of cooperation and free expression, which undoubtedly began with the researchers and academic fellows who were its first nonmilitary users. Although some shysters and charlatans can be found, their presence is markedly overshadowed by friendly and helpful colleagues in every discipline, ready to answer questions and generally share their knowledge with anyone who asks.

However, the opportunity to conduct monetary transactions over the Internet presents a greater challenge than sharing general information. Ways must be devised to provide privacy and security for consumers and for merchants.

As Lee Stein, CEO of First Virtual, says:

> *What's important is not that the Internet is changing—that's inevitable. More crucial is that change happens in a way that maintains the integrity of the Internet and its culture. The original design allowed for everyone to communicate on a completely equal footing. This shouldn't change, even with the addition of new services that enable commerce to take place in a market without walls or other boundaries.*

Internet Transactions Today

Internet transactions today are primarily credit-card based. Even so, warnings to consumers abound: Using your credit card over the Net (that is, without secure encryption) is a bad idea. Unscrupulous people have found ways of obtaining thousands of credit card numbers from Internet merchants and service providers. For the moment, *caveat emptor.*

Perhaps the biggest problem facing Internet-based businesses now is the lack of a single data security standard to shield their customers' credit card numbers from fraudulent use. Add to that the technical effort required to support transactions across a plethora of Internet browsers with different abilities and features, and it quickly becomes clear that all is chaos. For example, since some browsers already handle credit-card transactions securely and others don't, merchants are forced to respond differently to different browsers.

Over the next few years, however, the Internet community is likely to join together in creating standards to enable secure credit-card and cash-based transactions. Some efforts in that direction have begun. In fact several standards may arise and coexist, all to the benefit of the consumer.

For instance, two major secure-communications protocols already have arisen in the fledgling Internet/World Wide Web commerce market. One is called Secure HyperText Transfer Protocol (S-HTTP). The other, created by Netscape Communications Corp., is called Secure Sockets Layer (SSL). In April 1995, a group of Internet-related corporations joined together to fund an effort to combine the two protocols. America Online (AOL), CompuServe, Enterprise Integration Technologies Corp. (EIT), IBM, Netscape Communications Corp., and Prodigy Services are providing funding to a small company in Menlo Park, California, called Terisa Systems, to add the SSL protocol to its existing S-HTTP-based SecureWeb Toolkit product. Terisa formerly was a joint venture between RSA Data Security, Inc., an encryption specialist, and EIT, which administers CommerceNet.

Information Law Alert describes the difference between SSL and S-HTTP as similar to the difference between *an armored car*, which protects the channel, and *an envelope*, which secures the specific data being transmitted. This approach seems like a good combination. ILA goes on to say: "Practically speaking, this approach means that online purchasing and order systems built with a Terisa toolkit will be available to the largest possible base of users. . . . These two protocols can and will work side by side, provided the software on each end of a connection contains both protocols."

After Terisa delivers the new hybrid toolkit, compatible with both existing protocols, the company will work with Internet standards committees—the World Wide Web Consortium (W3) and the Internet Engineering Task Force—to get it approved, but that may take some time. Meanwhile, other vendors have stated they'll support secure credit-card transactions without S-HTTP or SSL. If Terisa's unified security protocol is a success, it will help online businesses deal with any customer's browser software uniformly.[4]

Although most Internet sales presently are credit-card based, one vendor, DigiCash, whom we will meet in Chapter 2, has created an experimental *ecash* demo currency redeemable for goods and services available at certain Web sites. Users who log in to DigiCash and open an account at their bank can get 100 *cyberbucks* to trade for t-shirts, mousepads, and novelty items.

Future of the Internet

With the recent and projected increase in size of the Internet (Figure 1.5), another transition has been proposed from the present 32-bit addressing scheme of the Internet, called IPv4, to a new

128-bit addressing scheme affectionately called IPng (Internet Protocol, next generation) or, officially, IPv6. The transition would take place starting when needed, sometime in the next three to seven years, and the new IPng addresses would coexist with older, 32-bit addresses. Since the Internet is so large, no coordinated rollout of the new addressing scheme is possible, so the changes must be made gradually and flexibly. Bill Fink, who is responsible for a portion of NASA's operational Internet, stated the importance of flexibility:

> *Being a network manager and thereby representing the interests of a significant number of users, from my perspective it's safe to say that the transition and interoperation aspects of any IPng is the key first element, without which any other significant advantages won't be able to be integrated into the user's network environment. I also don't think it wise to think of the transition as just a painful phase we'll have to endure en route to a pure IPng environment, since the transition/coexistence period undoubtedly will last at least a decade and may very well continue for the entire lifetime of IPng, until it's replaced with IPngng and a new transition. I might wish it were otherwise but I fear they are facts of life given the immense installed base.*
>
> *Given this situation and the reality that it won't be feasible to coordinate all the infrastructure changes even at the national and regional levels, it is imperative that the transition capabilities support the ability to deploy the IPng in the piecemeal fashion . . . with no requirement to need to coordinate local changes with other changes elsewhere in the Internet. . . .*

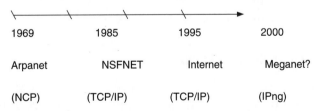

Figure 1.5   The future of the Internet.

I realize that support for the transition and coexistence capabilities may be a major part of the IPng effort and may cause some headaches for the designers and developers, but I think it is a duty that can't be shirked and the necessary price that must be paid to provide as seamless an environment as possible to the end user and his basic network services such as E-mail, FTP, Gopher, X Window clients, etc. . . .

Another way to look at this requirement for compatibility is by comparison to the product world. Vendors who do not provide backward compatibility for their products usually find they don't have many customers left. The beauty of the new scheme: It can provide approximately 665,570,793,348,866,943,898,599 addresses per square meter of the surface of planet Earth, assuming that the Earth's surface measures 511,263,971,197,990 square meters.[5]

That number of addresses should be large enough to allow the Internet to form the basis of a global communications infrastructure, don't you think? (The implications of which we will discuss in Chapter 10, *Technology in Service to Humanity.*)

A Few Notes on Terminology

Throughout the book, we use the terms *Internet commerce* and *electronic commerce* somewhat interchangeably. Although technically there are differences between them, the two seem to be merging as more banks and other financial institutions begin taking advantage of improving Internet security.

In general, throughout the book, Internet commerce, Internet value exchange, Internet transactions, and Internet business all refer to the same thing: exchanging goods and services for money using the capabilities of the Internet (Figure 1.6).

What Is an Electronic Transaction?

Any transaction is an exchange. In a common-sense definition, a transaction is a basic unit of measurement: You give X to me, and I give Y to you. Perhaps we make an exchange of goods or services

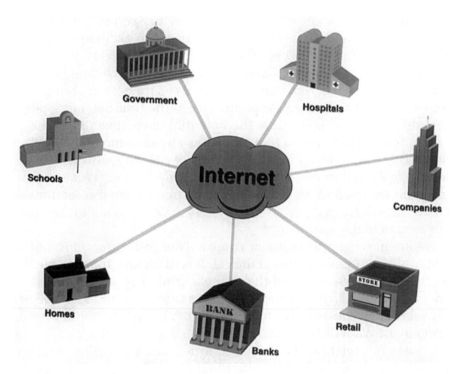

Figure 1.6   Getting the picture about Internet commerce?

for money, perhaps an exchange based on barter. In a technical sense, a transaction is a series of steps that must run to completion so that an exchange can be recorded, especially in an electronic transaction. Probably the most familiar example of an electronic transaction for people today involves an automated teller machine (ATM).

How does an ATM transaction work? You step up to your ATM, enter your PIN, and select the Withdraw Cash option. It may seem like the machine is taking a long time just to spit out some money. Actually, an involved procedure must be followed and every detail must be confirmed before the money can be released to you. Your PIN must be verified, your account balance must be checked, and the machine has to be certain it contains enough cash to grant your request. After that, a request can be sent to debit your account and the cash can be dispensed. If any of these steps fail, the transaction is aborted. *It is as if it never happened.* Thus this slightly technical definition of a transaction: An exchange is a process that must run to completion.

These steps in the ATM's process take place over secure banking networks. In fact, the banks have had secure networks in place for years. Now, with the new popularity of the Internet, more people and more businesses have the potential to create and use the secure transaction system that the banks already enjoy. The Internet must be brought up to the standards of security with which people feel comfortable sending their money around. What do we mean by secure, and what will it mean when online transactions are that way? A large part of this book is devoted to exploring the answers to that question.

We are moving into an era of *value exchange transactions*, not just traditional money turned digital. It will change the way we work, the way we play, and the way we think. For instance, the encryption and digital signature *architecture* used for exchange of digital money is capable of handling much more than money exchanges. We will find new ways to use this technology to exchange information about our identities, our credentials, online. But we must make sure that individual rights and civil liberties are protected in the process. Chapter 9, *Legal Questions*, looks at some of the issues involved in protecting our rights online. The book looks at many ways we will utilize this technology further, and the implications of all of it.

How to Read This Book

Certainly you can read this book cover to cover. But there are other ways. Each chapter is somewhat self-contained, so you can skip around. Here's a summary of what you'll find in each chapter:

Dramatis Personae gives a descriptive analysis of the main players in the Digital Money game, along with some other organizations you should know about.

For those who like a bit of technical discussion, *Cryptography: Secret Writing* starts off with some basic concepts in cryptography, then gives some details about the development and operation of cryptographic algorithms in use today.

Digital Money: The Cuneiform of a New Age describes the origins of money and banking as we know them today, gives a description of digital money and how we may come to carry it around (in smart cards and personal digital assistants), and speculates about the directions money and currency may take in the future.

New Business Concepts examines some new ideas that existing businesses may encounter when moving to the Internet, and it suggests some tantalizing possibilities for new types of businesses that may arise.

The Evolving Cyber Economy looks at how the Internet will shape our work through the development of a new information economy and new forms of transactions.

Electronic Information Exchange covers new types of business and personal information exchanges that will arise, and new ways of verifying our identities.

The New Wooden Nickel discusses new possibilities for fraud in the digital world.

Legal Questions takes a closer look at the issues of privacy in the electronic age, copyrights, U.S. legislation on cryptography, international laws, and precedents that are growing for using digital money.

Technology in Service to Humanity examines social and global questions attached to the New Era. It uses scenarios to illustrate how life might feel in the new era of Internet commerce.

At the end of the book, *Additional Readings* gives pointers to other books that provide hands-on information for setting up an Internet business. You could also contact any of several organizations mentioned in the book.

Classic Cryptography is an appendix that provides a little historical background about cryptography and some of the specific cryptographic algorithms.

There also is a *Glossary*, which contains some of the more commonly used terms and concepts introduced in the book. You can refer to it as you read.

chapter two

Dramatis Personae

Actually, Alice in Wonderland *does not run the industry, in spite of appearances to the contrary.*

—Einar Stefferud

What organizations are you likely to meet over the wires of the Internet? Who's making digital money? Who's regulating Internet commerce, if anyone? What government agencies are likely to get involved? This chapter will introduce you to many of the people and organizations that are playing a part in developing the new era of Internet commerce.

Summary of Digital Money Architectures

Recently, several corporations have begun to offer services that enable Internet commerce. Some offer credit-card purchasing or electronic bill-paying services, others offer digital cash. Who are the players in this digital money game? What are the distinguishing differences in digital money architectures? This section helps answer these questions so that you can make an intelligent choice about which existing architecture might work best for you.

The models for secure digital money transactions currently seem to fall into two basic categories: credit card sales, and digital *traveler's checks*. Online credit-card sales (and debit transactions) are pretty much as we know them, with the addition of encryption technology for security's sake. The digital *traveler's checks* model is more innovative, a different application of encryption technology. We'll meet companies that serve as examples of each model. In fact, there are numerous variations on these two themes, and each company has focused on meeting different market needs. Many of the companies we'll meet have licensed public-key encryption technology (which we'll describe in more detail in Chapter 3, *Cryptography: Secret Writing*) to provide for their security requirements.

What also is happening is that some vendors are creating *localized* digital money—and making sure that you can spend this localized money at their online location only. An example of this type of thinking today is coupons, which are actually just localized cash as we know it in 1995.

Although the field is changing rapidly, as this book goes to press some of the notable players seem to be those listed in Table 2.1.

The next few sections compare and contrast the basic viewpoints of each of these vendors.

Checkfree

Checkfree Corporation has been processing online credit-card and bill-payment transactions since 1983. It handles payments for

TABLE 2.1 Some of the Major Vendors in the Digital Money Game

Vendors	
◆ Checkfree	Columbus, OH, (614) 825-3000 http://www.checkfree.com
◆ CyberCash	Reston, VA, (703) 620-4200 http://www.cybercash.com
◆ DigiCash	Amsterdam, 011-31-20-665-2611 http://www.digicash.com/index.html
◆ First Virtual Holdings	San Diego, CA, (800) 570-0003 http://www.fv.com
◆ NetBill	Carnegie-Mellon University, Pittsburgh, PA (412) 268-2000 (information)
◆ Netscape Communications	Mountain View, CA, (415) 254-1900 http://mosaic.mcom.com
◆ Open Market, Inc.	Cambridge, MA, (617) 621-9500 http://www.openmarket.com

major online services, such as AOL and CompuServe, and for major access providers such as Netcom. Its software will validate Internet transactions using every major credit card. Essentially, Checkfree has individuals and merchants as customers, and it matches them up to make and collect payments: An individual signs up with Checkfree to pay bills electronically, and a merchant signs up to receive payments electronically, though there's no reason a merchant couldn't use Checkfree's services to pay their suppliers as well (Figure 2.1).

Here's how Checkfree's bill-paying service basically works. Using a touchtone telephone or personal computer and modem (not through the Internet), the subscriber sends payment information to Checkfree. Depending on the payee, Checkfree may send instructions using the existing U.S. Federal Reserve or MasterCard RPS system to transfer funds electronically from the subscriber's checking account to the creditor. For payments to smaller merchants or individuals, Checkfree may send a laser-printed check through the U.S. Postal Service. Payments are recorded on the subscriber's monthly bank statement or included in canceled checks, depending on how they're processed. For Checkfree sub-

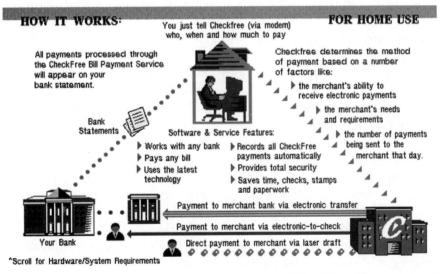

Figure 2.1   Checkfree's services. (Courtesy of Checkfree Corporation.)

scribers using personal computers, the software keeps a record of their transactions. Telephone service subscribers receive a monthly statement of transactions from Checkfree or from the financial institution offering the service. Checkfree offers security mostly because (so far) it relies on more traditional means of electronic funds transfer through telephone and modem, rather than on the Internet *per se.*

Checkfree's bill-paying software, CheckFree, is included in financial management packages such as Intuit's *Quicken* and Andrew Tobias' *Managing Your Money* from Meca Software. Recently, CheckFree has expanded its services to include what it calls the CheckFree Wallet. The CheckFree Wallet allows for cash, credit-card, check, coin, and micropayment transactions. (For more explanation of micropayments, please see Chapter 5, *New Business Concepts.*) Checkfree Corporation is partnering with CyberCash in the CheckFree Wallet venture: It has licensed Cyber-Cash's technology for encryption and authorization.

CyberCash

CyberCash was cofounded by Bill Melton and Dan Lynch. Bill Melton previously founded VeriFone, a company that achieved enormous success by providing a simplified system for processing credit-card transactions at the point of sale (Figure 2.2). (Those things you slide your credit card through are Bill's creations.) Dan Lynch previously founded Interop, which has grown to become the popular NetWorld + Interop networking show and exhibition. Their mutual goal was to "make the Internet safe for spontaneous financial transactions."

The banks have had secure electronic transactions across networks for years. Essentially, the Internet community has grown more sophisticated, and it wants these same capabilities. The banking networks as currently constituted could not and should not handle the number of transactions that could occur if everyone on the Internet had direct access to the secure banking networks for every exchange. Thus, CyberCash serves as a gatekeeper and bridge between the two communities essentially by linking the Internet to the banking networks as needed, and also by bringing Internet security up to the necessary standard.

Figure 2.2 CyberCash's home page on the World Wide Web.

The CyberCash architecture is notable because it handles credit-card, debit, and cash transactions equally well. It also works with any Web browser or server by calling consumers to download a free software module. The software module communicates with CyberCash's servers, which in turn communicate with the banks' own private networks.

For example, if you decide to make a credit-card purchase using CyberCash, the merchant sends you an *electronic invoice* over the Web. You can review the invoice and append your credit-card number to it. Then the CyberCash software module encrypts the credit-card portion of the invoice and returns it to the merchant. He appends his own confirmation number, encrypts the entire package, and forwards it to a CyberCash server for reformatting and encryption in banking formats, and then to the banking network, where it is then treated like a normal credit-card transaction. Notice that in this arrangement *the merchant never knows your credit-card number.*

For debit transactions, you would open a CyberCash account in advance. To make a purchase, you send an encrypted message to CyberCash requesting a funds transfer. If your merchant has a CyberCash account, the transaction is completed. If the merchant doesn't have an account, CyberCash creates one, then tells the merchant to download the free CyberCash merchant software, because there's money waiting.

For cash transactions, CyberCash doesn't actually accept cash deposits like a bank. Instead it works with the banks to create *pointers* to cash existing in customer's bank accounts. Basically, money that you've designated for your CyberCash account is held in escrow. In other words, your CyberCash account contains pointers to your money, and payments are completed by moving pointers, which enacts electronic funds transfers among these escrowed accounts. Currently, CyberCash is partnering with Wells Fargo Bank of California. For cash transactions, CyberCash customers have a noninterest-bearing, FDIC-insured trust account with Wells Fargo that holds their *cyber* funds. There is no need for customers to have any other Wells Fargo account to open a Cyber-Cash account (Figure 2.3).

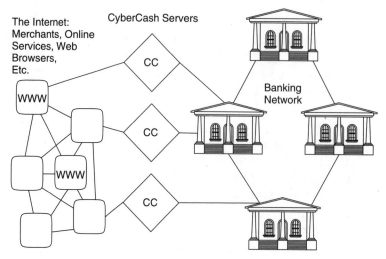

Figure 2.3   How CyberCash works with merchants and banks.

A general principle of the CyberCash architecture is that it stores a minimum amount of information about each transaction. For instance, CyberCash doesn't store a record of what you bought, only enough information to get paid for the transaction. Merchants do know your identity, however, and they may record what you buy. By the way, CyberCash never knows your encryption key, either. (See Chapter 3, *Cryptography: Secret Writing*, for more information about encryption keys.) Even if they are forced to turn over all your records to the government, the government still wouldn't have your key.

For debit and electronic cash transactions, CyberCash charges consumers a small transaction fee, comparable to the price of a postage stamp.

DigiCash

DigiCash was founded primarily by David Chaum, a cryptologist and notable member of the Internet community (Figure 2.4). Like CyberCash, DigiCash software also works directly with banks, in a model similar to purchasing a traveler's check. To use DigiCash, you can send money to a bank through a credit-card or automated-teller transaction, and the bank sends you an equivalent amount of E-cash as an encrypted E-mail message containing a list of 64-bit numbers (not easily duplicated). Each number corresponds to a specified amount of money, which is recorded by the issuing bank.

For instance, if you sent an E-cash bank $10, you would receive an encrypted E-mail message containing a 64-bit number. That number is now worth $10 on the Internet. If you want to buy something that costs $10, you send the merchant your number. The merchant forwards the number to the bank, and the bank credits his account $10 (Figure 2.5). The bank keeps track of numbers that are used or reported as lost.[1]

Dan Eldridge, DigiCash's vice president of business development, likens E-cash to travelers checks because it is a *bearer's instrument* that provides:

◆ Finality, which means that users cannot renege on E-cash transactions, as they might by stopping payment on a check or refusing payment on a credit-card transaction.

Figure 2.4 DigiCash's home page on the World Wide Web.

- ◆ Anonymity of payer and payee.
- ◆ Peer-to-peer transactions.
- ◆ Refundability if E-cash is lost or stolen.[2]

DigiCash provides for complete anonymity: The merchant never knows your identity, only that your E-cash is good. Anonymity may be E-cash's most controversial feature: It may be desirable except when an audit trail of transactions is required—say, for tax purposes—yet it raises concern for some people that the technology might be used for illegal transactions.

An advantage of DigiCash's system is that the lack of identity verification enables a low transaction cost. Compare DigiCash's plan at a penny or less per transaction with, say, First Virtual's cost of $.029 + 2 percent per transaction cost to the seller.

Figure 2.5 Your basic interaction with a bank that issues DigiCash's E-cash.

First Virtual Holdings

First Virtual Holdings, Inc. is the brainchild of Lee Stein, a San Diego lawyer, accountant, and financial advisor for celebrities; and Einar Stefferud, one of the most respected members of the Internet community (Figure 2.6). The story goes that they met in an airport when Stef, as he is sometimes called, was reading his E-mail on a portable computer, and the rest is history.

First Virtual may indeed be one of the first truly virtual corporations as well as one of the first Internet financial services corporations. The leadership staff of First Virtual is scattered from San Diego to Washington, DC, and they meet regularly by conference call and E-mail. "It would have been impossible to recruit all of the people we have if I'd had to relocate them," Stein said. When Mr. Stein feels his staff has been working too hard, he imposes an E-mail moratorium from Thursday night to Monday morning.[3]

Like the company itself, First Virtual's electronic transaction system is based on E-mail, not on specialized client software. When a new First Virtual customer wants to browse, she opens an account and is given a confidential identification number. When she wants to purchase a product or service, she sends an E-mail message containing her identification number to the merchant. The merchant sends the number to First Virtual by E-mail for verification and identification of the customer, and never knows the customer's personal identity. First Virtual then confirms with the customer by E-mail that she did indeed initiate the transaction and wants to make the purchase (Figure 2.7).

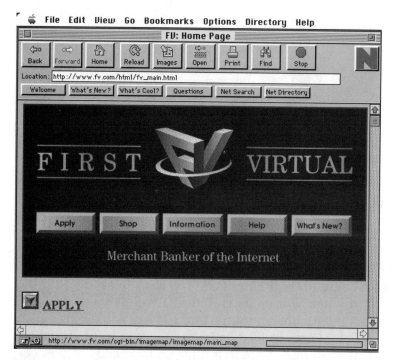

Figure 2.6   First Virtual's home page on the World Wide Web.

I personally remember Stef as one of the late-night login presences on the system at SRI International in the late 1970s, when I was a computer operator there, working for my coauthor Dan Lynch. —L.L.

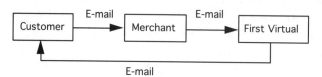

Figure 2.7   Basic schema of First Virtual Holding's Internet service.

The First Virtual system performs the most sensitive parts of financial transactions offline, utilizing Electronic Data Systems Corp. (EDS), a division of General Motors, to transfer the account information from the purchaser to the merchant over its own private network. First Virtual processes debit transactions of its U.S. merchants through the Automated Clearing House (ACH) network. Credit-card transactions are handled, again offline, through First USA Merchant Services, Inc., a fast-growing credit-card company in Dallas, that will issue a credit card for the new service.

Technically, First Virtual's model doesn't use the Internet *at all* for the financial transactions, only for placing and confirming orders. This offline approach to Internet commerce has met with quick acceptance; indeed, First Virtual had its first customer within hours of announcing the availability of its services, but Mr. Stein acknowledges that their approach may need to be altered as the Internet commerce market develops.

A distinguishing feature of First Virtual is its InfoHaus. First Virtual's InfoHaus system is a specialized Information Server that is excellently situated to provide a way for small businesses to sell information over the Internet. A First Virtual merchant account costs $10 to set up, and you must have an E-mail address; if you're selling information, rather than just handling orders online for products shipped offline, the InfoHaus handles all of the storage, distribution, and billing functions for you. The cost? First Virtual's normal transaction fees of 29 cents per transaction plus 2 percent of the transaction's value, plus an 8-percent InfoHaus service fee.

Apple Computer announced in April, 1995 that they will be selling QuickTime 2.0 over the Internet through First Virtual's Internet Payment System (available on the Web at http://quicktime.apple.com). Assuming this is a typical First Virtual transaction, Apple would be paying First Virtual 29 cents, plus 2 percent of the price of the software ($9.95 × .02 = 20 cents), for each copy sold.

Open Market, Inc. (OMI)

Open Market (OMI) is a startup company headquartered in Cambridge, Massachusetts. OMI has developed StoreBuilder, a software product for creating secure electronic storefronts on the Internet. The service is targeted specifically at small- to medium-size businesses.

Open Market was founded in 1994 by Shikar Ghosh, formerly CEO of Appex Corp., which developed an intercompany payment system for roaming across the cellular phone network. Mr. Ghosh teamed up with MIT Professor David Gifford and technology expert Lawrence Stewart from Digital Equipment Corporation to build security for Internet transactions.

Open Market says that a merchant, following simple computer commands, can open a store on its Internet Merchant Server for less than $1,500, not including regular monthly fees based on the store's size and transaction volume.

In contrast to how First Virtual built a payment system (for the InfoHaus server) around its initial application of selling electronic documents, Open Market connects its Merchant Server to a Payment Server. On the Payment Server, data are secured with personal identification numbers, passwords, data encryption, and, for large-dollar payments, a security code generated by a smart card (see Chapter 4 for more information about smart cards).

Open Market's system is limited initially to credit-card payments, which are processed through Litle & Co., but it plans to offer a full range of services, including debit cards, corporate accounts, digital cash, and automated clearinghouse options. "It's here, it's live, it's running today," said Gail L. Grant of Open Market, Inc.[4]

Open Market has been selected by Tribune Company, Advance Publications (owners of Conde Nast and Random House), and Time, Inc. to provide the environment in which they will publish their content electronically.

NetBill

NetBill is an alliance between Carnegie Mellon University and Visa International. It offers an Internet payment system designed to allow information, such as journal articles, book chapters, software, and video clips, to be bought and sold through the Internet at low transaction costs. For instance, a CMU student with some recipes or tips on automobile care could post her offerings on the Internet and receive a small payment each time the information is downloaded. CMU and other universities have a wealth of information to share. Visa, the credit card giant, plans to contribute payment system expertise as well as operating support and personnel.

Initially, NetBill customers who want to buy information will deposit a lump sum into a NetBill account. As the user buys information, NetBill will draw upon that account. Eventually, users will be able to charge their information purchases to their credit cards. There are no minimum purchase requirements.

NetBill clearly competes with First Virtual, but, says Nathaniel Borenstein, chief scientist at First Virtual, "there's room on the Internet for lots of payment systems."

In NetBill's trial period, during the summer of 1995, users had access to information from libraries at Carnegie Mellon, the University of Illinois, Massachusetts Institute of Technology, and the University of Michigan.[5]

Netscape Communications Corp.

Netscape Communications has formed an alliance with First Data's electronic funds services unit to create an online payment system. First Data, though not a household name, is the number-one processor of bank-card transactions. Like CyberCash and several other vendors, Netscape and First Data have licensed public key encryption technology from RSA Data Security, Inc. to provide secure transaction capabilities.

A Netscape transaction is credit-card based. All major credit cards will be accepted electronically. One drawback of Netscape's services is that it requires use of the popular Netscape browser which has some serious security flaws at this writing; other services, such as CyberCash, work with any browser software.

For approximately $5,000, Netscape offers a Commerce Server package that can accommodate secure online purchases and data exchange. Three customers already have signed up for First Data/Netscape's services: First Interstate Bank of California, which also is active in CommerceNet, Norwest Corp.'s Norwest Card Services unit, and Old Kent Bank and Trust Co. of Grand Rapids, MI. Mr. Randy Kahn, senior vice president of First Interstate says: "It is vital that payment services evolve along with technology."[6]

Analysis and Summary

Each of these companies has forged a unique identity and has started the process of bringing the future into the present. Some of them seem to group together, others stand apart. For instance, CyberCash and First Virtual seem to share the model of serving as gatekeepers between the Internet and the banking networks; yet First Virtual accomplishes the transactions by E-mail, and Cyber-Cash uses sophisticated client/server technology.

CyberCash's and First Virtual's systems both attempt to provide protection against the two types of credit-card fraud that are most prevalent today: stolen cards and merchant-perpetrated fraud. CyberCash protects consumers against stolen credit-card numbers with public-key encryption, and against merchant fraud because the merchant never knows the customer's credit-card number. First Virtual protects by requiring a confirming E-mail message from the customer. Of course, if someone has stolen a credit card, they may well have access to other secret information, and they could pose as the rightful owner of the card. Indeed, all bets are off if someone illegally gains access to another's private encryption key, as explained further in Chapter 8, *The New Wooden Nickel.*

Checkfree Corporation stands alone as a well-established inter-mediary between consumers and providers of all sorts. Their service existed before the Internet's recent explosion of popularity, and seems less dependent on it than the others. The CheckFree software definitely forces customers to rely on the trustworthiness of Checkfree as a company, and the fact that it has been in exis-tence longer than some of these other companies works to its advantage in that area.

DigiCash's identifiable difference is the fact that it offers com-plete anonymity. DigiCash stands outside the existing banking networks, whereas First Virtual and CyberCash make full use of them. Some users of digital money are uncomfortable with Digi-

Cash's dedication to the idea of anonymous cash transactions. In contrast to DigiCash's dedication to digital cash, Netscape seems to be solely directed at online credit-card transactions. Netscape's advantage is the popularity of its Web browser software, which continues in spite of recent publicity about several security flaws that have been discovered in it.

NetBill and First Virtual (through its InfoHaus server) share the ability to handle informationcentric transactions gracefully. The ability to track information sales will most likely prove very important in the development of electronic cottage industry. NetBill is commendable in its focus on making information available from universities.

Open Market sets itself apart by catering specifically to the growth of electronic storefronts and malls, where people can spend their digital money. The concept of *local* money that arises from OMI's approach is likely to prove important, since it is similar to the notion of national currencies today. Time will tell whether people want localized currency in cyberspace, or universal cyberbucks.

Table 2.2 summarizes the strongest offerings of some of the major vendors.

If this were a ballgame, which team would win? Actually, with each company carving out a uniquely identifiable service niche among businesses who want to offer online transaction services, there seems to be room on this ballfield for all the players. No single one of these models seems positioned to win the game for quite some time. Although all the companies are offering many of the same services—credit-card sales, digital money, debit

TABLE 2.2 Comparative Strengths of Various Online Digital Money Firms

Organization	Main Customer	Distinguishing Service
Checkfree	Consumers	Bill paying
CyberCash	Banks	Bank and merchant transactions
DigiCash	Consumers	Anonymity
First Virtual	Info Businesses	Microtransactions for selling info
NetBill	Consumers	Info from universities
Netscape	Consumers	Credit-card transactions
OMI	Businesses	Secure storefront

accounts, and so forth—each has a unique process (indeed, in the case of Checkfree, a patented process) and a unique style for getting things done.

In the long run, several models probably will coexist for Internet transactions, because each of the companies in Table 2.2 fits best with a certain portion of the market. For instance, as we will see in the case of Virtual Vineyards (see profile in Chapter 5, *New Business Concepts*), certain payment services had to be ruled out for business reasons; other Internet vendors will have different needs.

What also is happening is that, after the fashion of Open Market, *many* vendors may create *localized* digital money—and make sure that you can spend this localized money at their online locations only. An example of this type of thinking today is coupons, which are actually just localized cash as we know it today.

Also, there definitely seems to be a trend toward proprietary online commerce communities, referred to as *cybermalls*, and localized digital money may come into existence at the cybermall level or even at the level of the individual storefront. By the way, some of these cybermalls will be associated with existing online services, others will not—just pages on the Web pushing their *WebGuilders* or what have you. Overall, things in the digital cash arena may take awhile to settle down.

The prefix *cyber* is derived from the Greek word *kyber*, meaning *steersman*, a navigator of high rank.

The prefix was used by Norbert Wiener as part of his term *cybernetics*, which referred to the science of communications and control within a system, and how that system interacts intelligently with, or navigates through, its environment.

In science fiction, William Gibson used the term *cyberspace* to refer to the dimensionless world of computer data, through which a user must navigate.

In modern usage, the prefix cyber has acquired the connotation of something technologically fashionable, cool or hip. (Courtesy of *The CyberMedia Group*.)

By the way, perhaps the world's largest cybermall is the Internet Shopping Network (*http://shop.internet.net*), with over 600 companies listed at this writing. The Internet Shopping Network is a part of cable TV's Home Shopping Network.[7]

Where Is Microsoft in This Picture?

Microsoft has announced that it has formed an alliance with Visa International to provide Internet purchasing services, although Microsoft will say very little more about its plans specifically related to digital money. In fact, when one of the authors called Microsoft, their representative denied knowledge of any such plans. She said she'd get back to us.

However, with the release of Windows 95 and Microsoft Network in August 1995, Microsoft began to offer Interactive TV software, set-top boxes, video servers, online telecommunications services and Internet access, banking services, electronic payment services, entertainment, and wireless data communications.[8]

To get more specific, Microsoft paid NBC $4 million for an exclusive three-year agreement to provide financial, news, and sports content for the Microsoft Network. To sign on with Microsoft, NBC ended its partnership with America Online and Prodigy.[9]

Other new partners at the Microsoft Network include *The New York Times* Sports, *U.S. News and World Report*, QVC, Inc., and QVC's rival, The Home Shopping Network, Inc. Another new member of the Microsoft Network is Eastman Kodak's Kodalux film processing lab.

Other companies announced as content providers include American Greetings, Collector's Direct Network, C-SPAN, Hollywood Online, Jazz Central Station, Starwave Corp., Women's Wire, and Ziff-Davis Publishing Co. What are all these providers doing?

In the entertainment area alone, NBC produces CD-ROMs, interactive television services and products for the Microsoft Network, linked to its shows. Hollywood Online is an area that offers digital video clips, sound bites, photos, and electronic magazines. Starwave will provide multimedia sports information (ESPNET, SportsZone), entertainment news (Mr. Showbiz), and information about outdoor activities (Outside Online). DreamWorks SKG is a

Microsoft Network venture with Steven Spielberg, Jeffrey Katzenberg, and David Geffen to produce multimedia games.[10]

Microsoft displays its willingness to allow any number of competing content providers on the network, and "let the best company win." Over 70,000 homes have been involved in the Beta test for Microsoft Network, of which more than 30 percent were from foreign markets. That's more homes than the largest interactive TV test has had to date. Need we say more?[11]

Microsoft Network's Business Model

Microsoft Network has a new business model. Other online services are time-based: You pay a subscription fee and then pay hourly for any time spent over your allotted *free hours.* Microsoft network will be transaction-based: You pay a nominal monthly fee (probably under $5), and then you pay only for the services or transactions you are interested in. Microsoft also plans to limit the subscriber base to 500,000; however, as this book goes to press that limit has not been approached.

Here's Mr. Lee Stein of First Virtual's response to Microsoft's market entry: "I don't think the rest of the world will allow Visa and Microsoft to dictate the system." We agree with Mr. Stein. We think there's room for many business models.

The preceding sections have provided an overview of companies that currently are providing online transaction and data security services, with whom Microsoft will be competing. The next section provides an overview of the existing online services with which Microsoft will be competing as it enters the market.

Survey of Commercial Online Services

Online services began separately from the Internet proper, as self-contained, network-based communities through which subscribers could interact. So many online services sprang up in the 1980s that, as the Internet traffic grew, the old NSF backbone eventually was entirely replaced by private access providers and commercial online services. (See Chapter 1 for more information about the history and growth of the Internet.) Most of these services also offer Internet access and online banking services, or plan to do so soon.

America Online (AOL)

America Online recently surpassed CompuServe as the largest online service provider, forecasting over $1 billion in revenues in the 1996 fiscal year, compared with $394.3 million in 1995. Users like its clean, simple interface and good mix of content. AOL tends to be favored by online newcomers, Macintosh users, and computer *techies* who are interested in computer topics, downloadable software, direct support, and user forums. In recent years, AOL has made a push to establish strategic alliances with high-profile content providers.

America Online is a publicly traded company.

CompuServe

CompuServe's subscriber base recently exceeded 3 million online accounts. It is the oldest commercial online service. Its extensive offerings include stock quotes, travel services, a recently released Web browser, and diverse publishing offerings including *Fortune, Sports Illustrated, Rolling Stone, People*, and many technical forums. CompuServe is international in scope, with members from over 150 countries. It offers E-mail services, a CD-ROM supplement, libraries of free software, and worldwide Internet services. It has strong PC-oriented technical forums. CompuServe tends to be favored by executives, business users, and researchers.

CompuServe is a division of H&R Block.

Prodigy

Prodigy has over 1.2 million subscribers. It primarily targets families by providing a well-balanced offering of content—financial information, news, entertainment, and commercial wares. Prodigy specifically supports advertising.

Prodigy currently is involved in an interesting lawsuit that is testing the boundaries of an online service's responsibility for its users' postings. The case is discussed further in Chapter 9, *Legal Questions.*

Prodigy is a joint venture of IBM and Sears, Roebuck and Co.

Genie

Genie provides online games, bulletin boards, and downloadable software. It is popular with young users and hackers, mainly because online, multiplayer games are less readily available on other services. Over 40 percent of Genie's revenues are attributed to games. Genie has about 250,000 subscribers.

Genie is a division of GE Information Services.

Summary

These days, the online services are scrambling to offer Internet access in addition to their established bulletin boards, newswires, and so forth. They also are working to create unique brand identities, now that pricing has become fairly standard at $9.95 per month with five to ten hours of free time online. Without price competition, consumers have started to see the services as interchangeable, and they're switching services more.

As a result, America Online has chosen Chiat/Day to develop an ad campaign, and at this writing CompuServe is in the process of selecting between Omnicom and Martin/Williams. America Online is expected to produce an advertising campaign that emphasizes the "community and neighborhood atmosphere of America Online, not computers and modems," says Ted Leonsis, President of America Online. CompuServe hopes to play down its techie image in its new marketing campaign, without alienating its longtime customers. Prodigy is expected to aim for a niche market, with ideas including Prodigy for Kids and Prodigy for Seniors. Prodigy has a new television ad campaign in the works with Cliff Freeman & Partners, and it is revamping its graphics to suit the new image.[12]

Smaller Commercial Online Services

Many other online services exist that are too specialized, too new, or too small to group with the others. Many of these smaller services have been started by large corporations in an attempt to gain a foothold in the commercial online services marketplace. Notables include:

Women's Wire

Although not a large service itself, with 1,500 subscribers, Women's Wire is worth mentioning as the foremost provider of Internet services targeted to women. Women's Wire is available on Microsoft Network and on CompuServe. Women's Wire is privately held.

Apple Computer's E-World

E-World software is bundled with all new Macs sold. So far, E-World has met with mixed success, but it is a great attempt by Apple to capitalize on the loyalty of its customers. Apple has recently asked its employees to convert from the older Applelink service to E-World.

Imagination

Imagination is not a general-purpose online service, but a games-only network targeted toward children and seniors. It is a joint venture of Sierra Online and AT&T.

Many other small commercial online services exist, as well as a growing number of Internet access providers, who don't particularly provide an online environment, just a channel to the Internet and the World Wide Web. Judging by the growing list of participants in the commercial online services arena, it seems clear that anyone who is anyone is getting into the game. The trend toward online communications and commerce does not seem to be in any danger of diminishing, though there may continue to be consoli-

> ### *FTC Ponders Cybermarketing*
>
> The Federal Trade Commission is planning to set up its own Web site for gathering information and opinions about the need for policing advertising practices on the Internet. "I am not an advocate of fixing something that isn't broken," says an FTC Commissioner, "but I want to be wary of when they might break."
>
> Some analysts predict that commercial services may start charging a fee for the option of deciding how much advertising comes your way, and how much of your information goes back to marketers, resulting in a *privacy ghetto*, where only those who could afford to pay for privacy would have it, and those who couldn't would be at the mercy of marketers. (*Wall Street Journal*, 4/14/95 B5)

dation of smaller services into larger ones as we saw with Women's Wire.

We expect to see a proliferation of online services, especially some offering online chat environments and fantasy environments, such as *The Palace*, by Time Warner Interactive.

According to research completed in August 1995 by Inteco Corp., a Norwalk, Connecticut-based technology research firm, there is as yet little brand loyalty and significant customer dissatisfaction with all of the major online services. According to Inteco, over 6.2 million personal computer users have tried and cancelled subscriptions to the leading services.

There is lots more room for success in providing consumer satisfaction in cyberspace. One possibility is that, as online chat services become more sophisticated on the Web and on the Internet at large, brand-name online services will prove too limiting. People may wish to connect and form their own communities, unshaped by the corporate image of an AOL, CompuServe, or what have you. However, for the moment these large services are providing a terrific online home for millions of subscribers.

Online Banking Services

The larger commercial online services—America Online, Prodigy, and CompuServe—all are beginning to offer online banking services in cooperation with several banks, including BankAmerica, Wells Fargo Bank, and others. New collaborations are announced almost daily.

But the banks themselves also are developing the capabilities to offer their customers online services directly. "We're enthusiastic about it all," said Donald Ogilvie, Executive Vice President of the American Bankers Association.* Bankers also are afraid that, in the new world of electronic commerce, they'll get left behind and lose their customers to their rivals, who may be offering electronic banking services already.

In fact, once they get their software acts together, banks are in a good position to be technology providers and financial providers for electronic commerce. Why? The banks' existing expertise in payment systems is still unduplicated in the software industry, and the banks already control the existing payment systems.

As an example of things you can expect to see more and more of, a Kentucky bank, Security First Network Bank, announced in October 1995 that it will open its doors in cyberspace, offering savings accounts, certificates of deposit, and money-market accounts by the end of 1995, and credit cards and brokerage services beginning in 1996. Like Security First, banks across the country are eager to gain a foothold on the Internet, with its millions of users.

Other Internet Organizations of Interest

Several notable organizations exist that are furthering the growth and opportunities around online commerce, serving as watchdogs for consumer rights in the new era of Internet commerce, or working to establish standards. This section gives some details about

---

* [Quoted in *San Francisco Chronicle*, "Banking's Brave New World," Monday, October 9, 1995, B1.]

the groups that are arguably the most influential at this time: CommerceNet, the Internet Society (ISOC), the Electronic Frontier Foundation (EFF), Computer Professionals for Social Responsibility (CPSR), and several governmental organizations.

CommerceNet

CommerceNet's goal is to stimulate the growth of a communications and information infrastructure that is easy to use, oriented toward commercial use, and ready to expand rapidly (Figure 2.8). CommerceNet's charter is to:

◆ Operate an Internet-based World Wide Web server with directories and information that facilitates an open electronic marketplace for business-to-business transactions.

Figure 2.8 CommerceNet's home page on the World Wide Web.

- Accelerate the mainstream application of electronic commerce on the Internet by fielding member-driven pilot programs.
- Enhance existing Internet services and applications and stimulate the development of new services.
- Encourage broad participation from small, medium, and large companies; and offer outreach programs to educate organizations about the resources and benefits available with CommerceNet.
- Serve as a common information infrastructure for Northern California and coordinate with national and international infrastructure projects.

CommerceNet provides a forum for industry leaders and other people experimenting with developing procedures and protocols to discuss issues, deploy pilot applications, and from these define standards and best business practices for using the Internet for electronic commerce. Through these efforts, CommerceNet plans to help the emerging industry evolve common standards and practices so that users will see a seamless web of resources.

Here are some services CommerceNet provides to help companies participate in the Internet marketplace:

- Affordable, high-quality Internet connectivity (through BBN BARRNET) using a variety of options, including T1, 56K, Frame Relay, and ISDN.
- Online directories of CommerceNet members and subscribers, and of other electronic commerce initiatives.
- Online access to software tools for information providers that make it easy to set up their own electronic storefronts.
- Security mechanisms, including authentication and encryption, supported within applications, including RSA public key cryptography. Public key certification services also are provided to CommerceNet members.
- Services focused on making it easy for small businesses to participate as Internet information providers.

In short, CommerceNet's goal is to make public computer networks, such as the Internet, *industrial strength* for business use. CommerceNet addresses issues, such as low-cost, high-speed Internet access, using newly deployed technology such as Integrated Services Digital Network (ISDN) services and multimedia software. CommerceNet supports a range of commercial network applications such as on-line catalogs, product data exchange, and engineering collaboration. It also offers outreach services such as technical assistance to small- and medium-size businesses that want access to public networks.

CommerceNet is a nonprofit corporation. Half of the funds for CommerceNet are provided by the U.S. government's Technology Reinvestment Program (TRP). CommerceNet was awarded $6 million over three years. Matching funds are provided by the State of California and participating companies.

The TRP was created as part of President Clinton's program to revitalize the economy, create jobs, and help American industry remain on the cutting edge of technology. The TRP is sponsored by the Defense Department's Advanced Research Projects Agency (ARPA), the Department of Commerce's National Institute of Standards and Technology (NIST), the National Science Foundation (NSF), the Department of Energy (DOE), and the National Aeronautics and Space Administration (NASA). CommerceNet was one of 55 projects awarded TRP funding in November 1993 to promote the commercial use of defense-related technology.

The CommerceNet consortium is sponsored by Smart Valley, Inc. and the State of California's Office of Strategic Technology. Enterprise Integration Technologies (EIT), a local high-tech company specializing in electronic commerce, leads the CommerceNet effort.[13]

CommerceNet currently has nine active working groups: Connectivity, Network Services, Payment Services, Electronic Catalogs/Directories, Internet EDI, Engineering Data Transfer/Design-to-Manufacturing Integration, Internet Marketing, Collaboration Tools, and Public Policy.

CommerceNet's progress is a testimony to the viability of electronic commerce over the Internet. They now have over 100 member companies from the electronics, computer, financial service, and information service industries.[14]

CommerceNet's nine working groups are involved in 15 pilot programs, which are categorized as follows, with their corresponding mission statements:

Business Return Pilots

◆ End-to-end Commerce: Explore issues involved in deploying Internet commerce to small businesses, and examine the return on investment (ROI) of such deployment.

◆ Electronic Commerce Business Value: Define qualitative and quantitative metrics that can be built into electronic commerce applications (catalogs) to measure their benefit and effectiveness.

◆ CommerceNet User Demographics: Develop techniques and software tools to collect and analyze survey data on CommerceNet user behavior, attitudes, opinions, and demographics.

Security Pilots

◆ CommerceNet Server and Affiliated Individual Certification Authority (CA): Implement a reference deployment of server and individual CAs for CommerceNet members and pilots.

◆ Key Safeguarding: Provide a controlled means by which encrypted data can be decrypted even if the secret key is lost or unavailable. Deploy experimental services to recover merchants' private keys.

◆ Trusted Software Distribution: Provide means for trusted software distribution by allowing a software manufacturer to obtain an electronic certification of authority for its software.

◆ Secure Forms Administration: Demonstrate improvements in work processes involving government program administration and data exchange between a federal agency and private employers using secure Internet-based communications.

Catalog Pilots

◆ Smart Catalog (three pilot catalogs): Demonstrate the efficiencies and added capabilities afforded by making catalogs accessible on the WWW in a form that lets potential customers locate products based on descriptions of their specs. Data in the catalogs to include description of function as well as structure. Catalogs include: Test and Measurement Products, Electronic Components, and PC Products.

◆ Component Catalog Usability: Test, evaluate, and document the implementation of an online catalog of components (connectors).

Small Business/Connectivity Pilots

◆ Corporate Purchasing: Assess qualitative impact that Internet access has on corporate purchasing behavior, and determine obstacles that exist for new corporate users to use the Internet effectively. The pilot targets small businesses and subsidizes ISDN connectivity for participants, as required.

◆ Software Sales and Marketing: Assess qualitative impact of Internet access on software companies' sales, marketing, and software distribution activity. Determine existing obstacles to effective use of the Internet.

Other Pilots

◆ Payment: Explore issues involved in Internet payment systems, with focus on automated, secured, private credit-card transactions.

◆ CommerceNet WHOIS++ Testbed: Incorporate CommerceNet directories into the WHOIS++ Internet Directory Services Testbed.

The CommerceNet Server

The starting point for participation in CommerceNet is the server. CommerceNet's server provides access to all CommerceNet-related information and applications through the World Wide Web

(WWW), such as directories of participants, third-party services, Internet resources, member registration, tutorials, and examples. Information also is available by automated response to E-mail requests.

CommerceNet participants create home pages that are located on each participating company's WWW server. The home page serves as each participating company's storefront on the Internet. Users can reach participants' home pages by name, by a reference hyperlink from the CommerceNet directory pages, or by a document reference elsewhere in the World Wide Web.

Future Directions of CommerceNet

Future technologies under exploration at CommerceNet include intelligent shopping agents that can search through catalogs and negotiate deals; collaboration tools that support real-time interaction and videomail for distributed work teams; natural language search-and-retrieval techniques for large, distributed databases; and format translation services that enable engineering organizations to exchange product data even when they adhere to different standards.

CommerceNet organizers believe that the majority of companies and organizations in the United States may conduct business using the Internet within five years. CommerceNet is a step toward a *de facto* National Information Infrastructure capable of linking up with other electronic commerce projects in places such as Boston, Austin, and the University of Illinois. Potentially, such an infrastructure could support other national efforts in education, health care, and digital libraries.

You can contact CommerceNet at this address:

CommerceNet
800 El Camino Real
Menlo Park, CA 94025
Phone: (415) 617-8790
Fax: (415) 617-1516
E-mail: info@commerce.net
URL: http://www.commerce.net

Internet Society (ISOC)

Dr. Vinton Cerf, the very person who originally conceptualized the Internet and scribbled a design on the back of an envelope in the San Francisco airport, was the Founding President of the Internet Society (Figure 2.9). Larry Landweber is the current President. The Internet Society administers much of the technical standards-making activities of the Internet. The rather well-known Internet Engineering Task Force (IETF) is an affiliate of the Internet Society.

There is a consensus that the Internet would not be what it is today without the foresight and ability of the Internet Society. Perhaps the very openness and friendliness of the Internet is fostered by the processes used by the Internet Society when making technical decisions regarding the Internet. To quote Mr. Anthony Rutkowski, Executive Director of the Internet Society:

Figure 2.9   The Internet Society's home page on the World Wide Web.

The Internet standards development process is by far the best in the business. More than just a standards process, it is a distributed collaboration and innovation engine that has produced a thriving new field of electronic communication and a ten-billion dollar global marketplace growing faster than any communications technology yet devised. Its very uniqueness, however, suggests that it may not be easily applied to existing standards-making organizations and their proceedings.

It's worth examining the attributes of the Internet standards and the associated processes:

Individual participation. From the outset, the Internet standards process was based on individual as opposed to organizational participation. In fact, organizational views are not introduced or discussed. This significantly alters behavior at meetings because it creates an environment that emphasizes substantive issues.

Direct open participation by experts and innovators. Anyone may immediately access all relevant information and standards, or may participate in any Internet standards-making activity. This may be done via the global Internet at no cost, or by attending any of the triennial meetings at nominal cost. These meetings are also multicast live on two audio and video channels to more than 500 sites in nearly 20 countries. This exceptional accessibility has proven a magnet for experts and enthusiastic innovators, who freely share their ideas, expertise, and even their computer code. Many students and low-level researchers—who freely invent, criticize, and produce concepts and products—are also drawn into the activity. Much of the work itself progresses on the Internet—day and night.

Output consists of demonstrated working standards. Before Internet standards reach a certain point, at least two independent implementations must have been completed. This emphasis on working code and demonstrated interoperability is considered central to the process.

Emphasis on meeting real user needs. The use of preliminary interest groups to initiate a standards making activity, combined with participants who actually use the technology and the development of real implementations, produces products that generally meet actual user needs. This occurs predominantly through *bottom-up* rather than *top-down* standards-making.

A well-managed development process. Standards-making is closely followed by Area Chairs and forced to proceed rapidly or face termination.

Minimum institutional ossification. Working groups are created easily and terminated quickly upon completion of their specific tasks. This constant turnover prevents permanent committees, rigid institutional infrastructure, or semipermanent individual roles.

Internet standards must be accepted by both the Internet Engineering Steering Group and the Internet Architecture Board. This peer consensus is reached by people who are intimately familiar with the technology and have one principal motivation—making sure the standard will work. All formal standards actions are published electronically and on paper by the Internet Society—which also takes global international organization responsibility for the standards and peer liaison with other international organizations.

Standards and related materials are universally and instantly accessible and browsable. Internet standards (and frequently the associated code) are distributed and made available instantly on international Internet servers by mail-based and FTP services. Recently, the IETF secretariat has advanced the state of the art in standards making support by providing gopher-based and WWW-Mosaic hypertext browsing capabilities.

Activities are network based. Standards-making on the network also involves rather considerable support requirements. For each Internet Standards meeting, this support includes constructing a rather substantial enterprise Internet, obtaining scores of computers, providing docking stations, and assembling a multicasting facility. However, this allows attendees not only to accomplish their work, but also continue their personal professional endeavors.

Creating the right culture. Having the right institutional ambiance is very important to attract the best and the brightest in computer programming and networking. The right ambiance includes informality, network access, and the presence of a large peer group. Culture is also occasionally troublesome, as programmers and networkers have low thresholds of tolerance controls and influences perceived as unnecessary. Nevertheless, culture is often a critical factor in determining productivity and innovation.

The Internet standards process—although close to an ideal development model—is quite different from most existing standards making bodies. While it might be possible to adopt many of these Internet practices for a new organization, it is quite different to make over existing organizations to assume all of these attributes.

Standards bodies are more often homes for specialized industry or government constituents than they are neutral technological forums. As a result, even purportedly open governmental standards forums are usually effectively closed, with no incentives to admit outsiders. All of these factors limit propagation of the Internet model—even though its adoption would clearly be beneficial.[15]

RSA Data Security, Inc.

Founded in 1982, RSA Data Security is a major source of technology for public key cryptography all over the world (Figure 2.10). RSA's technology is licensed to many vendors seeking to offer data security, including secure online transactions. Licensees include Apple Computer, CyberCash, DigiCash, Digital Equipment Corporation, IBM, Microsoft, the National Aeronautics and Space Administration, Novell, Open Market, Sun Microsystems, and the U.S. Department of Defense.

The technology behind RSA's public key cryptography is discussed in detail in Chapter 3, *Cryptography: Secret Writing.*

Figure 2.10 RSA's home page on the World Wide Web.

You can contact RSA at this address:

RSA Data Security, Inc.
100 Marine Parkway
Redwood City, CA 94065
Phone: (415) 595-8782
Fax: (415) 595-1873
E-mail: info@rsa.com

Government Agencies and Politics

Over the next few years, several governmental agencies will have a major influence on the Internet. It's worthwhile to spend a few pages getting acquainted with these agencies and their potential to influence the online environment.

Again, we quote Mr. Rutkowski of the Internet Society:

> *Perhaps one of the principal roles of government in this envi-
> ronment is simply to follow and understand what is occurring
> both domestically and worldwide. This information can be
> made publicly available and used to enhance another impor-
> tant role—effecting open technology transfer. . . . A great deal
> can be done to encourage more open standards processes
> throughout the world, which will become increasingly impor-
> tant as a robust global marketplace emerges and WTO trade
> rules apply to the information infrastructure.*

Unfortunately, the government is likely to take a much more
active role in regulating the Internet than Mr. Rutkowski proposes.
With the recent passage of the Communications Decency Act by
the U.S. Senate, and ongoing debate throughout the Congress, a
precedent is set that may allow the government to gain control of
a great deal of communication that goes on over the Internet.

National Security Agency (NSA)

The National Security Agency (NSA), sometimes referred to as *No
Such Agency* and *Never Say Anything,* is the official security body
of the United States Government. President Harry Truman created
the NSA in the late 1940s under the Department of Defense, and
for many years even its existence was kept secret. The NSA's job is
to listen in on and decode any foreign communication that relates
to the security of the United States government.

The NSA is vitally concerned with cryptography. Indeed, the
NSA probably possesses cryptography expertise far ahead of the
public state of the art. Although most information about the NSA
is kept classified for security reasons, the NSA is known to be the
largest employer of mathematicians in the world. It also is the
largest purchaser of computer hardware in the world. With all of
this expertise and computing power, it can undoubtedly break
many of the systems used in common practice today.

The NSA works to restrict the availability of cryptographic algorithms, thereby preventing national enemies from using encryp-

tion methods that are too strong for the NSA to break. On the struggle between the NSA and academic or public research in technology, one prominent researcher writes:

> *If one regards cryptology as the prerogative of government, one accepts that most cryptologic research will be conducted behind closed doors. Without doubt, the number of workers engaged today in such secret research in cryptology far exceeds that of those engaged in open research in cryptology. For only about ten years has there been widespread open research in cryptology. There have been and will continue to be conflicts between these two research communities. Open research is a common quest for knowledge that depends for its vitality on the open exchange of ideas via conference presentations and publications in scholarly journals. But can a government agency charged with responsibilities of breaking the ciphers of other nations countenance the publication of a cipher that it cannot break? Can a researcher in good conscience publish such a cipher that might undermine the effectiveness of his own government's code breakers? One might argue that publication of a provably secure cipher would force all governments to behave like Stimson's "gentlemen," but one must be aware that open research in cryptography is fraught with political and ethical considerations of a severity more than in most scientific fields. The wonder is not that some conflicts have occurred between government agencies and open researchers in cryptology, but rather that these conflicts (at least those of which we are aware) have been so few and so mild.*[16]

Consider Mr. Zimmerman and the controversy surrounding the availability of PGP on the Internet. We doubt that it seems like a small conflict to the people involved, and we hope that it is resolved quickly and satisfactorily.

National Institute of Standards and Technology (NIST)

NIST, the National Institute for Standards and Technology, formerly was known as NBS, the National Bureau of Standards, until

1988. NIST is part of the U.S. Department of Commerce. Through its Computer Systems Laboratory (CSL), NIST promotes open standards and interoperability that it hopes will spur the economic development of computer-based industries. To this end, NIST issues standards and guidelines that it hopes will be adopted by all computer systems in the United States. These official standards are called Federal Information Processing Standards (FIPS).

To obtain copies of any NIST publication, you can contact this address:

> National Technical Information Service
> U.S. Department of Commerce
> 5285 Port Royal Road
> Springfield, VA 22161
> Phone: (703) 487-4650

NIST runs a publicly accessible dial-up bulletin board service related to computer security. It can be reached at (301) 948-5717. Settings are (2400 baud, n, 8, 1).[17]

Although NIST officially issues the government's standards for cryptographic functions, it works closely with the NSA, especially where cryptographic algorithms are concerned.

Securities and Exchange Commission (SEC)

As online investing becomes more commonplace, the SEC will undoubtedly begin to regulate stock and other securities transactions online. Currently, the SEC is not regulating online transactions, but a small SEC staff is monitoring exchanges on newsgroups such as *misc.stocks.*

As this book goes to press, discount brokerage houses, such as Fidelity Investments and Charles Schwab, are beginning to implement their online strategies but have not yet fully joined the frenzy. Small investors are enjoying the opportunity to communicate and trade without the presence of large investment firms.

According to a study by Forrester Research, Inc., a consulting firm in Cambridge, Massachusetts, the number of online brokerage accounts is likely to increase from 600,000 to 1.3 million over the next three years.[18]

World Trade Organization (WTO)

The World Trade Organization (WTO) is likely to become involved with the Internet in matters of International commerce. Although existing trade practices are likely to be followed to a first approximation, some new situations will inevitably arise that will require the WTO's involvement. In general, a great many international trade agreements may require modification to address the changing currency systems and jurisdictional difficulties that may appear in the coming world of global electronic commerce.

Human Rights Organizations and Electronic Commerce

Certain organizations deserve special mention for their role in preserving human rights and civil liberties in the new era. We cannot possibly mention them all here or thank them enough. We will start by thanking some of the largest and best known, but we hope our acknowledgment will go out to all who are doing this work.

Electronic Frontier Foundation (EFF)

The Electronic Frontier Foundation was founded in July of 1990 to ensure that the principles embodied in the U.S. Constitution and the Bill of Rights are protected as new communications technologies emerge.

The EFF has worked to shape the United States's communications infrastructure and the policies that govern it, thereby maintaining and enhancing First Amendment rights, privacy rights, and other democratic values. EFF has an overriding public goal of creating Electronic Democracy, so its work focuses on the establishment of:

- ♦ New laws that protect citizens' basic Constitutional rights as they use new communications technologies.

- A policy of common carriage requirements for all network providers so that all speech, no matter how controversial, will be carried without discrimination, and system operators are protected from liability for users' actions.
- An information infrastructure, where voice, data, and video services are accessible to all citizens on a nondiscriminatory basis.
- A diversity of communities that enables all citizens to have a voice in the information age.

EFF sponsors legal cases where users' online civil liberties have been violated. The Steve Jackson Games case, decided in March of 1993, established privacy protections for electronic mail and publications that are kept online.

EFF also is supporting the *Bernstein v. Department of State and NSA* case, which challenges the export restrictions on cryptographic products. These restrictions are a major roadblock on the way to online privacy and secure networks. EFF also submits *amicus* briefs and finds *pro bono* counsel when possible for important legal cases. EFF provides a free telephone line for members of the online community who have questions regarding their legal rights.

You can contact EFF at this address:

The Electronic Frontier Foundation
P.O. Box 170190
San Francisco, CA 94117
Phone: (415) 668-7171
Fax: (415) 668-7007

(510) 548-3290
Mike Godwin, staff counsel, CA

(301) 375-8856
Shari Steele, staff counsel, DC Area

Web: http://www.eff.org
Internet: ask@eff.org

CPSR

Computer Professionals for Social Responsibility (CPSR) is a national organization concerned with the application of technology and its social implications. CPSR tries to represent the public interest in policy debates that usually involve the government and large corporations. For instance, CPSR was involved in representing the public interest where the Challenger disaster was concerned.

As part of its project on Civil Liberties and Computing, CPSR is interested in cryptography. They desire that the development of policy relating to cryptography should be as open as possible to the public; therefore, they seek to obtain information from organizations, such as the NSA and NIST, about cryptographic policy. They have successfully sued NSA and NIST for information about their roles in developing DSA (Digital Signature Algorithm). CPSR also filed suit against the NSA in May 1993, seeking disclosure of documentation about the Clipper chip proposal under the Freedom of Information Act.

You can contact CPSR at this address:

Computer Professionals for Social Responsibility
P.O. Box 717
Palo Alto, CA 94301
Phone: (415) 322-3778
E-mail: cpsr@cpsr.org

Electronic Privacy Information Center (EPIC)

EPIC, the Electronic Privacy Information Center, is a public interest research center in Washington, DC. It was established in 1994 to focus public attention on emerging privacy issues relating to the National Information Infrastructure, such as the Clipper Chip, the Digital Telephony proposal, medical record privacy, and the sale of consumer data. EPIC is sponsored by the Fund for Constitutional Government and Computer Professionals for Social Responsibility. EPIC publishes the EPIC Alert and EPIC Reports, pursues Freedom of Information Act litigation, and conducts policy research on emerging privacy issues. EPIC also works closely with Privacy International, a human rights group, on domestic and international privacy issues.

You can reach EPIC at this address:

Electronic Privacy Information Center (EPIC)
666 Pennsylvania Ave. SE, Suite 301
Washington, DC 20003
Phone: (202) 544-9240
Fax: (202) 547-5482

General E-mail: info@epic.org

FTP: ftp.cpsr.org,/cpsr/privacy/epic/
            ftp.cpsr.org,/cpsr/alert/

Gopher: gopher.cpsr.org, 1/cpsr/privacy/epic/
            gopher.cpsr.org, 1/cpsr/alert

WWW: http://epic.digicash.com/epic
            http://cpsr.org/dox/privacy.html
            http://cpsr.org/cpsr/privacy/epic/
            http://cpsr.org/cpsr/alert/

League for Programming Freedom (LPF)

The League for Programming Freedom is a grassroots organization of businesspeople, students, professors, and others who are dedicated to restoring our personal liberty to write computer programs. For instance, they regard software patents as harmful to the computer industry. Some people among the business community may feel that LPF takes an extreme position, but it seems important to question certain assumptions that we hold, if indeed these assumptions could prove harmful to the industry.

You can reach LPF at: *lpf@uunet.uu.net* or (617) 433-7071.

The Privacy Rights Clearinghouse (PRC)

The Privacy Rights Clearinghouse has a gopher of useful legal and practical information about privacy. You'll find PRC under menu item 4, USD Campus-Wide Information System.

You can also reach PRC at this address:

> The Privacy Rights Clearinghouse
>
> Center for Public Interest Law
>
> 5998 Alcala Park
>
> San Diego, CA 92110
>
> Phone: (619) 260-4806
>
> Fax: (619) 260-4753
>
> E-mail: prc@teetot.acusd.edu
>
> Gopher: gopher.acusd.edu
>
> Hotline: (800) 773-7748 (California only)
>
> (619) 298-3396 (outside California)

Learning and Information Network for Community Telecomputing (LINCT)

The LINCT Coalition is a group of socially concerned not-for-profit organizations and affiliates dedicated to helping communities achieve electronic equity for all community members through the development of local telecomputing networks.

LINCT membership organizations are:

◆ The Center for Information, Technology, & Society, Melrose, MA

◆ The Educational Products Information Exchange (EPIE) Institute, Hampton Bays, NY

◆ Non-Profit Computing, Inc., New York, NY

◆ The Time Dollar Network, Washington, DC

Affiliated organizations:

- The National Urban League
- The Hispanic Federation of New York
- The New York Public Library
- The United Neighborhood Houses of New York
- American Association for the Advancement of Science, SLIC Project (Science Linkages in the Community)

LINCT's mission is to help communities to acquire both the technology and the know-how needed to make cost-effective, community-wide electronic networks accessible to all citizens, but especially to poor and economically marginal families, seniors, and the disabled.

While thinking globally, LINCT's mission is to help communities to act locally by applying a model that begins by assisting local people to establish and manage a not-for-profit, cooperative telecomputing network that is open to all community members.

You can reach LINCT at this address:

Ken Komoski, Director
W. Curtiss Priest, Policy and Systems Coordinator
The LINCT Coalition
The Hamlet Green
Hampton Bays, NY 11946
Voice: (516) 728-9100
Fax: (516) 729-9228
E-mail: KOMOSI@bnlcl6.bnl.gov (Komoski)
         BMSLIB@mitvma.mit.edu (Priest)

chapter three

Cryptography: *Secret Writing* as a Cornerstone of Digital Money

Where in the US Constitution does it say that the federal government has the right to tap your phone?
—*WIRED*, NOVEMBER 1994

Since cryptography is such an important part of making digital money and Internet commerce possible, it's worth taking a chapter to look into it in more detail. This chapter briefly covers the terminology of cryptography; some common cryptographic algorithms, such as DES and RSA; the distinction between public and private key cryptography; and gives some insight into why cryptography is important to Internet commerce.

What Is Encryption?

Throughout this book we talk about encryption. Encryption is the process of disguising a message in such a way as to hide its substance, a process of creating *secret writing*. Encryption is essential to creating a secure environment for digital money; it is essential to creating digital money *per se*.

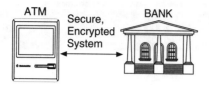

Figure 3.1   Banking transactions use encryption today.

For instance, suppose that a sender, in this case an ATM machine, wanted to send a sensitive message, containing your PIN number, to a second party, your home bank. The ATM machine needs a way to make sure that no one else can affect the message—specifically, that no one could intercept and read the message, intercept and modify the message, or substitute another message. The machine would use encryption to protect the message (Figure 3.1).

The ATM machine *encrypts* its message using a *key*. The key is a set of rules for substituting one character for another, or on a computer, a key can be a special string of characters that is *combined* with the message by multiplying, logical *XOR*, or some other set of mathematical steps (an *algorithm*). By processing the message with the key, it is effectively disguised.

The unencrypted message is called the *plaintext*. Once encrypted, the message is called *ciphertext*. The ATM machine sends the ciphertext of your PIN number and your request for cash to your bank. In fact, encryption is only half the process: Turning ciphertext back into plaintext is called *decryption*. The bank *decrypts* the message containing your PIN number (Figure 3.2).

Encryption and decryption are part of the art and science of keeping messages secure, of creating *secret writing*, which is called *cryptography*. Cryptography is practiced by cryptographers.

The art and science of breaking (deciphering) ciphertext is called *cryptanalysis*, which is practiced by cryptanalysts. The

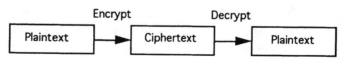

Figure 3.2   Encryption and decryption.

branch of mathematics that embodies cryptography and cryptanalysis is called *cryptology*. Cryptology is practiced by cryptologists, who nearly all are theoretical mathematicians, because ciphers (encryption algorithms) all are based on certain extremely difficult mathematical problems and the underlying number theory.

For many years the discipline of cryptography was conducted behind the closed doors of secretive governmental agencies. But the new popularity of the Internet is bringing cryptography into the public's awareness in new ways. For the first time, state-of-the-art computer cryptography is being practiced outside the walls of governmental and military agencies. It is now possible for businesses and individuals to employ security that can protect even against these agencies themselves (although in some countries it may not be legal, as we will see in Chapter 9).

The Need for Security

During the battle between Boris Yeltsin and the Russian Parliament, with Russian freedom hanging in the balance, software author Philip Zimmerman received an E-mail message from Latvia. It read: "If dictatorship takes over Russia, your PGP is widespread from Baltic to Far East now and will help democratic people if necessary. Thanks."*

PGP stands for Pretty Good Privacy. It's a program Mr. Zimmerman wrote for protecting computer messages. Because it is so secure, PGP has generated a lot of controversy, which we will examine elsewhere in this book.

Does an Internet business really need this kind of security? Absolutely. To gain the trust and loyalty of its customers, a business must be able to guarantee that sensitive personal and financial information about them is not accessible to outside parties. The issues and controversy about personal privacy in our technological age will no doubt increase, and a business must be able to offer its customers a level of privacy commensurate with their needs.

*Wall Street Journal, April 28, 1995.

Five Basic Principles of Encryption

Encryption systems are often referred to as *strong* or *weak*. The strength of an encryption system can be expressed in five basic principles. Any truly secure encryption system must uphold all of these principles:

- Identification
- Authentication
- Nonrepudiation
- Verification
- Privacy

The next few sections discuss each principle in more detail.

Identification

Identification in cryptography is the process of verifying that the sender of a message truly is who they are stated to be. In cryptography, since there is no place for sealing wax and signet rings, identification rests on the notion that some part of the encoded information must positively identify its source. In public key systems, *digital certificates* provide identification: They can prove that Alice is who she says she is. (For more information about digital certificates, please see the section in Chapter 7 called "Certification.")

One of the most common ways to fulfill the need for identification is by requiring a password or a PIN number—traditionally, passwords or PINs are secret pieces of knowledge known only to the individual in question.

So, when Alice steps up to her ATM machine, how does the machine know who she is? Answer: She enters her PIN.

At the risk of digressing, one worry that system administrators used to have is about someone breaking into a machine and stealing a list of passwords. Then a cryptographer realized that the computer doesn't have to know the passwords, only to distinguish valid passwords from invalid passwords. Today, instead of storing passwords, most computers store one-way functions of passwords. The ATM machine's identification process works something like this:

1. Alice enters her PIN.

2. The machine performs a one-way function on her PIN.

3. The host bank's computer compares the result of the one-way function with a stored value.

Stealing the list of one-way function values stored in the bank's computer is useless, because the one-way function cannot be reversed to recover the actual PIN numbers.

Authentication

Authentication is the process of verifying the true sender of a ciphertext and verifying that the text of the message itself has not been altered. In public key systems, authentication requires *digital signatures.* (Identification, in contrast, requires digital certificates, which affirm the credentials of the sender, not just listing his or her *name.*)

To perform authentication, the public key is applied to decrypt a message, which presumably has been encrypted with the private key. If authentication fails, it is impossible to tell whether the sender is illegitimate or the message has been altered. Notice that since the public exponent of a key pair is usually much smaller than the private exponent, authentication is much faster than encryption. Conveniently enough, a document usually is signed only once, but it may be verified many times in the course of Internet commerce.

Digital signatures are self-authenticating; that is, if a single byte of the digitally signed message has been altered, the decryption process will reveal that alteration. How is authentication accomplished? In the RSA protocol, for example, the message is retrieved twice: once from the decrypted digital signature and again by recomputing it directly from the input data. If the two messages don't match, the text has been altered.

(Actually, it is the message digest that's retrieved twice. For more information about the message digest, see the section "MD5," later in this chapter.)

Verification

Verification is the ability to positively identify *and* authenticate a particular encrypted communication. Both must be true before a message can be trusted completely.

Nonrepudiation

Nonrepudiation is the quality of a secure system that prevents anyone from denying that they sent certain files or data, when in fact they did. To achieve non-repudiation requires a fault tolerant communications system. The equivalent in U.S. Postal mail would be to send a letter Certified, Return Receipt Requested. In a networked secret-key authentication system such as Kerberos (which originated at MIT), many keys are stored (and generated!) on a single volume. Kerberos may not provide as much security as some other key management systems, but it does provide for non-repudiation: A user cannot deny that he or she had access to the Kerberos server, because the server keeps a record log of every transaction. (The drawback of Kerberos is that if the server were compromised, the entire system would fall.)

Privacy

Privacy is the ability of a cryptosystem to shield communications from prying eyes effectively.[2] In general, strong cryptosystems (those with longer keys) provide more privacy than weak cryptosystems.

Encryption Today

Traditional cryptography is based on having the sender and the receiver of a message know and use a secret key; the sender uses the secret key to encrypt the message, and the receiver uses the same secret key to decrypt the message. This method is known as *secret-key* cryptography. (For more information about traditional cryptography, please refer to the Appendix, *Classic Cryptography.*)

The main drawback to secret-key cryptography is getting the sender and the receiver to agree on the secret key without anyone else finding it out. If they are in separate physical locations, they must trust a courier, a phone system, or some other transmission system not to disclose the secret key while it's being transferred. For instance, anyone could overhear a secret key while it's in transmission, and later use it to read all message encrypted with that key.

The alternative to secret-key cryptography is called *public-key* cryptography. In this section, we'll compare these two kinds of cryptography, both of which are commonly in use today. Probably the most commonly used encryption methods today are DES and RSA. DES is a secret-key system, and RSA is a public-key system. We'll also specifically examine several other common encryption algorithms that you're likely to encounter in your journeys into Internet commerce.

DES

Data Encryption Standard (DES) has been a worldwide standard for over 15 years, and it has a fascinating history. It has held up to cryptanalysis by the most powerful of adversaries, and probably will continue to do so for a while yet. The security of DES is based not on the secrecy of its encryption algorithm, but on the secrecy of the key used to encrypt a given message. Encryption with DES and related algorithms is known as *secret-key* or *symmetric-key* cryptography, since the same secret key must be used to encrypt and decrypt a message (Figure 3.3).

DES is based on an algorithm developed at IBM in the early 1970s, and its final development was assisted by the NSA. At first, many cryptographers were leery of the NSA's *invisible hand* in

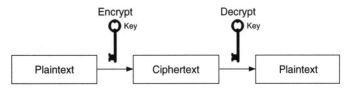

Figure 3.3 DES encryption and decryption use the same (secret) key.

developing the DES algorithm. They were afraid the NSA had installed a trap door, perhaps something like the trap door in the proposed Clipper chip (see the section on Clipper later in this chapter). Nevertheless, after some controversy, DES was adopted as a federal standard by the NBS in November of 1976, authorized for use on all unclassified government communications. DES has twice been readopted as the federal standard, the most recently in 1992.

DES can be used for encryption in several officially defined modes. Some of these modes are more secure than others. The simplest mode, called *electronic codebook* (ECB), simply encrypts 64-bit blocks of plaintext one after another, using the same 56-bit key. *Cipher feedback* (CFB) mode allows code blocks less than 64 bits in length. In *cipher block chaining* (CBC) mode, each 64-bit plaintext block is XORed with the previous ciphertext block before it is encrypted with the 56-bit key. Each 64-bit block depends on the previous block; therefore, the same 64-bit block yields different ciphertext, depending on its location within the message.

In practice, CBC mode is the most widely used mode of DES. It is specified in several DES-related standards. For increased security, one could use triple encryption with CBC mode, but single DES in CBC mode usually is considered sufficiently secure (Table 3.1).

One way DES is being used effectively today is on smart cards, since the DES algorithm was designed to be implemented in hardware. Often, a card will contain DES hardware that does most of

TABLE 3.1 DES Speeds on Different Processors[5]

Processor	Speed in Mhz	Bus Width in Bits	DES Blocks per Second
8088	4.7	8	370
68000	7.6	16	900
80286	6.0	16	1100
68020	16.0	32	3500
68030	16.0	32	3900
80286	25.0	16	5000
68030	50.0	32	9,600
68040	25.0	32	16,000
68040	40.0	32	23,200
80486	33.0	32	40,600

the encryption, alongside RSA hardware for encrypting the key. (See Figure 3.5 in the section called, "Using RSA and DES Together.")

Public Key Cryptography and RSA

In contrast to private-key cryptography, the concept of public-key cryptography is based on the notion that cryptographic keys can come in pairs, and that one key cannot be derived from the other. One key of the pair is used to encrypt a message, the other to decrypt; only that specific key of the pair decrypts a message encrypted by its complementary key. Whitfield Diffie and Martin Hellman first presented this idea in 1976 at the National Computer Conference, and a few months later their seminal paper, "New Directions in Cryptography," appeared in the *IEEE Transactions on Information Theory*. Independently, the concept of public-key cryptography was invented by Ralph Merkle, but due to the slow publishing pace of the *Communications of the ACM*, his contribution was not apparent until 1978. Until recently, the Diffie-Hellman patent was regarded as the basic patent on all of public key cryptography; however, a court case was in process at the end of 1995 attempting to render that patent invalid, in which case Diffie-Merkle will move to the fore.

The primary advantage of public-key cryptography over secret-key (symmetric-key) cryptography is the potential for increased security, since the private half of the key pair need not be transmitted or otherwise revealed to anyone. By contrast, in a private-key system such as DES, there is always the chance that an interloper could discover the secret key while it is in transmission. This whole problem of how to create, store, and transfer keys securely is referred to as *key management*, and it is a topic of ongoing discussion in the cryptographic community.

At the same time public-key cryptography was being invented, DES was under consideration as a standard. Thus arose some partisan political differences within the cryptographic community. Diffie and Hellman criticized DES on the grounds that its key was too small to provide true security, but their criticism was seen as an attempt to disrupt the standards-making process in favor of their own work. Public key cryptography was attacked in sales literature and in technical papers. All the same, the NSA claimed credit for inventing public-key cryptography a decade earlier, although they offered no public evidence to support their claim.

Although many public-key algorithms have been proposed, only a few are both secure and practical. Some have extremely large keys, others generate extremely large ciphertext in comparison to the plaintext they encode. Only two algorithms are suitable both for encryption and for digital signatures: RSA and ElGamal.

All public-key algorithms are slow, usually too slow to support encryption of large data sets, which is called *bulk data encryption.* Of all the public-key algorithms, the easiest to understand and implement is RSA.[6]

RSA

RSA stands for Rivest, Shamir, Adleman, who are the inventors of RSA (Figure 3.4). It was introduced in 1978. RSA is the first full-fledged public-key algorithm, meaning an algorithm that works for encryption as well as for digital signatures. Also, RSA is by far the easiest algorithm to understand and implement of all the public-key algorithms proposed over the years.

Figure 3.4 Drs. Rivest, Shamir, and Adleman, the inventors of RSA. (Courtesy of RSA Security, Inc.)

RSA gains its security from the difficulty of factoring large prime numbers. The public and private keys in RSA are a function of a pair of large prime numbers, of at least 100 to 200 digits. The difficulty of recovering the plaintext from one of the keys is conjectured to be equivalent to factoring the product of the two large primes. How is it done? First we'll give you the summary version, followed by an example to clarify:

For every user who needs a pair of keys, take two large primes, p and q, and find their product n, which is called the modulus. Choose a number e, which is less than n and relatively prime to $(p-1)(q-1)$; that is, it has no factors in common with them. Then find the inverse of e, call it d, mod $(p-1)(q-1)$ such that $ed = 1$ mod $(p-1)(q-1)$. (Euclid's algorithm, a traditional mathematical theorem, can be used to determine d.)

After all these calculations are done, the pair (n,e) becomes the public key, and the private key is d. The two large prime factors p and q must be kept secret or destroyed, since if anyone could factor n into p and q, the private key, d, could be obtained.

Example: Finding a Key Pair

A simplified example may serve to illustrate the key-finding process clearly. Remember that, in actuality, these numbers usually are more than 100 digits long.

To begin, select two (large) prime numbers, p and q. For the sake of example, let $p = 7$ and $q = 13$.

Thus, $p \times q = 91 = n$.

The encryption key, e, must have no factors in common with $(p-1)(q-1)$:

$$(p-1) \times (q-1) = 6 \times 12 = 72$$

Select e at random to be 43. Choose d such that:

$$ed = 1 \bmod 72$$

Using Euclid's algorithm, d is calculated to be 67.[7]

The public key is the pair (n,e), in this case (91, 43); the private key is d, in this case 67. The factors p and q are kept secret or destroyed.

Using the New Key Pair

How would I encrypt a message using my new key? Suppose Bob wants to send me a message, call it m. Bob would use my public key (91, 43) in this way:

Bob creates the ciphertext c by exponentiating: $c = m^{43}$ mod 91. To decrypt the message, I also exponentiate, using my private key: $m = c^{67}$ mod 91. Since I am the only one who knows d, my private key (in this case 67), I am the only one who can decrypt Bob's message.

Using RSA and DES Together

RSA is not an alternative or replacement for DES. It is intended to supplement DES (or any other fast bulk encryption cipher), and it is used together with DES in a secure communications environment. RSA allows for two functions that DES doesn't provide:
1. secure key exchange without prior exchange of secrets, and
2. digital signatures.

Used together, RSA and DES provide a secure *digital envelope* for sending encrypted messages (Figure 3.5). RSA and DES are usually combined as follows: First, the bulk of the message is encrypted with a random DES key. Then, the DES key (which was used to encrypt the message) is encrypted with RSA. The DES-

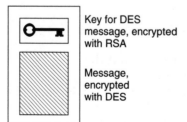

Key for DES message, encrypted with RSA

Message, encrypted with DES

Figure 3.5   A digital envelope.

encrypted message and the RSA-encrypted DES key are sent together as a secure digital envelope.

In some situations, DES alone is sufficient. For instance, if two parties can agree on a DES key in a private meeting, they would not need to exchange a DES key over public communications channels, and they would not need RSA. Also, an individual could use DES without RSA to encrypt personal files just by keeping a personal key or using a personal password as a key.

Because it is fast, DES is well suited for encrypting large sets of data. Its weakness is the requirement to transmit a secret key. In general, public-key cryptography such as RSA is best suited to a multiuser environment, or an environment where digital signatures are required, because it does not require sharing of secret keys. RSA's weakness is that it is about 1,000 times slower than DES. Actually, these two encryption methods complement each other perfectly.

TIP: You probably won't want to use DES by itself over the Internet. Although it is about 1,000 times faster than RSA, DES used alone may not be secure enough in the new environment of Internet commerce, primarily because it requires the sharing of secret keys. Since DES uses the same key for encryption and decryption, everyone who has access to DES-encrypted messages must know the key. Thus, DES-encrypted communication can take place only between individuals who have some prior relationship, be it personal or professional. A key-sharing system like DES works well in a small workgroup or within a federal agency, but it could not provide the same security for large environments like the Internet as a two-key system such as RSA, in which the private key is never revealed to anyone. Try using a *digital envelope*, shown in Figure 3.5.

Whitfield Diffie writes about the wisdom of combining these two methods:

In viewing public-key cryptography as a new form of cryptosystem rather than a new form of key management, I set the stage for criticism on the grounds of both security and performance. Opponents were quick to point out that the RSA system ran about one-thousandth as fast as DES and required keys about ten times as large. Although it had been obvious from the beginning that the use of public-key systems could be limited to exchanging keys for conventional cryptography, it was not immediately clear that this was necessary. In this context, the proposal to build hybrid systems was hailed as a discovery in its own right.[8]

Obtaining a Key

To utilize RSA on a widespread basis, each user would generate his or her own public and private keys, then register them with a certifying authority (CA). (See the section called "Certification of Public Keys," in Chapter 7.) People may have more than one key pair. For instance, someone might have a key for use at work as well as a separate personal key. Entities such as corporate departments, hotel registration desks, or university registrars also are likely to have keys. Electronic entities, such as modems, workstations, and printers, may have their own keys as well.

Some people have expressed concern that if everyone generates a pair of keys, two people could end up with the same key pair; or worse yet, that we might run out of prime numbers, or we may select a large number and have it turn out not to be prime, thus compromising the integrity of our encryption keys.

In fact, there are enough prime numbers that RSA users will never run out of them. For example, the number of primes that are 512 bits or less in length exceeds 10^{150}. That number is larger than the number of atoms in the known universe. And there are probabilistic primality tests with an error factor of less than 2^{-100} that can be performed relatively quickly to help users identify and utilize these prime numbers.

It would be tempting to create a centralized key-generating authority as well as a key certifying authority. However, such a setup would create a tremendous security risk. It would involve transmitting private keys over a network, and it would provide a centralized repository of keys as a target for an attacker. On a network, each node should have the ability to generate keys so that no private keys are ever transmitted over a network and no external key source need be trusted. Smart cards undoubtedly will need to generate keys for their owners. (See the discussion of smart cards in Chapter 4, *Digital Money: The Cuneiform of a New Age.*)[9]

RSA in Hardware

The RSA algorithm currently is available in a number of hardware implementations. Table 3.2 shows a partial list of RSA chips that are available. If nothing else, the table gives a good feel for the variety of hardware technologies available and a list of manufacturers.

RSA in Practice

In practice, as we have seen, RSA often is used in combination with DES. To create what is commonly referred to as digital signatures, RSA also is used in practice with a hashing algorithm (such as MD5, described later in this chapter). This process is illustrated in Figure 3.6.

TABLE 3.2   Partial List of RSA Hardware Available[10]

Company	Speed	Baud Rate per 512 Bits	Clock Cycles to Encrypt 512 Bits	Technology	Bits Per Chip	Transistors
Alpha Tech.	25Mhz	13K	.98M	2 micron	1,024	180,000
AT&T	15Mhz	19K	.4M	1.5 micron	298	100,000
British Telecom	10Mhz	5.1K	1M	2.5 micron	256	NA
Business Sim., Ltd.	5Mhz	3.8K	.67M	Gate array	32	NA
Calmos Sys., Inc.	20Mhz	28K	.36M	2 micron	593	95,000
CNET	25Mhz	5.3K	2.3M	1 micron	1,024	100,000
Cryptech	14Mhz	17K	.4M	Gate array	120	33,000
Cylink	16Mhz	6.8K	1.2M	1.5 micron	1,024	150,000
Pijnenburg	25Mhz	50K	.256M	1 micron	1,024	400,000
Plessy Crypto.	NA	10.2K	NA	NA	512	NA
Sandia	8Mhz	10K	.4M	2 micron	272	86,000

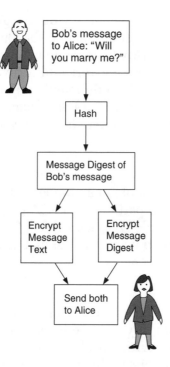

Figure 3.6 A message sent using the RSA encryption process with digital signatures.

The process goes something like this: Suppose Bob wants to send Alice a digitally signed message. First, he uses a hash function on his message to create a *message digest*.

You can think of a message digest as the *fingerprint* of a message; given an adequate hashing algorithm, it is essentially accurate to say that no two messages will have the same message digest. A small change in a message, such as adding or deleting a space, will create a significant change in the message digest.

Then Bob encrypts not only the original message, but also the message digest with his private key. *The encrypted message digest is what we commonly refer to as the digital signature.* He sends the encrypted message along with its encrypted message digest, or digital signature, to Alice.

Alice decrypts the message text using Bob's public key. Then she decrypts the digital signature with Bob's public key to recover the message digest. Finally, she hashes the decrypted message text using the same hashing function that Bob used, and compares the message digest she gets to the message digest she obtained by decrypting Bob's digital signature. If the two message digests match, the message has been verified. Alice can be confident that the message did indeed come from Bob. If the message digests do not match, she can be confident that the message was altered and therefore did not come from Bob (Figure 3.7).

Bob may also have sent along one or more certificates with his message and digital signature. A certificate is a signed document which attests to the identity and the public key of the person who digitally signed the message. Without certificates, Ralph might

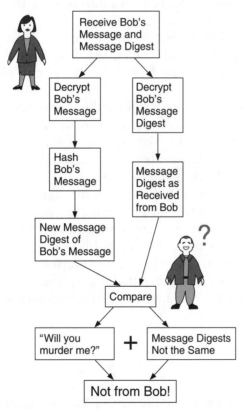

Figure 3.7 Details of RSA decryption process, as used in practice with digital signatures.

impersonate Bob by using a phony key pair. (Cyrano de Bergerac goes digital?)

For more information on Certificates, see Chapter 7, *Electronic Information Exchange.*

RSA and Standards

RSA has become a part of many standards worldwide. For instance, ISO 9796 (from the International Organization for Standardization) cites RSA. So does the International Telecommunication Union (ITU) X.509 digital certificate standard. (The ITU was formerly called the Consultative Committee for International Telegraphy and Telephony, or CCITT.)

RSA has become a *de facto* standard in the financial community. It is included in France's ETEBAC 5 and Australia's AS2805.6.5.3 standards for digital signatures and electronic funds transfer.

The existence of a *de facto* standard is important to the development of Internet commerce, regardless of what official standards may also exist. If one public-key system is available everywhere, then signed digital documents can be exchanged among users in many different nations, using different software on different platforms. It there is an accepted standard for digital signatures, it becomes possible to have, for instance, leases, wills, passports, college transcripts, checks, and voter registrations that exist only in electronic form. A paper version would be a copy of the original electronic document, rather than the other way around.

RSA and DES also provide a major cryptographic engine for another standard, ARPA's Internet Privacy-Enhanced Mail (PEM) standard.

PEM

PEM is the Internet Privacy-Enhanced Mail standard. It has been designed, proposed, and all but adopted by the Internet Activities Board as a means to provide secure electronic mail over the Internet. PEM is designed to work with existing Internet E-mail formats.

PEM includes encryption, authentication, and key management. It allows for use of public-key and private-key encryption systems. PEM supports multiple cryptographic tools, because the specific ciphers (encryption algorithm, digital signature algorithm, and hash function) used in a message are encoded in its header. Currently, PEM explicitly supports DES for message encryption, and both DES and RSA for key management. PEM also supports the use of certificates.

RSA Encryption and Export

The U.S. Department of State considers encryption technology extremely sensitive. It places export restrictions on the shipment of encryption technology overseas. Applications that contain only authentication technology are not restricted, but software that incorporates encryption is heavily regulated and in many cases barred from export. In particular, the DES encryption algorithm is not approved for export outside the United States.

To help alleviate problems caused by these restrictions, RSA Data Security, Inc. has developed two algorithms, RC2 and RC4, that are approved for use in applications for export. RC2 (colloquially known as Ron's Code 2) is suitable as a *drop-in* replacement for the DES algorithm. RC4 (Ron's Code 4) is suitable for real-time encryption applications, such as secure telephony, modem, and link encryption.

If you wish to license RC2 or RC4, you can contact:

Ed Franklin
RSA Data Security, Inc.
10 Twin Dolphin Drive
Redwood City, CA 94065
Phone: (415) 595-8782

Products that implement RC2 or RC4 with a 40-bit key have, by special agreement between the Software Publishers Association (SPA) and the U.S. government, a simplified export approval process. Some of the more cynical cryptographers believe that the

U.S. government would not allow export of any algorithm it could not, at least in theory, break. Rumors in the industry indicate that RC2 and RC4 are also approved for export with 48-bit keys. If true, it would imply that the NSA has sufficient computing power to break such a cipher, which would require 256 computers running in parallel.[11]

Patents and Intellectual Property Rights on Encryption

A U.S. patent lasts only 17 years. After that, the invention covered by the patent becomes part of the public domain. Many patents that were granted on public-key cryptography are about to expire. Some of the most important patents are shown in Table 3.3.

As Table 3.3 shows, Cylink licenses several public-key encryption algorithms, and RSA licenses RSA and its derivatives. If you are interested in licensing any patents on public-key cryptography, you can contact Cylink at this address:

Robert B. Fougner

President

Cylink Corporation

910 Hermosa Court

TABLE 3.3   U.S. Patents on Public-Key Cryptography, Held by Cylink and RSA

Patent #	Granted	Expires	Inventors	Invention Covered	Held By
4,200,700	3-29-80	3-29-97	Hellman, Diffie, Merkle	Diffie-Hellman Key Exchange	Cylink
4,218,582	8-19-80	8-19-97	Hellman, Merkle	Merkle-Hellman Knapsacks	Cylink
4,405,829	9-20-83	9-20-00	Rivest, Shamir, Adleman	RSA	RSA
4,424,414	3-3-84	3-3-01	Hellman, Pohlig	Pohlig-Hellman	Cylink

Sunnyvale, CA 94086

Phone: (408) 735-5893

Fax: (408) 735-6642

E-mail: fougner@cylink.com

RSA is not patented outside the United States, but some other public-key encryption algorithms are.

PKCS

In early 1991, RSA Data Security, Inc., along with other computer organizations and educational institutions formed a consortium to create a standard for certificate-based encryption, called Public Key Cryptography Standards (PKCS).

The members of the PKCS Consortium are:

Apple Computer

Microsoft

Lotus Development

Digital Equipment Corporation

Sun Microsystems

Northern Telecom

Fischer International

Massachusetts Institute of Technology

PKCS is essentially a package of algorithms and extensions to choose from when designing applications. It is compatible with the Internet's Privacy-Enhanced Mail (PEM) specifications. Applications developed using PKCS are certificate-based, secure, interoperable, and platform-independent. PKCS itself is based on OSI, and it meets OSI's X.411 security recommendations.

According to the PKCS standard, every digital signature must point to some certificate that validates the public key of the signer. Specifically, each signature must contain the name of the issuer of the certificate and the serial number of the certificate. Thus, even if no certificates actually are enclosed with a message, the recipient can use the signature to trace the certificate chain and determine the status of the signer's public key. (Please refer to Chapter 7 for more information about certificates.)

Cryptography Standards

Many standards bodies have developed standards in the area of public-key cryptography; ANSI, ITU, Internet PEM, and PKCS are a few of them. As with any emerging technology, public-key cryptography can be applied in various ways. Table 3.4 lists some of the more widely-accepted standards at this writing.

Public Domain Toolkit

At least one public domain developer's toolkit for data security is available on the Internet. RSA Data Security has developed a reference toolkit, called RSAREF, for developers who want to utilize public-key encryption technology. The toolkit is available from RSA using anonymous ftp. Table 3.5 shows the commands and their descriptions. Portions of the commands shown in boldface are typed by the user.

Other Important Algorithms

This section describes some prevalent and important encryption algorithms other than RSA and DES. Throughout the section, a major algorithm or project, such as PGP or Capstone, is described first, then all of its component algorithms or parts are described in accompanying subsections. The projects and algorithms described in these sections have created considerable controversy, and knowing what you now know, you soon will begin to understand why.

PGP

Pretty Good Privacy (PGP) is a public-domain encryption algorithm designed by Philip Zimmerman. It uses IDEA for data

TABLE 3.4   Standards Related to Public-Key Cryptography

Relevant Standard	Area of Coverage	Benefits
ANSI X9.F.1 (Draft)	Certificate management for financial applications	Maintains compatibility with X.509 standard for future financial applications.
ITU X.500	Distinguished names	Standard format for names within certificates.
ITU X.509 (1992)	Digital certificates	Standard format of digital certificates that promotes interoperability among applications.
Internet Privacy-Enhanced Mail (PEM) RFC 1421	Message encryption and authentication procedures	Defines a generic framework for incorporation of encryption and authentication into Internet E-mail.
Internet PEM RFC 1422	Digital certificate-based key management	Defines a supporting key-management architecture and infrastructure based on public-key digital certificates.
Internet PEM RFC 1423	Algorithms, modes, and identifiers	Defines different algorithms that may be used to implement PEM.
Internet PEM RFC 1424	Key certification and related services	Defines procedures and basic services related to key management.
Public-Key Cryptography Standards (PKCS)	Most aspects of public-key cryptography	Most popular public-key cryptography standard among international corporations.

encryption (see the upcoming section called "IDEA"), RSA (with a 512-bit, 1,024-bit, or 1,280-bit key) for key management, and MD5 as a one-way hash function. PGP also compresses files before encrypting them. Messages encrypted with PGP have layered security; the only thing cryptanalysts can learn about the message

TABLE 3.5 Anonymous ftp Commands for Retrieving the RSA Toolkit[12]

Command	Description
%ftp RSA.com Connected to rsa.com 999 chirality FTP server (SunOS 4.1) ready	Connection to the anonymous ftp link.
Name (rsa.com user_name) : **anonymous**	Log in as the anonymous user.
Password : **Your Email Address** 999 Guest login ok, access restrictions apply.	When using anonymous ftp, the convention is to give your E-mail address as a password. (Notice that whatever is typed will not be displayed.)
ftp> **cd rsaref**	At the ftp prompt, change your directory to RSAREF.
ftp> **get README**	Get the README file. It provides further instructions about which files to transfer.
ftp> <get whatever files are of interest to you>	Refer to the README file to see which files are of interest to you. Be sure to read the licensing restrictions and understand them before you use RSAREF. Licensing information is contained in the file license.txt.

is the recipient, provided that they know the recipient's key ID. The recipient himself learns who signed the message, if it is signed, only after decryption.

A unique aspect of PGP is its system of distributed key management. There are no key-certification authorities for PGP. Instead, all users generate and distribute their own public keys. Users can sign one another's public keys, thereby adding confidence about the key's validity. Someone who signs another's public key becomes an introducer for that person. When a PGP user receives a new public key, he examines the list of introducers who have signed it. If any one of the introducers is someone he trusts, he has a good reason to accept the validity of the key. PGP is the closest any individual is likely to get to military-grade encryption.[13]

Precisely because it is so good and it's in the public domain, PGP has stirred up a lot of controversy. Though it may be furthering the cause of freedom in Latvia, PGP encryption also blocked police from reading the computer diary of a convicted pedophile in Sacramento, CA, in 1994.

Because PGP is close to unbreakable, a federal grand jury in San Jose, CA, is examining whether Mr. Zimmerman broke the U.S. laws against exporting encryption codes, which are considered to be munitions. He may be facing a term of between 41 and 51 months in a Federal prison. Mr. Zimmerman was awarded a prestigious Pioneer award by the Electronic Frontier Foundation in April 1995 for his efforts to preserve Americans' privacy rights.[14]

Freeware versions 2.5 and 2.6 of PGP have been released by posting them on a controlled ftp site maintained by MIT. This site has restrictions and controls that have been used at other sites to comply with export restrictions on other encryption software, such as Kerberos and RSA software.

PGP 2.6 currently is available in the United States under the terms of the RSAREF license. It can be freely distributed for non-commercial use. The ftp address is net-dist.mit.edu and the directory is /pub/PGP. Previous versions of PGP also are available in some areas.

You can contact Mr. Zimmerman at this address:

Boulder Software Engineering

3021 Eleventh Street

Boulder, CO 80304

Phone: (303) 541-0140 (10 A.M. until 7 P.M., Mountain Time)

E-mail: prz@acm.org

Meanwhile, in the summer of 1993, Mr. Zimmerman made an exclusive agreement with a company, ViaCrypt, to create a version of PGP that licenses the RSA patent from Public Key Partners. Actually, ViaCrypt already had obtained a patent license from PKP, and they offered a way to help PGP penetrate the commercial, corporate environment.

To obtain ViaCrypt's version of PGP, which is fully licensed in the United States and Canada, you can contact this address:

ViaCrypt
2104 West Peoria Avenue
Phoenix, AZ 85029
Phone: (602) 944-0773
Fax: (602) 943-2601
E-mail: viacrypt@acm.org

ViaCrypt has a version of PGP for MS-DOS and a number of UNIX platforms. Other versions are under development. ViaCrypt has obtained all the necessary licenses from PKP, Ascon-Tech, and Philip Zimmerman to sell PGP for use in commercial or government environments. ViaCrypt PGP is equally secure as the freeware version of PGP, and the two are entirely compatible.[15]

The next few sections describe the individual ciphers used by PGP.

IDEA

IDEA stands for International Data Encryption Algorithm. IDEA is a relatively new cipher, first available in 1992. It may be the most secure block cipher available in the world today.

A block cipher is a cipher that divides the plaintext to be encoded into blocks before encrypting them. IDEA operates on 64-bit blocks. Its key is 128 bits long—over twice as long as the key for DES.

IDEA mixes operations from different algebraic groups. All of the groups it uses are easily implemented in hardware or software. It uses:

- XOR
- Addition modulo 2^{16} (addition that ignores any overflow)
- Multiplication modulo $2^{16} + 1$ (multiplication that ignores any overflow)

IDEA uses the same key for encryption and decryption; it is a private-key algorithm similar to DES. There are a few weak keys for IDEA, but they are unlikely to be generated at random.

The IDEA block cipher is patented in Europe, and it is patent-pending in the United States. The patent is held by Ascom-Tech AG. No license fee is required for noncommercial use of IDEA. Commercial users may contact:

Dr. Dieter Profos

Ascom-Tech AG, Solothurn Lab

Postfach 151

4502 Solothurn, Switzerland

Phone: +41 65 242-885

Fax: +41 65 235-761

MD5

MD5 is a one-way hash function. A hash function is a computation that takes a variable-size input and returns a fixed-size string, called the *hash value.* A one-way function is a function that's significantly easier to perform in the forward direction than in the inverse direction. For example, the forward computation of a one-way function might take minutes, but the inverse computation might take *years.* If a hash function is hard to invert, like MD5, it is also called a *message digest function,* and the result is called a *message digest.*

MD5 is one of several functions commonly used to encrypt messages and passwords. MD2, MD4, and MD5 are like the three bears: too slow to be effective, too fast to guarantee security against attack, and *just right.* MD5 with sample code is available in Internet RFC (Request for Comments) 1321.

Although hash functions have many uses in computer programs, in cryptography they are used to generate a small string, the message digest, that can represent a much larger string securely, such as a file or a message. A hash function for cryptographic use must have certain properties that make it secure:

- ◆ It must be infeasible to find a message that hashes to a given value.
- ◆ It must be infeasible to find two distinct messages that hash to the same value.

If an attacker finds a message (M) that hashes to a given value, he or she can substitute a fake message (M') for one that is already signed. In other words, such an attacker has the ability to violate the nonrepudiation property of digital signatures in general by claiming that he or she actually signed a different message that hashes to the same value.

If an attacker can find two messages that hash to the same value, he or she can trick someone into signing a message that hashes to the same value as a message with quite a different meaning. (Note: This attack is sometimes referred to as the *birthday attack.* Compared to the chances of finding a message that hashes to a given value, the chances are much greater of finding two messages that hash to the same value. It's analogous to the difference between finding someone in a roomful of people who shares *your* birthday, versus finding *any* two people in the room that share a birthday.)

For example, suppose Alice has the ability to find two messages that hash to the same value with Bob's hash function:

1. Alice has two electronic contracts, one that is favorable to Bob and one that takes him for all he is worth.

2. She makes several subtle changes to each document, such as replacing a space with space-backspace-space, adding an extra space before a carriage return, and so forth. Alice can generate 2^{32} different versions of each document by making such changes (or not making them) on 32 different lines.

3. She hashes all these documents and compares their hash values, looking for a matching pair. Mathematically speaking, if Alice had 2^{32} different versions of each document, she probably would find a matching pair if Bob's hashing function outputs 64-bit values.

4. Alice has Bob sign the version of the contract that is favorable to him.

5. Alice substitutes the version that is favorable to her, and she can convince an adjudicator that Bob signed it![16]

To prevent attackers from finding such messages, the hash function must create a message digest that is long enough to prevent the attacker from finding such a pair by exhaustive search. If a hash function produces a 100-bit string, an exhaustive search for any message that hashes to a given value will take approximately 2^{100} attempts. It would take approximately 2^{50} attempts to find two messages that produce the same message digest.

A *strong* hash function usually is considered anything requiring more than 2^{64} operations, which would produce a 128-bit hash value (referred to as a *digest*). For instance, the Secure Hash Standard (SHS) proposed by NIST produces a 160-bit digest. With 2^{64} operations, an attacker could find two messages that hash to the same 128-bit digest under any of the MD functions. That effort is comparable to the effort required to break 512-bit RSA encryption. Thus, the two ciphers MD5 and RSA form a good pair, since neither presents an obvious *weak link*.[17]

Capstone

Capstone is the U.S. Government's long-term project to develop a set of standards for publicly available cryptography, as authorized by the Computer Security Act of 1987. The primary agencies responsible for Capstone are NIST and the NSA.

All parts of Capstone offer cryptographically strong 80-bit security; that is, all the keys involved are 80 bits long, and other aspects are designed to withstand anything less than an 80-bit attack (2^{80}). Eventually, the government plans to place all the Capstone operations onto a single chip, much like the Clipper chip, which is described in the next section.

The Capstone specification covers all the features of the Clipper chip. It also includes specifications for the Digital Signature Algorithm (DSA), a Secure Hashing Algorithm (SHA), a general-purpose exponentiation algorithm, and a general-purpose random number generator that uses a pure noise source. The key exchange protocol has not been announced.

Clipper

Clipper is a topic of great controversy. Clipper is an NSA-designed VLSI chip that uses the Skipjack encryption algorithm, which has not been made public by the NSA. The Clipper chip is designed for the AT&T commercial secure voice products. Each chip is uniquely programmed before being sold to customers. The chip's programming environment writes the following information into a special memory (called VROM or VIA-link) on the chip:

♦ A serial number, unique to the chip
♦ A unit key, unique to the chip
♦ A family key, common to a family of chips
♦ Any specialized control software

Each chip has a special key that is not needed for encrypting messages. The special key is used to encrypt a copy of each user's message key. Anyone who knows the chip's special key can decrypt any communications that are protected by this chip. This decryption feature gives government personnel the ability to conduct electronic surveillance, such as wiretapping, with ease. The claim is that the government alone will know this key, and that they will use it only if authorized by a court. More specifically, government representatives claim that the special key will be split in two and deposited with two *key escrow* databases established by the Attorney General. For more information about key escrow, please see "Key Escrow Issues," later in this chapter.

To prevent anyone from circumventing this scheme, the chip can be programmed not to enter secure mode if the fields have been tampered with. The chip also is resistant to reverse engineering "against a very sophisticated, well-funded adversary."[18]

Skipjack

Skipjack is the encryption algorithm developed by the NSA for use in the Clipper chip. The algorithm is classified Secret, but it is known to be a symmetric algorithm that uses an 80-bit key. For each single encryption or decryption operation, Skipjack processes 32 rounds. The NSA worked on developing and analyzing Skipjack for five years, from 1985 until 1990. In a preliminary report published by several experts from outside the government, who examined Skipjack:

> Under an assumption that the cost of processing power is halved every 18 months, it will be 36 years before the difficulty of breaking Skipjack by exhaustive search will be equal to the difficulty of breaking DES today. Thus, there is no significant risk that Skipjack will be broken by exhaustive search in the next 30–40 years.
>
> There is no significant risk that Skipjack can be broken through a shortcut method of attack, including differential cryptanalysis. There are no weak keys; there is no complementation property. The experts, not having time to evaluate the algorithm to any extent, instead evaluated NSA's own design and evaluation processes.
>
> The strength of Skipjack against a cryptanalytic attack does not depend on the secrecy of the algorithm.[19]

DSA

Digital Signature Algorithm (DSA) is part of the Digital Signature Standard (DSS) proposed by NIST in cooperation with the NSA as part of the Capstone project. DSS has been advocated as the digital signature standard for the United States Government. DSS is used for authentication only.

For the most part, the computer industry has looked upon DSA unfavorably, hoping that the government would adopt RSA as the standard. Criticism of DSS has focused on a few main issues: that it lacks the capability for key exchange, that the underlying cryptosystem is too recent to merit trust in its strength, that verification of signatures with DSS is slow, that vendors have already standardized on RSA, and that the process by which DSS was chosen was too secretive, with too much influence by the NSA.

The most serious criticism of DSS involves its security. Originally, DSS was proposed with a fixed 512-bit key size. After much criticism, NIST revised DSS to allow key sizes up to 1,024 bits.

Also, the algorithm has not yet received much public study. Sometimes serious flaws in a cryptosystem are discovered only after years of scrutiny by cryptographers. RSA has already undergone over 15 years of examination for weaknesses.

In DSS, it is faster to sign a message than to verify a signature; in RSA, verification is faster than signing. NIST claims it is an advantage of DSS that signing is faster; cryptographers say that faster verification is preferred. Government folks sign a lot of documents; cryptographers verify a lot of documents. You say tomato. . . .

Key Escrow Issues

Key escrow is another topic of controversy related to the Capstone project in general and the Clipper chip in particular. Those in favor of escrowed keys see it as a way to provide secure communications for the public at large while permitting law-enforcement agencies to monitor the communications of suspected criminals. Those opposed to escrowed keys see it as an intrusion into the lives of private citizens; they argue that it infringes on their rights of privacy and free speech.

It has not been determined which organizations might serve as key escrow agencies for the Clipper chip keys. Certainly no law enforcement agency would serve as a key escrow agency, to prevent potential conflicts of interest, and it is possible that at least one escrow agency would be an organization outside the government.[20]

Key escrow also is a major area of controversy in relation to escrow of software keys, not just the Clipper chip hardware keys.

The U.S. government currently proposes to allow general use of longer encryption keys on the Internet, provided that the keys are filed with an approved escrow agency and that certain other (difficult) computational requirements are met. In general, the government's key escrow goal is to allow interception and decryption of communications as needed. Another facet of key escrow is the need to store sensitive data securely. One company, Trusted Information Systems, proposes a commercial key escrow system designed to allow long-term storage of sensitive data by keeping the keys safe. In general, for hardware or software keys, the key databases must be kept extremely secure, since they could become targets for break-ins.

chapter four

Digital Money: The Cuneiform of a New Age

. . . and I will give him a white pebble, and on that pebble a new name written which no one knows except the one receiving it.

—Revelation 2:17

What is digital money? Digital money is an electronic replacement for cash. It is storable, transferrable, and unforgeable. It is the cuneiform of a new age. As it is written on the DigiCash home page, digital money is "Numbers that are money."

Using digital money, lobbyist Alice can transfer money to Senator Bob so that newspaper reporter Eve cannot determine who contributed the funds. Bob can deposit Alice's money in his campaign account, even though the bank has no idea who Alice is. But if Alice uses the same piece of digital money to bribe two different members of Congress, the bank can detect that. And if Congressman Bob tries to deposit Alice's contribution into two different accounts, the banks can detect that, too.

What Is Currency?

In trying to understand where digital money is taking us, it helps to create a *conjectural history* of currency, so we gain a better understanding of what currency means to us now. Currency probably began in a primitive barter economy, which is driven by the interest of individuals. For instance, a trader might seek to avoid problems by exchanging his own goods—say, apples—for an easily disposable (salable) intermediary good, such as cowrie shells. After he trades his apples for cowrie shells, he looks to trade with someone who has another item he wants, and who is willing to accept cowrie shells in return. Cowrie shells are a sort of *intermediary good* for the apple trader.

If many other traders decide to accept cowrie shells in return for their goods, cowrie shells are likely to become a generalized *medium of exchange*; a form of currency.[1]

Currency Standards?

In modern societies, gold remained the generalized medium of exchange for centuries. Since gold is heavy to carry, gold coins gradually gave way to paper currency redeemable for gold, then to paper currency not redeemable for gold. Our paper currencies of today are circulated on trust, a trust that has been built by the banking systems over the past three centuries. Today, we feel entirely comfortable with paper money as our standard. Or do we?

Internet commerce is about to push us to the limit on any questions about what makes money worth what it is commonly agreed to be worth. We are confronting questions here that are related not just to the Internet, and not just to digital money. These questions are the new-age cousins of questions people asked when the first coins were struck, when the first paper currency was circulated, and when the first credit cards were offered. Part of the excitement of digital money is that it frames our questions for us in a pure, almost conceptual form: Digital money has no intrinsic value, and the barest trace of physical existence.

It is helpful here to distinguish between the two main functions of money: as a medium of exchange and as a store of value. Digital money is potentially a perfect medium of exchange. Because it can transfer financial claims at incredible speed, because it can create instant settlement of transactions, digital money could help simplify the complex network of interlocking loans and liabilities that characterize modern commerce. For instance, small companies that wait months for their large customers to pay their bills

Figure 4.1 Money as a medium of exchange.

would benefit immensely from a system in which instant payment was the norm.

The most disputed aspects of digital money's future are related mainly to its other role, as a store of value. People like money to have a tangible form, when necessary (Figure 4.1). In times of crisis, what value would their money have if it cannot be exchanged for food, clothing, or shelter? So far, the concept of *legal tender*, or national currency, which in most countries by law cannot be refused as settlement for a debt, has served to alleviate popular concern of this nature. With the acceptability of cash guaranteed by law, most people are happy to leave their money in the bank and settle most of their bills by check or electronic funds transfer. They are confident that they can obtain legal tender (cash) on demand.

What if, to create confidence, every unit of digital money must be guaranteed convertible into legal tender on demand? Then for every unit of digital money, there would have to be a unit of cash reserved in the *real* economy. Or, to look at it the other way, there would be a supply of cash in the real world for which digital proxies are created and made available for purposes of electronic commerce (Figure 4.2). (That is exactly how CyberCash plans to

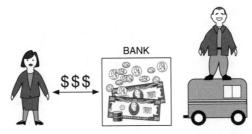

Figure 4.2 Money as a store of value.

operate, since banks working with CyberCash must hold cash converted into digital money in an escrow account.)

This subject is complex and has not yet been worked out among the banks and the proponents of digital money at this writing. However, an expanded discussion of the issues involved is beyond the scope of this book.—D.L.

In that scenario, in an efficient system, if one unit of digital money represents an immobilized unit of *real* money, then positive balances of digital money will earn no interest; that's right, funds converted into digital money will earn no interest, because any interest they might earn would be offset by interest foregone on the real cash that is backing them. It follows that people would keep only small amounts of their assets as digital money in such a system, much like the cash in a wallet or pocketbook. It also follows that there would be no virtual lending in such a system: Such action would increase the stock of digital money without a corresponding increase in the stock of real money, thus undermining convertibility. The new digital money economy would be free of usury at this stage of its development!

General Properties of Payment Systems

Eric Hughes, cofounder of the cypherpunks group and designer of payment systems through his company, Open Financial Networks, offers this helpful characterization of payment systems into a set of mostly independent axes.

The *debit/credit* axis refers to the order in which the intermediary, such as a bank, receives and remits payments from the parties in a transaction. In a credit payment, the bank would remit payment before receiving it. In a debit system, the bank receives funds before they are remitted. Debit systems also are referred to as pre-paid systems.

Continued

The *immediate/delayed* axis refers to the time lag between clearing and settlement. Float and credit cost are important elements along this axis. Also, long settlement times increase risk. Characteristically, two time lags are represented here: payer/intermediary and payee/intermediary.

The *gross/net* axis expresses the relationship between clearing and settlement. In a gross payment system, the relationship is one-to-one; that is, each cleared transaction generates its own settlement action. In a net payment system, multiple transactions are batched together for a single settlement action. Net payment systems have lower operational costs because they perform fewer settlement actions, but they have higher risk because of the unavoidable settlement lag during the accumulation phase of the process.

The *anonymous/identified* axis expresses the degree of identity substantiation or substitution present. Anonymous systems work well for small transactions. Large transactions are inherently riskier; therefore, they require more robust (that is, expensive) proxy services, possibly involving actual identity.

The *fixed/fraction* axis specifies the fee structure of a transaction. Fixed fees generally are used to pay for the infrastructure required for a transaction. Fractional transaction amounts are more appropriate for risk fees and short-term credit fees. Fractional fee percentages generally go down as transaction systems become more efficient and the technology reduces the risk of failure.

Adapted from Eric Hughes, "A Long-Term Perspective on Electronic Commerce," *Release 1.0*, Esther Dyson's Monthly Report, March 31, 1995.

Because banks could not create new money by lending in the digital world, they might see digital money as unproductive. They might charge a fee for converting it, or take an agency fee for issuing it, but competition tends to make this a low-profit activity. Conventional banks might make less from this new business than they lose if customers drift away from traditional services. Banks may not be happy about digital money at first![2]

Banking Systems, Old and New

In the United States and in most European countries today, the government retains the exclusive right to print money. We call our systems *centralized banking* systems. However, we have not always had centralized banking. How, where, and why did centralized banking evolve? Once again, as we look to the future, it helps to examine the past.

History of Central Banking in Britain

Central banking began in Britain in 1694 with the establishment of the Bank of England. The Bank of England, properly known at that time as the Governor and Company of the Bank of England, was established by William III when he needed money to wage war against France but was faced with the embarrassment of a poor credit record because his predecessor, Charles II, had repudiated a debt to the London goldsmiths in 1672.

William III was highly receptive to the suggestion of a Scottish financier, William Paterson, that Paterson and a group of other financiers would advance the government a loan in return for the right to set up a bank to issue loans and print bank notes. Originally, the bank loaned the government 1,200,000 pounds in return for the right to issue notes in the same amount. These amounts were extended in 1697, when it was also stipulated that the bank should enjoy "a monopoly of chartered banking in England and the privilege of limited liability for its shareholders." These were the beginnings of the Bank of England's monopoly on issuing money. The bank's notes were made legal tender in 1812. Gradually, through a series of bank failures (of smaller banks) in the late nineteenth century, the Bank of England accepted the role of lender of last resort and custodian of the nation's monetary system (Figure 4.3).

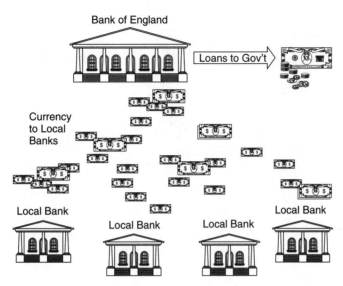

Figure 4.3 Britain's centralized banking model.

Another Historical Banking Model

In contrast to banking in England, banking in Scotland took a different turn. The first Scottish bank was the Bank of Scotland, which received its charter from the Scottish Parliament in 1695. This charter gave it the right to limited liability and a monopoly of note issue in Scotland until 1716. Unlike the charter of the Bank of England, however, the Bank of Scotland's charter prohibited the bank from lending to the government.

Shortly after the Bank of Scotland was founded, the Act of Union in 1707 merged the Scottish and English Parliaments. The new Westminster Parliament was unsympathetic to the Bank of Scotland because of its suspected Jacobite leanings. Parliament therefore ignored the bank's pleas not to charter a rival bank—the Royal Bank of Scotland, which was founded in 1727 (Figure 4.4).

Warfare between the banks broke out on the same day the second bank opened. Each bank tried to drive the other out of business by collecting the other's notes and presenting them for redemption in gold. Although these note duels inflicted considerable damage, it

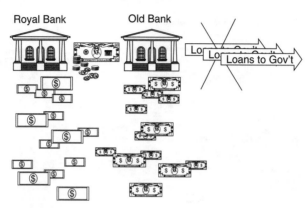

Two Currencies in Circulation

Figure 4.4   Free banking: the Scottish banking system, circa 1727.

became apparent that neither bank was going to put the other out of business. The banks gradually developed a more peaceful note exchange, which led to a formal agreement in 1751.

Their competition led to some other major banking innovations. In 1728, the Royal Bank instituted the cash credit account. This account was a form of overdraft protection that individuals could use if they presented evidence of sound character and two or more co-signatories who accepted liability for the loan. In this way, individuals were able to borrow money without extensive collateral of their own.

In the same year, the Bank of Scotland (the "Old Bank") began offering interest on its deposits. In 1729, it introduced a cash credit account of its own. In 1730, it introduced an option clause to protect itself from sudden demands for redemption.

New banks entered the field until the early 1760s. Each issued its own notes. At first the rivalry was extreme, but an uneasy coexistence prevailed. Each bank followed the Old Bank's practice of inserting option clauses into their bank note contracts to protect their liquidity. (The bank retained the option to redeem the notes at a later date, payable with interest.)

In 1771, all Scottish banks agreed to accept each other's notes at par, and to exchange them at a regular clearing. This agreement helped to promote the demand for each bank's notes, and it contributed to the stability of the banking system because it created an effective check on any bank that sought to overissue its notes. Branch banking also began to be successful in Scotland in the 1770s.[3]

Scottish bank notes were widely accepted, not just in Scotland, but in much of northern England as well. The esteem in which the Scottish bank notes were held is illustrated by this message sent to Parliament by representatives from the border areas of northern England in 1826:

> *The natural consequence has been that Scotch notes have formed the greater part of our circulating medium, a circumstance in which we have reason to rejoice, since, in the course of the last 50 years, with the solitary exception of the Falkirk bank, we have never sustained the slightest loss from one acceptance of Scotch paper; while, in the same period, the failures of banks in the north of England have been unfortunately numerous, and have occasioned the most ruinous losses to many who were little able to sustain them.[4]*

An estimate of all losses from all Scottish banking failures up to 1941 is only £32,000. The losses in London alone for the previous year were reported to be twice that amount.[5]

An Emerging Banking Model for Internet Commerce?

In some respects, the development of digital money for Internet commerce seems to parallel the development of the Scottish banking system (Figure 4.5). Several providers of Internet value transaction services have sprung up, each in competition with the other. Each presents certain advantages to its customers. Will Digi-Cash choose to honor CyberCash's digital money? Will First Virtual honor E-cash? Are these meaningful questions?

William M. Randle, senior vice president of Huntington Bancshares, Inc. in Columbus, Ohio, is crusading to preserve a central role for today's banks in guiding customers into Internet com-

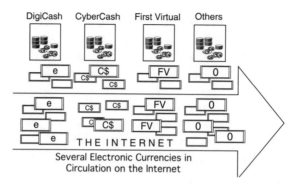

Figure 4.5 Is the Internet commerce model similar to the Scottish banking system?

merce. "Things are happening so fast, there is no way to keep up with it all," he says. "The effect on the banking industry is total confusion. . . . If [we] wait for a clear path to emerge, it will be too late."[6] Banks are eager to begin offering Internet services. With their traditional conservatism, banks may help bring a new level of respectability and credibility to online commerce.

What we'd like is for a system to evolve that's the best for customers: a reliable, rock-solid currency that happens to be digital. What qualities would digital money need to have to gain people's trust?

Guiding Principles of Digital Money

Six properties of an ideal digital money system have been identified:

1. Independence: The security of digital money must not depend on its existence in any singular physical location.
2. Security: Digital money must not be reusable. That is, it must not be possible to spend the same digital money more than once. Thus Alice cannot bribe two different Congressmen with the same piece of digital money.
3. Privacy (Untraceability): Digital money must protect the privacy of its users. It must not, of itself, allow for trac-

ing of the relationship between a person and a purchase. Thus, lobbyist Alice can transfer campaign funds to Congressman Bob and the bank will not know the identity of the contributor.

4. Offline Payment: Merchants who accept digital money must not depend on a connection to a network so that a transaction can be made. Alice could transfer digital money to Congressman Bob simply by plugging in her smart card to his computer; the digital money is independent of the means of transporting it.

5. Transferability: Digital money must be transferable to others. When Alice transfers digital money to Congressman Bob, her identity is completely removed from the money.

6. Divisibility: A quantity of digital money must be divisible into smaller amounts, and they must total up again when recombined. If Alice transfers 100 digital pennies to Congressman Bob, he gets a digital $1.00.[7]

Some of the digital money *dramatis personae* we met in Chapter 2 have created systems that meet most of these requirements. Table 4.1 summarizes the offerings of each of the companies we met in Chapter 2, as they've currently characterized themselves, in terms of these six requirements. On analysis, it seems that some of the groups are not offering a form of true digital money, but an intermediate form of convenient electronic payment. True digital money may be a future stage for them.

The two cryptographers who formulated these six requirements, Tatsuki Okamoto and Kazuo Ohta, also have designed a system that meets all six, but it has not been implemented to date.[7A]

A Basic Digital Money Transaction

Suppose that Alice wants to send Bob some digital money, essentially the digital equivalent of a check. How would that exchange work? Here is a typical digital money transaction:

1. Alice uses her computer to generate a random number worth, say, $10. She chooses to generate a 100-digit

TABLE 4.1   Six Requirements of Digital Money Systems

Company	Independence	Security	Privacy	Offline Payment	Transferability	Divisibility
CheckFree	Yes	Yes	No	Yes, by check	Sort of (EFT)	No, only standard denominations
CyberCash	Yes	Yes	Yes	Yes, on smart cards	Yes	Yes
DigiCash	Yes	Yes	Yes	Yes, on smart cards	Yes	Yes
First Virtual	Yes	Yes	No, it's designed to link them	No, E-mail is required	Somewhat (credit cards aren't transferable; we'll count EFT)	No (possibly yes at InfoHaus)
Open Market	No, only at designated cybermalls	Yes	No	No	Probably, within a cybermall	No
NetBill	Yes	Yes	No	No	No, credit cards only	Yes
Netscape	No, requires Netscape	Yes	No	No	No, credit cards only	No

number to represent her $10, since larger numbers are less likely to be duplicated. (See Chapter 3 for detailed discussion about why larger numbers are needed when creating digital money.)

2. Alice encodes the 100-digit number using her secret key.

3. Alice transmits this encoded number to her bank, along with her digital signature. (See the section called "RSA in Practice" in Chapter 3 for a full explanation of how the message and the digital signature work together through the use of hash functions.)

4. The bank uses Alice's public key to decode the number and the signature, thus verifying that the message is indeed from Alice. The bank removes Alice's digital signature from the number.

Digital Signature Technology

Digital money is possible today because of a cryptographic technology called the *digital signature.* In fact, digital money may be one of the most interesting and esoteric applications of digital signature technology. Certainly it has the potential to change the world.

Digital signatures were first proposed in 1976 by Whitfield Diffie, who was at Stanford University at the time. The work culminated in 1977 with the patent of Diffie-Hellman key exchange. A digital signature guarantees that anyone who reads a digitally signed message can be certain of who sent it. Digital signatures employ a pair of keys: a private key, used to sign messages; and a public key, used to decode them. Only a message signed with the private key can be decoded and verified using the public one. For example, if Alice wanted to send Bob a digitally signed message, she would encode it using her private key. When Bob applies Alice's (previously established) public key, he learns the content of the message. Not only that: By the very fact that he was able to decode it, Bob can rest assured that Alice actually sent the message.

For more detailed technical information about public-key cryptography and digital signatures, please see Chapter 3, *Cryptography: Secret Writing.*

How reliable are digital signatures? Says David Chaum, founder of DigiCash, "The best-known methods for producing forged signatures would require many years, even using computers billions of times faster than those now available."[8]

See also Hellman, Martin E., "The Mathematics of Public-Key Cryptography," *Scientific American,* August 1979.

5. Seeing that Alice has specified an amount of $10, the bank debits Alice's account for $10.

6. The bank signs Alice's number with its private key, denoting that the number is worth $10. (The bank might have a special key for each currency denomination it needs; for example, a worth-one-dollar key, a worth-five-dollars key, and so forth.)

7. The bank sends the digitally signed number back to Alice.

8. Alice sends the number to Bob.

9. Bob verifies the bank's digital signature on Alice's number.

10. Bob sends the number to his bank.

11. Bob's bank uses Alice's bank's key (in the proper $10 denomination) to reverify Alice's number.

12. Bob's bank checks Alice's number against a list of *already spent* numbers.

13. Bob's bank credits Bob's account for $10.

14. Bob's bank add's Alice's number to the *already spent* list.

15. Bob's bank sends him a digitally signed deposit slip for $10.

Notice that since everyone has a receipt to verify the portion of the transaction that is crucial to them, none of the three parties can cheat: Bob cannot deny that he received the money (because Alice can check that her number is on the *spent* list), the bank cannot deny that it issued the money to Alice or accepted it from Bob for deposit, and Alice cannot deny that she withdrew the money from her account, nor can she spend it twice. This system is beautifully secure, but it is not private.

Digital Money and Privacy

What if Alice decides to rent an adult video? Even though the Video Act protects the privacy of video rentals and sales from disclosure by the merchant, if the bank keeps track of the note numbers, it might link the video shop's deposit with Alice's withdrawal.

The Mathematics of Digital Signatures

In the RSA public-key encryption system Alice is using, encryption and decryption are accomplished by raising her 100-digit number (let's call it x) to a power that is the appropriate key.

Alice's exponentiation is done in a modular arithmetic system. It saves only the result, not the remainder, of division by a fixed number, called a *modulus.* (Alice's modulus must be quite large, at least 150 digits.)

When Alice opened her account at the key-making bank (a duly authorized certifying authority), the bank generated two large prime numbers for her: p and q. The product of p and q, pq is now the modulus for all of Alice's exponentiations.

The basis of the two-key system is that:

$$x^{(p-1)(q-1)} = 1 \pmod{pq}$$

(Provided that x is not divisible by p or q, which is a possibility that Alice and the bank can safely ignore.)

Next, the bank chose values e and d such that:

$$ed = 1 \pmod{(p-1)(q-1)}$$

Without looking at it, the bank assigns Alice d, which is her private key. It keeps a record of e, which is Alice's public key. Anything encrypted with d can be decrypted with e, using this formula:

$$(x^d)^e = x \pmod{pq}$$

Alice tells all her friends her public key e and her modulus pq. But she never tells anyone p, q, or her private key, d.

See Chapter 3 for a specific, simplified example of key generation and digital signatures.[9]

An extension of digital signature technology, called blind signatures, restores privacy to transactions made using digital money. When blind signatures are used to create digital money, the *digital bank notes* are untraceable; even if the shop and the bank collude, they cannot determine which notes Alice spent. However, if Alice wishes she can reveal the numbers so that the money can be stopped or traced.

Basically, blind *notes* are used exactly like ordinary digital money, except the number Alice uses is multiplied by a random blinding factor before it is digitally signed; then that factor is divided out at the end. The additional steps show how the transaction between Alice and Bob would change if Alice used blind signatures:

1. Alice uses her computer to generate a random number that represents, again, $10. She chooses to generate a 100-digit number to represent her $10, since larger numbers are less likely to be duplicated.

1a. Alice multiplies her 100-digit number by a random factor.

2. Just as before, Alice encodes her 100-digit number using her private key.

3. Alice transmits the encoded number to her bank.

4. The bank uses Alice's public key to decode Alice's digital signature, thus verifying that the message is indeed from Alice. The bank digitally signs Alice's message, knowing nothing about it except that it carries Alice's digital signature. The bank knows that the message is from Alice, but it doesn't know anything else about it.

5. The bank debits Alice's account for $10.

6. The bank signs Alice's number with its private key, denoting that the number is worth $10.

7. The bank sends the digitally signed number back to Alice.

7a. Alice divides out the blinding factor.

8. Alice sends the number to Bob.

9. Bob verifies the bank's digital signature on Alice's number.

10. Bob sends the number to his bank.

11. Bob's bank uses Alice's bank's key (in the proper $10 denomination) to reverify Alice's number.

12. Bob's bank checks Alice's number against a list of *already spent* numbers.

13. Bob's bank credits Bob's account for $10.

14. Bob's bank add's Alice's number to the *already spent* list.

15. Bob's bank sends him a digitally signed deposit slip for $10.

The Mathematics of Blind Digital Signatures

Here's how Alice creates her blind signature:

1. She chooses a blinding factor r, and she presents her bank with xr^e(mod pq), where x is her original 100-digit number.

2. Alice's bank signs it: $(xr^e)^d = rx^d$ (mod pq).

3. Alice divides out the blinding factor: $(rx^d)/r = x^d$ (mod pq).

4. Alice gives x^d to the video store.

Since r is random, Alice's bank cannot determine x. Therefore, it cannot connect the signing with Alice's payment.

Chapter 3 includes a simplified example of key generation and digital signatures.[10]

Smart Cards

Cryptographic techniques are such that digital signatures can be created with paper and pencil just as easily as with a computer. We assume that Alice and Bob use computers to carry out all of their digital money exchanges a lot more speedily. What might their computers look like? They might be a lot smaller than you'd think.

Smart cards are wallet-size cards, much like credit cards, that contain stored value. Perhaps the best-known smart cards are the telephone cards used in France, where they can be purchased at any newspaper stand. Smart cards sometimes are referred to as PCMCIA cards, because they are designed to fit into PCMCIA slots on portable computers.

Varieties of Smart Cards

Four basic types of microcircuit cards exist for use as smart cards. In historical order, they are:

- *Memory cards* have data storage space and require a password or PIN for access. Most telephone cards, such as those commonly used in France, are of this type.
- *Shared-key cards* store a secret key and can communicate with other cards that share this key. They use standard microcontrollers.
- *Signature-transporting cards* contain a ready-made supply of *blank checks,* which are large pregenerated random numbers that can be assigned a denomination and signed to use as digital money, one *check* at a time.
- *Signature-creating cards* contain a dedicated coprocessor, which makes them capable of generating the large, random numbers (that is, the *blank checks*) to be used as digital money.

Smart Card Hardware and Relative Costs

The simplest of the smart cards, memory cards, are well suited to systems in which there is little incentive for fraud: either because they are closed systems (only a few authorized users) or because the transactions involved are small (as in phone calls). Memory cards are quite inexpensive to produce.

Signature creating cards, the most complex cards, are correspondingly the most expensive cards to produce. They may not in fact be cost-effective, because they provide only an incremental improvement in functionality over the shared-key and signature-transporting types. Also, signature-creating cards tend to be slow in generating signatures (signing takes longer than validating), too slow even for some telephones.

Shared-key cards and signature-transporting cards both are relatively low-cost: about $1.00 to $1.20 to buy the chips in quantity, plus $.50 to $2.00 for assembly and printing of the card. Shared key cards require validation of the secret key at the point of sale, which means there must be a relatively sophisticated piece of equipment at the point of sale.

Since the *blank check* smart cards are loaded in advance and the *checks* need not be reverified, signature-transporting cards do not require point-of-sale validation. Therefore, not only are the cards reasonably priced, the point-of-sale system can be simpler and less costly. These cards also maintain privacy for their users. For all these reasons, the cards that carry *blank checks* currently seem to provide the best all-around solution in terms of low card cost and low system cost, with adequate security and convenience. These cards may prove to be the ones that proliferate in all our pockets and personal data assistants.

The CAFE Project

A number of countries have already announced national prepaid smart card systems that combine public transportation, public telephones, merchants, and vending. Soon it will be possible to pay road tolls in Europe at full highway speed using a handheld radio-controlled device. One example of a project that's making this type of digital money possible is called CAFE (Conditional Access For Europe). Mr. David Chaum, founder of DigiCash, is Chairman of the CAFE project.

The CAFE project is being carried out by a consortium of companies acting together with some leading research organizations on their vision of digital money and electronic payment systems. CAFE also is supported financially by the European Commission (EC). CAFE is developing an electronic wallet, designed as a pan-European device for consumer payments and even for identification. After a trial period, the technology should come to market in

1996. The CAFE project uses smart cards of the type described in the previous section, onto which *blank checks* can be downloaded and stored for later use.

The electronic wallet itself will be a small handheld or pocket-size device, with an infrared interface. Some will be simple, with no more than two buttons; some will have fancy displays and LCD screens (sometimes these devices are called personal digital assistants, or PDAs for short). The wallets will not use proprietary technology, and they are likely to be sold in consumer electronics shops.

Participants in the CAFE Project

Center for Mathematics and Computer Science (CWI), The Netherlands

Aarhaus University, Denmark

Cardware, United Kingdom

Catholic University of Leuven, Belgium

DigiCash, The Netherlands

France Telecom and Post Research (SEPT), France

Gemplus, France

Ingenico, France

Institute for Social Research, Germany

Royal Dutch PTT Research, The Netherlands

Siemens, Germany

SINTEF-DELAB, Norway

University of Hildesheim, Germany

For more information about the CAFE project, you can contact this address:

CWI CAFE, kruislaan 413
1098 SJ Amsterdam

The Netherlands

Phone: +31 (0) 20 592 4049

Fax: +31 (0) 20 592 4199

E-mail: cafe@cwi.nl

France

In a small way, France has had digital money for a long time. At most any newspaper stand you can buy a phone card. The Metro in Paris issues small cardboard coupons with a magnetic stripe—you can't get a ride with a coin.

Even hard currency must adapt to changing times. For instance, there are no more centimes in France. They've been pulled out of circulation because you can't buy anything for a centime any more. In a similar vein, the United States has considered taking pennies out of circulation. Expect more of this, as small transactions probably will be the first ones that people begin to carry out in digital money.

As a proof-of-concept for the usability of smart-card technology in ordinary environments, DigiCash has set up two office buildings in Amsterdam so that the copiers, fax machines, cafeteria cash registers, and even the coffee vending machines accept digital money.

DigiCash also has been working with MasterCard International to develop a smart card that uses DigiCash's underlying technology, integrated into a smart card that conforms to the joint Europay, MasterCard, Visa (EMV) specification. DigiCash has licensed RSA Data Security's RSA encryption technology for the chip. For the project, DigiCash has developed a hardware technology that uses minimal silicon, only 1,000 bytes of EEPROM memory; and that preserves its data in case of power failure or some user errors. This DigiCash chip was demonstrated for the first time in London, February 14–16, 1995. The chip costs less than $1.[11]

Digital Money on Existing Devices

As we've seen, digital money can be stored on or created with several kinds of smart cards. To spend their digital money, Alice and Bob might carry cards in their pockets, they might carry laptop computers or personal digital assistants (PDAs) reminiscent of Dick Tracy's famous watch, or they might be sitting at their home computers, dialed in to the Internet.

Private Money

Digital money raises another fascinating issue: Who has the right to print money? Who ultimately authorizes the digital dollars that go onto our smart cards? Again, it's all a matter of trust. As we discussed earlier in this chapter, banks and governments have gained our trust historically, so now they primarily control the making of money. What if something else becomes a de facto standard? For example, could E-cash become the cowrie shell of the Internet? Remember, money can be anything that's widely valued and accepted. Some digital money might be backed by governments, or, as has long been the case in the international bond markets, certain private issuers might prove to have better names than many governments.

For instance, a nearby car wash distributes coupons through the mail every week offering a full-service wash and wax (a $29.95 value) for $7.50. They're trying to bring in new customers to their car wash, of course. But now, all the car washes in the neighborhood are announcing, "We accept that other car wash's coupons." Isn't it just as if those coupons were money? I can go to any car wash in the neighborhood and get a $29.95 value for $7.50 if I have a coupon.

At the very least, these particular coupons are an interesting, abstract form of barter. One could go a step further: What if people accepted these car-wash coupons in trade for other coupons, or for other services? The coupon-based economy could grow quite large! Still more interesting is the potential for transactions based on microcurrency, pennies, and fractions of pennies, that can enable a worldwide economy based on cottage industry. Anyone could establish an Internet server and use it to sell small products or bits of information at micro-prices.

On the Internet, it could happen that money gets associated with specific places, such as Web pages (WebGuilders); or specific cybermalls, such as the one that Open Market and First Data are trying to create (see Chapter 2, *Dramatis Personae*). Or perhaps currency will come to be associated with specific products that it can buy, much like coupons are today. In other words, digital money creates the new possibility that currency will gradually become specialized and differentiated. There could be many kinds of currency. Yet at the same time a single, global currency becomes feasible.

Digital Money and World Currency

Currently, many world currencies exist: dollars, yen, marks, francs, guilders, lire, sheckels, rupees, pesos, piasters, rubles, punt (Irish money), pounds sterling, yuan (Chinese money), to name a few. How might existing world currencies be affected by the emergence and adoption of digital money?

It is important to realize that digital money has a great potential for bypassing the transaction costs of the foreign-exchange market. If you pay yen for digital dollars in Tokyo, then buy something from a merchant based in Paris, a currency conversion has taken place. Most governments today feel highly defensive about such activity. If digital money started creating its own gray market for settlement of foreign-exchange transactions, the government might begin to clamp down on it.

In the beginning, digital money certainly will be held in equivalents of national currencies: It will be yen in yen out, dollars in dollars out. It will be denominated in familiar units and exchanged at conventional market rates (Figure 4.6), even though there is still the possibility for microtransactions. Eventually, people are likely to want virtual credit, and therefore it must find its price. In that case, digital money will evolve further, toward an overarching monetary system in which convertibility into legal

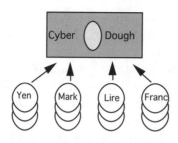

Figure 4.6 At first, digital money is likely to be exchanged at conventional rates.

tender (as we know it) ceases to be a condition. Digital money will become indistinguishable from older, more traditional sorts of money. Money will be money, whether it is a string of digits, a piece of paper, or an entry in a ledger.

As every world currency comes to have an equivalent value in digital money (as with cowrie shells), the natural tendency is to move toward a singular world currency. The ideal form of digital money will be a currency without a country, or of all countries, infinitely exchangeable, without the expense or inconvenience of exchanging among local denominations.[12]

The idea of a single, global currency makes sense when paired with a global information infrastructure that can move digital money around easily. Certainly goods, services, and information have value on a global scale. Information in particular, is a global commodity, is naturally suited to digital means of exchange, and could be priced in a global currency.

Digital money is fast becoming the currency of a new era. In 50 years or so, we probably will feel comfortable relying on the cyber standard, and today's currencies will be in collectors' collections. Paper dollars will be something to show our grandchildren, the way our grandparents once showed us gold coins. As we have seen, digital money may in fact be leading us away from the banking and monetary systems we are most familiar with today. Digital money technology permits people to experiment with trusting each other in new ways. Naturally, all of this will take a while to sort out.

chapter five

New Business Concepts

Remember that time is money.
—BENJAMIN FRANKLIN, *ADVICE TO A YOUNG TRADESMAN,* 1748

Remember that this isn't a hands-on book, so we won't cover the details of setting up an Internet business here. For your convenience, we've compiled a list of Additional Reading at the end of the book, which includes books with specific information about HTML, Web Servers, Internet Marketing, and so forth. What this chapter does provide is general advice about how to succeed in this market, examples of real-life businesses that are operating today on the Internet, and suggestions for potential businesses that could be enabled by Internet technology.

Who Will the Customers Be?

Are Americans ready for the new era of electronic commerce? Research by Checkfree Corporation, MasterCard International, Inc., and other organizations indicates that people are ready for easy-to-use remote banking and commerce services that save time and money.

Three major trends are converging to create this new market: First, Americans are running out of time in their daily lives. A recent study showed that Americans are now working 13 months a year, that's 158 hours per year—four extra weeks—more than the typical worker in 1969. Not only that, more of us are working. Most households today have two wage-earners. Paid time off dropped from an average of 19.8 days in 1981 to an average of 16.1 days in 1989. European workers, by contrast, had paid vacations of at least five weeks.[1]

Second, the technical and financial barriers to remote access banking and commerce are dropping. A study by Anderson Consulting showed that home banking services launched in the early 1980s achieved only limited success, because consumers found personal computers either too intimidating or too expensive. Personal computers are cheaper and easier to use than ever.

Third, whether they realize it or not, Americans today are much more comfortable with remote access and electronic financial transactions than they were a decade ago. Direct deposits, pre-authorized payments and ATM transactions all are forms of remote-access banking.

Internet Commerce May Be Lukewarm in Europe

Some Europeans seem to have a different reaction to Internet commerce. Europeans in general may be far less interested in the glitz of interactive services than their counterparts in the United States. A recent survey of European countries by Inteco Corporation, based in Norwalk, Connecticut, found fewer Europeans are engaging in so-called *precursor behaviors* to Internet commerce, such as video rental, mail-order purchases, ordering tickets by phone, and pizza home delivery.

Consider:

♦ Just 19 percent of consumers in France and Britain say they're "very interested" in video on demand services, compared with 43 percent in the U.S.

♦ While 75 percent of VCR-owning households in the U.S. rent at least one video per month, that number drops to less than 40 percent in Western Europe.

♦ The less gourmet-minded Germans are the most likely to order food for home delivery, but only 2 percent actually do, compared with 45 percent in the United States.

In anecdotal surveys, Europeans say that the rash of multimedia services has little relevance to their lives and lifestyles. Even the most techno-literate are wary about allowing the electronic network into their living rooms. "Are we going to be a society of everybody just staying at home, doing home working, home banking, home shopping?" asks Alexander Heintz, a 30-year-old German businessman who owns a software design company, but who recently decided to get rid of his home personal computer.

On the other hand, Rupert Gavin, director of British Telecom's ICE program, which is the information, communications, and entertainment division that conducted consumer trials in the summer of 1995, responds, "We wouldn't be doing all we're doing if we didn't think there was a genuine consumer interest in this type of service."

The consumers' reactions seem to depend on which specific service they are examining. For instance, in the United States, video on demand is the biggest consumer attraction. But in Europe, the TV schedule already is full of movies that run commercial-free, therefore, video on demand is expected to have a more difficult time there. Instead, analysts expect that home shopping with CD-ROM catalogs, home banking, and other convenience services will do better. Overall, multimedia companies are hoping that services designed to help companies sell their goods and services will get a good reception.

For years, the French have had access to home services through their Minitel phone terminals, and indeed, the French seem most interested in home shopping. In France, 37 percent of consumers regularly use mail-order to buy clothes or footwear—about the same number as in the United States.

At least one German businessman finds the idea of ordering groceries by computer appealing. Store hours in Germany are restrictive, and 32-year-old Marc Breddleman usually comes home from work well after the stores are closed. Are you listening, Peapod?[2]

In spite of Mr. Breddleman's interest, a European Union-wide survey in mid-1995 showed that Germans were among the least multimedia-literate in Europe, with 64 percent saying they weren't familiar with the terms *data highway* or *information soci-*

ety. In fact, when Chancellor Helmut Kohl was asked about the *infobahn* in a television interview during the 1994 campaign, he began talking about highway construction plans until he was interrupted and told what infobahn means.

To raise German awareness and inspire new thinking, Mr. Juergen Ruettgers, Germany's new Minister for the Future, has organized a series of high-level round tables about down-to-earth topics. Topics have included: What will happen to publishers and authors if fully digitized libraries mean that only one copy of a book can supply the world? (Indeed!) What will future universities look like as multimedia and online classrooms make large lecture halls obsolete?

One of the thorniest issues is how *virtual workplaces* will affect Germany's well-entrenched system of strong labor representation and consensus management. If employees work from their computers at home 300 miles away, are they still considered full employees? Do they accrue the same social-security benefits?

Naturally, Germany does not want to be considered a laggard on the Infobahn. Mr. Reutters states, "We have the densest network of fiber optic cables and ISDN connections in the world. . . . We Germans don't get so excited about new things as quickly as Americans do." Mr. Reutters attributes much of the American excitement about the information highway to Vice President Al Gore: "Mr. Gore's approach is fascinating to kick off a new topic; when you want to implement it, it is not enough." Germany plans to take a well-considered approach to its entry of the infobahn.[3]

Differing Social Mores

Social mores in Europe may also contribute to the Europeans' less enthusiastic response to the idea of (their children) obtaining interactive entertainment from the Internet, since it crosses international and cultural boundaries with equal ease. Even some video games are causing a stir. Recently, video game manufacturers have begun providing ratings of their games in terms of suitability for certain age groups. Each country has come up with a different rating scheme based on national cultural preferences. No two countries seem to agree. For instance, even a joint U.S./U.K. ratings standard causes disagreement.

"In terms of the erotic content of the software, we're probably very close to the standards that would apply in the U.S.," says Roger Bennett, managing director of European Leisure Software Publishers Association, Ltd. "But in terms of violence, that wouldn't be the case. It's much more acceptable for people to watch violent scenes in America that would not be acceptable here."

According to some software games officials, the Germans don't enjoy the sight of blood. On the other hand, too much skin is much more likely to offend the British than the French.[4]

Survey in Canada

The second annual Gallup survey indicates that 69.9 percent of Canadians have heard about the info highway, but 61.8 percent fear it represents a threat to Canada's cultural identity and say they want the federal government to assume responsibility for protecting that identity. Three and a half million Canadians, or 11.9 percent of the population, have used the Internet. (*Toronto Globe & Mail,* April 20, 1995, B1.)

That being said, if we wish to create a realm of successful Internet commerce, what may be needed is a deeper understanding of what merchants and customers both want and need to make them feel comfortable doing business online. This section presents an examination of some basic questions that are worth examining again in the context of electronic commerce. In this chapter we'll present some profiles of specific, existing businesses that are facing these questions today.

Question 1: What Does Exchange Really Mean?

When exchanging money, the basic issue involved is trust. If you don't trust the people involved in an exchange (for instance if they are strangers), you certainly need a system that you can trust.

In the real world we have a trustworthy system; let's start by examining its features.

In the real world, commerce takes place within constraints that don't exist in the digital world. Probably the most important of these constraints is about physical location: The real world has real places. So when a customer buys a pair of jeans at Macy's that turn out to be defective, she can return them. Macy's has a clear return policy, a persistent physical presence, and a persistent identity. When the customer returns to the store, she finds clerks she can talk to, maybe the same one who sold her the jeans. And there's a manager who can interpret and enforce Macy's policies in case a dispute arises. The customer knows in general what to expect.

Macy's also exists within a clear legal and social framework. Macy's has relationships it must uphold with other customers, consumer organizations, suppliers, and banks that can serve to validate its credibility and reliability as a store, and to help anchor its presence in physical reality. Should legal action ensue, Macy's can have court judgments enforced against it by the State.

In contrast, Internet commerce today takes place between electronic addresses, physically unlocatable. An electronic address is designed only to route messages for delivery among computers. When an address is fed into a machine, it disappears into the Internet. It is beyond anyone's ability to control or even to know where it actually goes. Later, a message returns from somewhere out there, from places unknown. This part of one's experience of using the Internet is very disassociated and slightly disturbing.[5]

To create the same confidence about Internet purchases that customers have about Macy's purchases, Internet merchants need to establish clear policies that merit their customers' trust. Some issues of trust, such as returns, have been handled quite well by some of today's catalog sales businesses. However, new issues will emerge in the new business medium. Certainly, we'll need new mechanisms for creating a persistent sense of place, for verifying reputations, and for resolving disputes.

So trustworthy Internet commerce requires much more than methodologies for secure payment. It requires ways of checking credentials, building and verifying reputations, and fostering trust among merchants and consumers.

Question 2: What Makes Trust Difficult Online?

In a simple business exchange, trust is fairly easy to define. From a customer's viewpoint, trust usually means that:

♦ I'm getting what I think I'm getting.
♦ I know I can return it if it's damaged.

Another good thing about shopping at a major department store is that I can try on my jeans before I buy them. I know what I'm getting. That creates trust.

From the merchant's point of view, trust also is relatively easy to define:

♦ Will I be paid for my merchandise?
♦ Will I be paid on time?

As a customer over the Internet, it can be difficult to know what I'm getting before I pay for it, and it could prove difficult to return it. In fact, certain kinds of goods and services (things often found on the Internet) are harder to return than others, which complicates the picture of trust.

From the merchant's point of view, it could prove more difficult to check credentials and provide delivery of some salable goods over an international network.

Question 3: What Sells Best Online?

Basically there are three categories of salable goods:
Hard goods: All hard goods are basically returnable. Some are resellable, which is a boon to the merchants. Interestingly enough, hard goods may prove to be the most difficult products to sell in the electronic environment, because they themselves are not fundamentally electronic. There always has to be a separate shipping process. Certain hard goods are regulated by law, such as tobacco and alcoholic beverages.

Services: Services are not returnable. How can I return a shoeshine or a massage, much less a consulting agreement? With regard to inspiring trust in services, service businesses must establish policies for resolving disputes online, perhaps even including online mediation if needed.

Information: It's meaningless to return digital bits. Once I've seen them, they are in some sense mine forever. Information is much more like a service than a product, although people tend to think of it like a product. In spite of its nonreturnability, information may prove to be the easiest thing to sell electronically. Why? It is intrinsically suited to the medium: It is digital. Information can be paid for instantaneously and transferred to the buyer instantaneously, using digital money.

Question 4: Will I Get Paid Reliably Online?

In Internet commerce, the question arises again of exactly when the payment for goods or services should be made. It's possible to transfer the value before, during, or after receiving goods, services, or information. Good questions each merchant should consider in setting up an Internet storefront:

> When do things get paid for?
> When do they get delivered?
> What are ways of unwinding a deal?

Many electronic storefronts offer customers a chance to browse books, articles, and magazines. Sellers worry that the customers will browse but will not buy. However, customers risk losing their browsing privileges if they download from a service too many times without paying—sort of a *de facto* online credit rating system.

One author has had a good experience so far: Bob Rankin, a columnist for *Boardwatch* says: "I decided to put two of my $5 publications on [First Virtual's] InfoHaus server, even though I was concerned about people downloading them and deciding not to pay. Even though I have done practically no publicity, I have been notified by the InfoHaus server that a number of people have downloaded and purchased my information. The really cool thing is that not one person has refused to pay! This beats the heck out of the shareware scene, where a very small percentage of the users actually register and pay the fee."[6]

Question 5: What Other Factors Affect Trust?

Besides the potential for problems with nonpayment and returns, here are a few other important factors that will affect the development of trust in a system of Internet commerce.

Anonymity

Internet merchants may or may not wish to allow anonymous purchases. For instance, anonymous sales of any regulated product, such as alcohol or cigars, probably wouldn't be allowed.

Consumers, on the other hand, may wish to purchase things anonymously. For example, what about downloading adult videos (if indeed adult videos could exist online in the aftermath of the Communications Decency Act)—could it or should it be done anonymously? Anonymity creates value for customers because it retains their privacy, preventing their names from being circulated on unwanted mailing lists, and preventing dossiers from being compiled about their spending habits.

Mistakes Policies

Internet businesses also must learn to deal with lost money problems: If our money is stored digitally, what happens if a disk crashes? How can we arrange to give honest citizens their money back?

Also, people will accidentally spend money twice—not dishonestly, but as honest mistakes. Merchants will need to figure out a policy for dealing with these types of mistakes.

Trust Takes Time to Develop

What will it take to create the same level of trust in Internet transactions that we already have in transactions arranged through our banks? Remember when you got credit card slips? Remember when your mother warned you always to tear your carbons? Now we don't usually get slips. Carbons are a thing of the past. As it was with credit cards, people will want to see how the new system works at first. After a while, they'll get comfortable. If the system works, they'll trust it eventually.

Question 6: Why Bother to Develop Trust in a New System?

For exchange at a distance, we've already worked out a system through the banks involved: check writing. Why not stick with what we've got? Today, checks are the most common way to exchange value at a distance. The problem with checks is that it takes time to get your money. Usually, a merchant who accepts a check gets paid in 3 to 15 days.

(Cash, in contrast to checks, takes no extra time to collect. But cash is good only in person, not at a distance, unless the sender is willing to accept a great risk of pilferage along the way.)

Over the last five years, electronic funds transfer has also become nearly as popular checks as a way of exchanging value at a distance. Again, the trust we have in electronic funds transfer is an outgrowth of the trust we already have in our banks and banking system. But electronic funds transfers cannot be made among private individuals.

The new system has many benefits. It builds on the Internet's properties so that it combines the best aspects of checks and cash: a person-to-person (digital money) transport mechanism. Transactions across the Internet offer speed and assuredness. Specifically, if the customer wants any *bit-oriented* goods, he gets them in a short time, and the merchant need not wait to collect the payment. You might say that the combination of digital money with Internet commerce creates a way of providing for hand-to-hand payments across space in zero time.

Successful Internet Sales

Several online advertising services have begun to offer tips for businesses that want to be successful on the Internet. Hyojong Kim, a director of I . . . PRO, a digital advertising company, stresses that to really understand the effectiveness of online marketing, you must see online sales in terms of these five key components: promotion, one-to-one contact, closing, transaction, and fulfillment.

Promotion

The Internet environment excels at promotion, which consists of advertising and otherwise creating product awareness. On the Internet, an advertiser can post to a server, where the information can potentially be seen by millions of customers.

However, to succeed at online promotion, one must understand that the demographics of the Internet community are not the same as the demographics of an audience that would be reached in print or through other electronic communications media. An advertiser must also come to understand the habits of Net surfers, so that information can be presented in a way that will hold their interest.

With TV and radio advertising, a viewer has a reason to hang around for the commercials: He's waiting for the program. On the Internet, as with print advertising, there's no reason to linger over information that does not hold one's attention. With the click of a mouse, a potential customer can leave an ad site. For these reasons, some advertisers have begun to create interesting environments such as SGI's Silicon Surf, or Zima Clearmalt's Zima.com site.

One-to-One Contact

Unlike a retail store or a telephone sales call, the Internet environment doesn't offer opportunities for *real time* one-to-one communication with customers. In fact, it doesn't even offer the customer an opportunity to examine the products in person or to speak with a sales representative.

What the Internet does offer is an opportunity to create customer relationships by asynchronous means, such as electronic mail. For example, the Internet Shopping Network (ISN) has a salesperson standing by at all times to answer E-mail as soon as it arrives. The goal of one-to-one contact is to create a comfortable place to shop, even if it is in cyberspace.

Closing

Closing a sale is the process of settling on a price and striking a deal. In general, buying on the Internet is a lot like catalog ordering—closing is an activity of the buyer alone. Sales talk designed for this medium has to be effective in an E-mail message, rather than in a phone conversation or in person.

The Internet is an excellent place to take repeat orders, and it has the advantage of easily maintaining a written (electronic) record of the sale.

Transaction

Until recently, few sales could be consummated over the Internet because of lax security measures. As Chapter 2 of this book discusses in detail, several companies now offer secure transaction and digital cash services. Transactions will only get easier.

The ability to create spontaneous transactions is crucial to the Internet sales process. It gives a customer less time to change his mind about a purchase.

Fulfillment

Fulfillment is the delivery of goods. Online delivery can be accomplished most naturally for digital products, such as software and electronic books, although for larger software programs customers still prefer having diskettes or CD-ROMs sent to them along with manuals.

Fulfillment is more than just shipping of goods. Excellent fulfillment involves fast and accurate processing of ordering and billing information. An electronic ordering system, in which the customer enters relevant information, could prove superior to order processing in which a staff takes the customer orders. What is essential is that the necessary information be transmitted to all the relevant parties quickly and accurately.

In a similar vein, Mr. Brian Ek, director of communication for Prodigy, reports that the service now has 30 or 40 merchants, who sell everything from stocks and bonds to discount pantyhose. Mr.

Ek expects that Internet merchants will share the success that Prodigy merchants have begun to enjoy if they keep these four tips in mind:

- Offer a fully representative product line; don't treat the Internet as a liquidation medium.
- Be competitively priced; online shoppers are not willing to pay a premium for convenience.
- Provide excellent fulfillment services.
- Use the online medium to develop better relationships with your customers; use E-mail and keep a full staff.[7]

A Real-Life Example: Virtual Vineyards

One of the first retail businesses to be created using a new Internet business model is Virtual Vineyards, founded by Mr. Robert Olson. As the name implies, Virtual Vineyards sells wine through the Internet (Figure 5.1).

How does an Internet business grow? When Mr. Olson left SGI, he knew he wanted to get into business in the Internet arena, but he didn't know exactly what he wanted to do there. His first thought was to start a software business. "But software is an arms race," he says. Software doesn't hold its value over time, and it's easily copied. So he decided to go into a hard-goods business. These were his criteria for starting Virtual Vineyards:

Well, the first thing is that information had to be crucial to the sale. I believe that most people on the Internet today are infor-

Figure 5.1 Virtual Vineyards' online logo.

*mation professionals. They're trained to be analytical, they like
to make considered choices. The second thing is that it had to
be a business that could hold its margins. Of course in software
the margins are nonexistent. In wine, your price umbrella is
Draeger's [an upscale market in the area]. Also, whatever
you're selling needs to have a distribution problem, so you're
not competing with Safeway. Finally, it had to be something
that I could find an expert about. As it happened, I was talking
to my brother-in-law, Peter [now the sommelier at VV], and he
told me my description fit the high-end wine business perfectly.
The small wholesalers and retailers are getting squeezed out.
These wines aren't carried by the large retailers—a whole vin-
tage might be 5,000 cases. What's that, 100 cases per state? It's
not worth their time or their shelf space.*

The original plan was to use wine as a first product, to keep
finding experts in new businesses and build a group of businesses that share a core engineering team, which is the major cost
factor in setting up a business on the Internet from Mr. Olson's
perspective. But now he believes their company can make it on
the wine and food business they already have. "We're meeting
our plan," he says. "By the way, most people think of the Internet
as a low-cost option. In fact, it's a high-cost option. By the time
we're cash-positive, we'll go through about 1.5 to 2 million dollars. People getting into this area today need to figure out how to
leverage the characteristics of the medium to get 1. volume *and* 2.
premium prices. It's possible to do the Internet inexpensively, but
it usually looks it. To get a quality product, you have to spend the
money. In the future that may change, since there will probably
be a lot of off-the-shelf solutions, which will cut down the labor
costs. But your personality always shows through."

According to Mr. Olson, Virtual Vineyards's thinking about how
to get volume and premium prices went like this: In any business,
there are two possible models. The first model would go something like "we got it all at rock-bottom prices but you'd better
know what you want. The wine industry equivalent of that would
be The Liquor Barn."

The second model is what Mr. Olson calls the *discretionary*
model, in which "we are responsible for the choice you make. We

put Peter's first-person voice on our Web pages, and Peter responds well to that. He thinks about the wines he's recommending—he's got a reputation to uphold. Also, people who like this discretionary model often regard recommending some smoked salmon to go with their Torres Chardonnay as a *value add* to the process. They'll come back because they like what we recommended the first time."

As far as the technical details: Virtual Vineyards runs its own Web server, a Micron Pentium running BSDI UNIX, and NetSite Commerce Server software. Their databases and CGI scripts are homegrown, thus the engineering cost. Their Internet connection is a T1 line. Says Mr. Olson, "It's important to be snappy if you want repeat traffic, much more than being beautiful. It's also good if it's easy to find things when you're there."

Their staff: an operations manager, a source person, two engineers, a designer, and a founder. At that size, their monthly expense rate is about $75 to $80K. Their goal is to maintain a 30-percent gross margin, which means they must generate approximately $250K per month in revenue to break even.

How did Virtual Vineyards come to select CyberCash for its digital cash transactions? It fit their business model best. DigiCash couldn't be considered, because Virtual Vineyards is selling a regulated product and therefore didn't want to offer anonymous transactions. First Virtual "seemed to offer mostly information-oriented, small-sized transactions, and our customers didn't want to spend 10 minutes to transfer $120 dollars from their account over to First Virtual before they could transfer it to us," Mr. Olson says. "Our only problem with CyberCash is that some customers don't want to take time to download and install the CyberCash client software."

How much CyberCash business does Virtual Vineyards do? Mr. Olson concludes: "Probably about ten times the number of cash and credit transactions over CyberCash [digital money] transactions at this point."

Flowers, Anyone?

Bill Tobin's PC Gifts and Flowers shop on Prodigy, an online service with about two million members, rang up over $4 million in sales last year. That's a success. However, Mr. Tobin's World Wide Web site is chalking up only about 200 orders per month, even though it gets 25,000 to 30,000 hits a day. Compare that to 150,000 orders per year he receives through Prodigy. Apparently, there are a lot of browsers on the Web, but few people are buying.

Mr. Tobin won't consider his Web site a success until it generates $10 million or more in sales. To enhance his presence on the Web, Mr. Tobin has developed links with cybermalls, such as MecklerWeb and Open Market, as well as Prodigy, since they recently rolled out their Web browser. He says he pays a 5-percent sales commission to cybermalls or online services that send him business. His strategy? "I'm going to have 150 sites on the Web pointing at us within the next six months. On the Internet, you don't own that right like you do on an airline service."

And that's not all Mr. Tobin is planning to do. To keep his customers coming back, he has created a searchable database that contains "everything they ever wanted to know about roses." Later, he plans to add "communities of interest" about gardening, cooking, sports, and other topics. By the end of the year, he plans to add a virtual guide who meets shoppers at the door and helps them select products and services. (Shades of Peter, the [real] sommelier at Virtual Vineyards!)

Mr. Tobin adds, "A lot of companies are just going on the Web for public relations reasons. Nobody knows where they are, and nobody will ever find them. Unless you have all the pieces of the puzzle, don't go on the Web, because you're just wasting your time."

An analysis of Mr. Tobin's difficulty with the Web? Right now:

◆ It's not easy to find the shops—it's still easier to pick up the phone.

◆ It's hard to comparison shop.

◆ Security is lax.

◆ There aren't a lot of bona fide shoppers; more are browsers and students.

◆ It's not a comfortable place—where are the benches and ice cream shops?[8]

> ### *Voices of Dissent*
>
> Many of the marketers developing commercial sites on the World Wide Web have unrealistic ideas of the costs and benefits of an effective Web site, with at least one merchant expecting to pay $10,000 for an operation that would realistically cost ten times that much. Web enthusiasts are worried by the excessive hype, and one ad agency executive said, "Everybody points to 1-800-Flowers, with 30,000 hits a day and 25 orders. I fear the possibility that people are going to use the medium badly—as they already are—and then the prevailing sentiment will send Web sites to the Old Fad Graveyard to rub shoulders with the CB radio and Nehru jackets."
>
> [Internet Business Report, June 1995, p.1/Edupage 6/18/95.]

Another Example: Peapod, Inc.

Although slightly less cutting-edge than Virtual Vineyards or PC Gifts and Flowers, Peapod is another example of a business dedicated to making it easy for people to shop from home: a grocery delivery service (Figure 5.2). Thousands of items at the local supermarkets have been meticulously entered into a database. Sale items are even marked with an asterisk, and you can sort the selections by unit cost to get the best price.

Once you're online with Peapod, you can roam the aisles electronically, you can search for items generically, as in "potato chips,"

Figure 5.2 Peapod, Inc.'s online logo.

or you can shop by brand name. You're automatically taken to the aisle that holds the item you are searching for. The Peapod software has a number of other user-minded conveniences, like a Personal List feature to let customers keep track of items they buy regularly.

When an order is complete, you send it to Peapod by modem and choose a 90-minute delivery window, usually later the same day. Courteous drivers in bright green polo shirts even carry in your groceries for you! The basic delivery service subscription in the San Francisco Bay Area currently costs $35 per month (by electronic funds transfer), no matter how many deliveries are made per month. Other pricing structures are available as well. Groceries are offered at regular store prices, no special markup.

Peapod circumvents the problem of transferring sensitive information over the Internet by providing a mail-in registration service. Credit card information and other personal information is not transmitted online, and the customer pays the driver directly when the groceries are delivered, either in cash or by authorizing a standard electronic funds transfer. Peapod could be a good candidate for one of the Internet transaction services, once the security kinks are ironed out.

In the Not-Too-Distant Future . . .

Here's a scenario presented by CommerceNet about what life will be like for a small business owner in the new era of Internet Commerce.

Bill owns a small company that designs printed circuit boards. His four-engineer design group is located ten miles outside Boulder Creek in the mountains near Santa Cruz, California. This morning, he checked his Internet mail and found a message from Irene, a design engineering manager at a large computer company in San Jose, California. She asked him to look at a sensitive Request for Quotation (RFQ) she had just posted. The RFQ was open only to three firms, and the message was encrypted in such a way that only those three firms could read it.

After analyzing the RFQ, Bill again used the Internet. He checked the current prices for the integrated circuits (ICs) he would need to build Irene's board. He examined several online catalogs for IC manufacturers, and he made rough estimates of the cost of materials. There was one thing left to deal with: a design issue he didn't quite understand.

Bill queried several engineers at Irene's company, as well as an engineer in Amsterdam he had met at Comdex. The Amsterdam engineer referred him to an article in a back issue of an electronics association journal, which Bill promptly downloaded from the journal's Internet forum.

After lunch, Bill prepared his quotation and sent it to Irene, encrypted. Not only was the bid secret, it was a legally binding offer. Bill mused about how his access to the Internet enabled his company to get jobs that used to go to the big boys on the other side of the hill.

Bill's quotations are extremely accurate; he can always look up the most up-to-date prices and inventories in the online catalogs. His designers are very efficient, because they have access to the latest applications and utilities from colleagues all over the world. And Bill's company cash flow is improved because he sends his invoices and remittances over the Internet.

Irene, at the other end of the electronics food chain, remarks about how using the Internet has helped her company's profitability. The publications group cuts printing costs by putting its data sheets, catalogs, and data books online. Her engineering group takes advantage of the special strengths of different board designers, no matter their location: The other two firms bidding on this RFQ were in Oregon and Taiwan.

The bottom line: For Bill and Irene, the Internet is secure and easy to use. It provides access to services and information around the globe. It is a commercial tool, as fundamental as a spreadsheet or a telephone, that they both use to stay competitive.

Women Online

It has been said that women are the great shoppers of our society. However, men outnumber women online about 2 to 1. Women who are active online have reported feelings of harassment and exclusion, which creates a certain barrier to trust and Internet commerce.

One solution to the problem of getting more women online is to create some sheltered environments where E-women feel secure. Some service providers are doing just that. An example is Women's Wire, which became available on the Microsoft Network when it began operating in August 1995, and also is available on CompuServe.

So far, Women's Wire has not provided Internet shopping services, only E-mail and active online discussion, a virtual water cooler. Of course, Women's Wire women could make use of their E-mail capabilities to go shopping online right now, through First Virtual Holdings, whom we met in Chapter 2, *Dramatis Personae*.

The Future: Possibilities for New Businesses

Electronic commerce opens up a host of possibilities for some altogether new businesses. This section lists a few tantalizing possibilities, categorized according to our three basic business types: Hard Goods, Services, and Information Businesses.

What's also interesting to consider is that any of these businesses can be set up in a bargain-basement or a top-floor fashion, depending on how much you want to spend. Remember what Robert Olson of Virtual Vineyards said: "It's possible to do the Internet inexpensively, but it usually looks it—your personality always shows through."

Hard Goods

Blind Broker: A blind broker buys and sells merchandise over the Internet for parties who wish to remain anonymous. For instance, a company may wish to purchase a large number of specialized computer chips, but such a purchase could reveal too much about its corporate strategy. Using a blind broker, the transaction could be made without revealing too much strategic information.

A variation on the blind broker is an *international broker.*[8A] An international broker provides information about products or materials that may be available overseas, categorized into areas such as semiconductor chips, new consumer products, raw cotton, and so forth. If a company expresses interest in purchasing a quantity of these goods, the international broker helps arrange for international letters of credit to be exchanged between the parties. He makes a commission on the sale.

Service Businesses

Web Architect: A Web architect, either as an employee or as an independent consultant, designs and constructs Web pages for business and personal use. Right now, that job involves using HyperText Markup Language (HTML) to create pages that can be read on the World Wide Web (WWW). The interesting thing about this business in particular is that it's easy to pursue online. A Web architect gives potential clients pointers to Web pages he or she has designed that are currently in use on the Web.

Internet salesperson: Oh, how to be an Internet salesperson without spamming? Answer: This job involves getting people onto the Internet for the first time. (By the way, *spamming* means sending unwanted advertising or sales-related messages simultaneously to large numbers of people on the Internet.) This job might be more difficult to pursue online, since your new customers are offline. But with the growth of the Internet, one way to find new business is to send E-mail to people who have online accounts and ask them for the addresses or phone numbers of those who don't yet. Beware of overusing the MCI "Friends and Family" model, however.

Interactive Actor/Actress: Special talents are required to act out alternative, branching sequences of a story. Interactive actors and actresses will be a special group. An interactive actress would most likely refer potential clients to games or CD-ROMs in which she played one or more feature roles.

New Information Businesses

Information-related businesses are perhaps the most naturally suited to Internet commerce. Almost any information can be represented as a set of bits to be downloaded.

Advertising

Internet commerce creates the potential for huge changes in the techniques of advertising. Advertising is likely to expand in many ways, thereby giving more value to Internet users. Image advertising and fluff advertising probably will not entirely die, but infomercials and hard-fact advertisements are likely to increase dramatically. A large part of what advertising agencies are likely to do in the new era of Internet commerce is provide on-demand information about specific products. As one futurist put it: "Advertisers may become almost *sales counselors*—something of a cross between the Shell Answer Man and Marian the Librarian. They will have to answer tough questions and perform comparison shopping."[9]

Entertainment

Here is a standard example of an opportunity for electronic commerce: Working for a major studio distributor such as Paramount, as a local distributor storing movies on servers for download on demand, and tracking all of that: downloading, payment, billing, and so forth. What counts as a transaction? Whenever a customer buys a digital videotape by downloading it, not necessarily for viewing right away. The model: The Internet is the transport system.

One possibly related model for books: Perhaps it costs no money to download (buy) the book, and you get charged only each time you *read* a page. That amounts to creating a smaller modularity of charging for the information in the book. Journalists doing research for a book or an article might appreciate this model.

Another Idea: A Mailing-List Management Company

Today, a number of companies exist that buy and sell mailing lists. The new model is a bit different: The customer gets a choice about what mailing lists to be on. In the prevailing Internet culture today, interested parties add themselves to special-interest mailing lists. (These lists are not sold, as is common today with offline mailing lists.) This new Internet mailing-list company maintains the list on behalf of companies that make money by selling subscriptions to their list, as to a magazine. The company sends out the "Snowbird update of the week," or what have you, to the mailing list's members. The list management company earns its keep by charging the selling company a small fee (microtransaction) for each message sent, and possibly also by charging the customer a small fee. For the selling company, it's a cost of advertising. For the customer, it's a cheap subscription. Everyone wins.

Other Possibilities

Each of these potential businesses, though primarily based on selling information to customers, has a service component:

Cybrarian: A cybrarian searches the Internet for sources of information on behalf of a customer or client.

Mailing List Manager: A mailing list manager is like the mailing list management company outlined previously, but performing the service within a larger corporation.

Information Brokerage: An information broker sells or resells information, usually to wholesalers such as news services or online services, usually in a *Digest* form. The beauties of an Information Brokerage business are many. Here are two:

- It can be any size: It can be performed as a cottage industry or within a major corporation.
- It has lots of depth: It can involve *mining* the Internet for *raw* information all the way through *refining* and packaging the information for presentation.

An Era of Mass Customization

Something that the preceding examples demonstrate is the ease of getting specialized, personal service over the Internet. An existing example: In May of 1995 the *Wall Street Journal* announced its Personal Journal service. A reader can get selected sections of the *WSJ* and filtered searches for specific keywords daily for $12.95 per month. We are entering the era of Mass Customization, in which almost everyone can get products customized specifically to meet their needs.

chapter six

The Evolving Cyber Economy

"Well, in our country," said Alice, still panting a lit-
tle, "you'd generally get to somewhere else—if you
ran very fast for a long time, as we've been doing."

"A slow sort of country!" said the Queen. "Now, here,
you see, it takes all the running you can do to keep
in the same place. If you want to get somewhere else,
you must run at least twice as fast as that."

—Lewis Carroll, *Alice Through the Looking Glass,* 1872

Classical economics created a zero-sum transaction model for
our global economy. In the new era of Internet commerce, an
information-based economy, old models for transactions no longer
seem to apply.

Let's consider a normal economy. Suppose I have five bushels of
apples. If I sell one bushel to you, I now have four bushels and
you have one. And if my friend Marlene were making applesauce,
she could make only a fixed amount of applesauce from my
apples, somewhat less from four bushels than from five.

In an information economy, suppose I have five facts. I sell one
to you. Now a still have five facts, and you have a new one. The
entire process is additive: My pile has not shrunk, but your pile
has grown. Not only that, given all the facts you knew before,
maybe that new fact is the one that makes you a millionaire.

Unlike bushels of apples, information doesn't come in discrete
units. It multiplies and grows unpredictably. Information is never
depleted, although some of it may become outdated. The value of
the information you have depends on what other information you

have, and the relationships among *piles* of information can be complex.

An entire industry, the so-called information industry, has evolved based on these interesting properties of information, on moving all kinds of information around, and in some cases on selling the same information again and again: From telephones to video tapes, from desktop publishing to MIDI, from Fax machines to CD-ROMs, the information industry has grown. With the widespread availability of Internet commerce, more business opportunities than ever will be arising.

How Do I Adapt?

What steps should companies take to begin adapting to this new information-based economy? Here's some advice from The CyberMedia Group, a consulting firm in Silicon Valley (Cupertino, California):

> Most companies today have a variety of databases that they use to run their business, but most of the databases are disconnected. For instance, marketing's database may not talk to engineering's database. An individual employee may have access to several of these databases, but in general, access is limited. For greater efficiency in this age of self-directed teams and corporate downsizing, it makes sense to give employees access to as much information as possible, even across departments.
>
> First, begin to link your databases together so employees have access to your information in a timely manner. Second, consider using EDI or other standards to connect suppliers and service providers to your database. Such a connection is likely to improve responsiveness, inventory control, and quality control. Third, start setting up interactive links to individual customers or clients. That way, you are enabling direct, interactive sales to consumers.[1]

As Nicholas Negroponte is apocryphally attributed with saying: "The world of bits is a world of abundance." With an understanding of where the economy is likely to grow as a result of Internet commerce, businesses can position themselves to take advantage of this new world of abundance. This chapter can give you a start on the understanding you'll need.

Digital Convergence

In large part, this new arena for business development is fueled by what some have called *the digital convergence*, which is the convergence of telecommunications, computers, media, and consumer electronics industries. The increasing tendency to digitize information is causing a rapid conjoining of many products and services. The five figures in this section graphically illustrate the phenomenon of digital convergence.

These figures depicting digital convergence appear courtesy of The CyberMedia Group. If these figures look familiar to you, it's because you may have seen them in *The New York Times*, *Forbes*, or *The Economist.* They've been widely used and reprinted since they were first developed in 1974, the result of over a decade of work at Harvard's Center for Information Policy Research. These versions were newly updated for 1995.

Figure 6.1 depicts in words the huge array of information products, services, content, and containers that combine to make up the information industry. The vertical axis shows a spectrum ranging from tangible products at the bottom, to intangible services at the top. Thus, hard, tangible items, such as file cabinets, are at the top; and services, such as libraries, appear at the bottom. The horizontal axis suggests a continuum from container to content. It measures information according to its value and what happens to it as it is used or consumed. Specifically:

◆ Items that are merely containers for *storing* information, such as file cabinets and floppy disks, appear at the far left.

Basic Info Industry Map

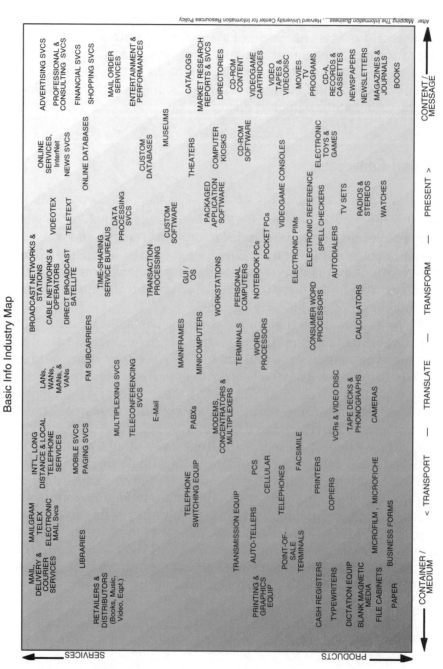

Figure 6.1 Basic information industry map. (Courtesy of The Cybermedia Group.)

- Devices that *transport* information without modifying it, such as telephones and copiers, appear one step to the right.
- Devices that *translate* information from one form into another, such as VCRs and CD players, appear farther to the right.
- Devices that *transform*, *modify*, *manipulate*, or *process* information, such as calculators or computers, appear in the middle of the continuum.
- Devices that *present information*, such as TV sets, appear to the right of the middle. In this area, some value is retained in the quality of the presentation, though the information presented is more important than the container.
- Finally, devices such as newspapers, where the message is by far the primary focus, appear in the far right column of the figure.

As you move from lower left to upper right, notice that the elements become increasingly customized and personalized.

As Figure 6.2 shows, the information industry in the 1970s consisted of seven subindustries that were essentially separate and parochial. Each subindustry was focused inward and concerned with its own growth. Naturally, little or no energy was spent forming alliances among the subindustries.

It is interesting to note that where the industries did overlap, such as in the areas of PBX, modems, teletext, and videotext, they met with little success—precisely because the infrastructure to support them had not yet been developed.

By the end of the 1970s the worldwide market for all the products and services shown in this figure totalled approximately $150 billion.

Figure 6.3 shows that between 1980 and 1990, telecommunications, personal computing, and consumer electronics have experienced tremendous growth and are beginning to intersect. During this period, deregulation and the breakup of AT&T occurs. Telecommunications and consumer electronics begin to encroach on the office equipment industry; everyone seems to be making telephones, answering machines, and so forth.

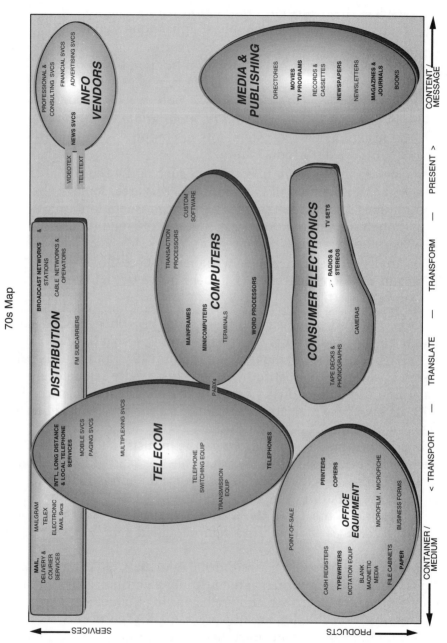

Figure 6.2 The information industry, 1970 to 1980. (Courtesy of The Cybermedia Group.)

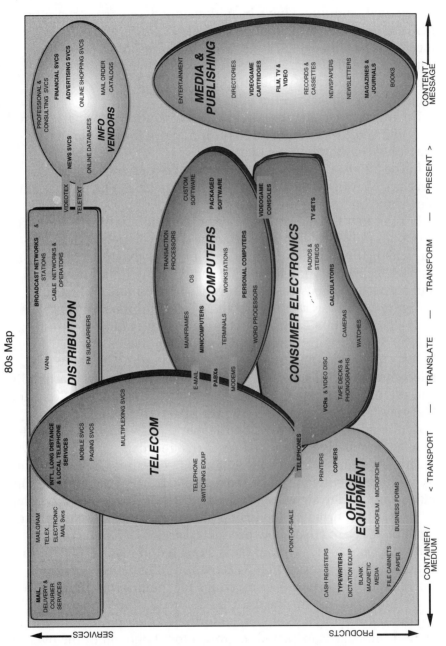

Figure 6.3 The information industry, 1980 to 1990. (Courtesy of The Cybermedia Group.)

Personal computers have been developed and are surpassing mainframes and minicomputers in sales. New devices are arising, most notably videogame consoles, that represent the overlap between personal computers and consumer electronics. Meanwhile, the media and publishing industry is growing without much interactions with the others.

During this decade, the worldwide market for information products and services reaches $500 billion, more than triple in comparison with the previous decade.

In the 1990s, these industries begin to experience significant overlap. New, multifunctional products, such as Fax phones and electronic books, are introduced.

For the first time, a company can take a popular book and turn it into an innovative, interactive novel, encyclopedia, or dictionary, using the miniaturization and low-cost expertise of the consumer electronics industry combined with the microprocessors and software database capabilities of the computer industry.

Figure 6.4 shows clearly that the office equipment industry is losing ground to telecommunications and consumer electronics. Consumer electronics, fueled by new technologies of videogames, VCRs, CD players, and low-end PCs, is extending its reach into telecommunications and the computer business, as well as media and publishing. (For example, recall the acquisitions by Sony and Matsushita of Columbia and MCA, respectively.)

By the mid-1990s the worldwide market has reached $1.5 trillion; again, nearly tripling the previous decade.

The last figure in this series, Figure 6.5, examines how the industry will likely evolve through the year 2001. All of the information industries overlap significantly, and growth is *fusion-powered;* that is, growth is spurred by the fusion of these technologies and their functionalities to create new products, services, and markets.

By the year 2001, this market is expected to reach $4.5 trillion, another tripling. Notice that $4.5 trillion refers to the total, projected, worldwide end-user revenues for the information industry as a whole, not just for the multimedia market, the PDA market, the interactive TV market, and so forth. In other words, the information industry is expected to grow 5 to 10 percent of the overall world market.

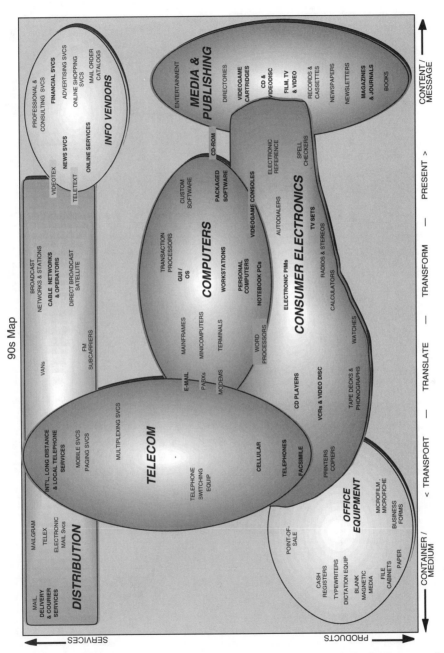

Figure 6.4   The information industry, 1990 to present. (Courtesy of The Cybermedia Group.)

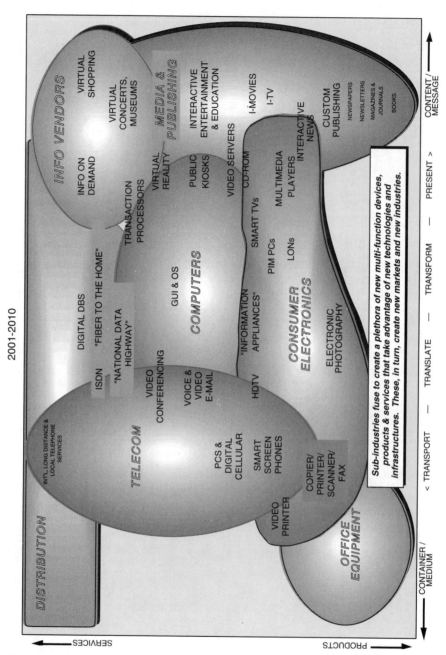

Figure 6.5 The information industry, in the new millenium. (Courtesy of The Cybermedia Group.)

Partly because of the Internet's commercial development, perhaps the biggest opportunities lie in the overlap of the computer industry with all the other industries. Operating systems and interface software will drive the acceptability, usage, and therefore the growth of these technologies. Excellent business opportunities are likely to exist in these areas, which are not mutually exclusive:

◆ Home control and monitoring

◆ Interactive TV, entertainment, and news

◆ New kinds of communication networks, including very local networks

◆ Public information kiosks or systems, including database inquiry systems

◆ The national information infrastructure

TIPS: Key advantages in software will arise through creating products that are modular, scalable, object-oriented, and have multiple platform capability. Key advantages in content will stem from well-known brand names, characters, broad multiplatform product lines, crossover characters from other media, and, as ever, having a good story to tell.

Alliances, joint ventures, and licensing agreements are imperative in the New Era; acquisitions are not as important (despite the recent high-profile acquisitions of ABC by Disney, and CBS by Westinghouse). If you pick a niche and go for it now, early dominance can give your business the skills it needs to transfer to another arena. Nothing beats experience.[2]

Ten Great Myths of the Information Industry

Along the road to experience, everyone makes mistakes. Let's take a few paragraphs to address some common misconceptions about factors that will shape the cyber economy going forward. Here are the myths we'll address:

Myth 1: Soon all information will be digital.

Myth 2: If it's digital, it's interactive.

Myth 3: Digital information is the ultimate form of information.

Myth 4: Selectivity plus choice equals interactivity.

Myth 5: Interactivity is the key to a huge market.

Myth 6: Information at your fingertips is the *killer app.*

Myth 7: Current platforms are too expensive—consumers won't pay more than $500.

Myth 8: Digital convergence means that companies and industries will collide, cannibalizing each other.

Myth 9: Content is king. To win, you must own it.

Myth 10: The *real winners* will be (fill in the blank).[3]

Let's examine and debunk these myths one at a time, with a nod to The Cybermedia Group.

Myth 1: Soon All Information Will Be Digital

Many people find a paper document more permanent, more trustworthy, and more final than its digital counterpart. At present, nothing beats paper for ease of use (no interface to learn), mobility, and readability. Most software engineers still prefer paper documentation to online documentation, since it doesn't take up screen real estate. For many people, paper always will carry more weight than an onscreen display. Someone took the time and spent the money to get that thing printed, after all.

By the way, some people feel that digital money will never entirely replace hard currency for this very reason. We all might like to keep some permanent, hard cash around, just in case.

Myth 2: If It's Digital, It's Interactive

The vast majority of information is digitized primarily for storage or transmission. We digitize things so that our computers can handle them. Today, most digital information is not even readable by humans, much less interactive.

Myth 3: Digital Information Is the Ultimate Form of Information

Consider the quality, reliability, convenience, and low cost of 35mm photographic prints. By comparison, digitizing images is a time-consuming and expensive process. Not only that, if we had analog or holographic optical computers, we probably wouldn't choose to digitize things. Many modern composers, musicians, and audiophiles lament the limitations of digital sound: 4-bit samples, 8-bit samples, 16-bit samples, slow sampling rates, incompatible playback formats—whatever the state of the art, there's something to complain about.

Myth 4: Selectivity Plus Choice Equals Interactivity

If your idea of interactivity is surfing 500 channels of cable, choosing pay-per-view movies, or searching an electronic database, you've set your sights too low. Better examples of interactivity include the ability to change camera angles on a movie scene (adjacent angles carried in a multiplexed manner), provide commentary or feedback to an editor or artist, or interrupt a storyline to get more information.

Myth 5: Interactivity Is the Key to a Huge Market

Although Myth 5 may become a truism in the near future, for the moment it applies only to a small subset of the population of developed countries. Today's Nintendo kids may indeed become the interactive adults of tomorrow. However, people always will need and enjoy the opportunity for passive entertainment.

Myth 6: Information at Your Fingertips Is the *Killer App*

Perhaps partly true, but there's no way to identify a single killer app. In business, E-mail, document preparation, and presentations are primary uses for computers. At home, PCs and video equipment are used for games and edutainment. Interactive TV, smart phones, electronic yellow pages, multimedia online services, and other devices are just as likely to be used for shopping, games, security, and communications as for information services.

Myth 7: Current Platforms Are Too Expensive—Consumers Won't Pay More than $500

Consumers pay for value. Tens of millions of consumers spent between $1,500 and $2,000 on personal computer systems last year. The first TVs, VCRs, CD players, and camcorders cost thousands in adjusted dollars. And the biggest consumer item of all—automobiles—cost $10,000 to $50,000 (or more) each.

Myth 8: Digital Convergence Means that Companies and Industries Will Collide, Cannibalizing Each Other

Digital convergence creates many opportunities for new technologies, products, and services. Companies can look outside their industries for the right expertise, raw materials (mainly content), branding, and distribution. No one company has all the right ingredients for success. Licensing agreements, OEM agreements, and other small alliances can work as well as some of the grand alliances we've seen—maybe better.

Myth 9: Content Is King; to Win, You Must Own It

The first statement is partially true: Content is important. Key content owners can spread their content to different platforms—comics, clothing, videotape, TV, movies, books, whatever comes along. Their challenge is finding new outlets for their content; thus the purchase of ABC by Disney. But the second statement doesn't hold water. Owning content is silly if you aren't already in the content business. Virtually all content is available for licensing, so why spend money to buy it? A lot of content will be generated by customers of services as well: A major part of the *content* of a chat service is just the ability to chat!

Myth 10: The *Real Winners* Will Be (Fill in the Blank)

In fact, cooperation and multiple partnerships will be the key, not competition. Most players will be winners because there will be thousands of networks—local, national, regional, special-interest, expensive, free—all intertwined. They will coexist in all sorts of variations and permutations like these:

Technology: Wired and wireless, switched and broadcast, copper and fiber

User Locations: Office, home, school, car, handheld

Functionality: Shopping, learning, playing, working, socializing

Who will the real winners be? The real winners will be anyone and everyone who watches the confluence of information technologies and responds quickly with innovative products and services. Here is some more advice about ways that business transactions might change for companies entering the New Era.

Stay Ahead of Collapsing Chains

Because it can enable direct sales to customers, online commerce is likely to collapse some existing value chains and distribution chains. It may drastically alter the roles of the people along those chains. One of the most interesting effects may prove to be the elimination of the middleman for many transactions. Who needs a middleman when you can sell directly to the consumer online? The role of the retailer will always be retained, since certain people will always want to look at goods before purchasing, and a low-resolution picture can't take the place of looking and touching. However, the retailer's role may evolve to more of a showroom and order-taker, or a customer service center. There would be no need for the retailer to hold (much) inventory, since products could be shipped directly from the manufacturer upon receipt (and, of course, immediate payment with digital money) of the order.

When linked directly with consumers, companies won't need sophisticated market research in the way we think of it today. What will be needed is a way to track and record every transaction (within the limits of any privacy legislation that may be in effect). The focus of market researchers is likely to shift toward tracking large databases that are updated in real time. In fact, market researchers may need help from automated agents to analyze the large amounts of database information quickly and accurately.

Related to privacy concerns, customers may be willing to grant the kind of information needed for these new databases in return for something of value to them. Generally, if you offer something of value to a customer, they will allow you to gather all kinds of information about their purchases, previous purchases, demographics, and usage preferences. Make it worth their while. For instance, free subscriptions, product guarantees, and discounts all can serve as incentives to your customers.

It will be essential for companies to follow the development of the Internet marketplace, so they can stay ahead of these collapsing value and distribution chains. Look closely at the impact of the new cybereconomy on your business models and business plans.

Growth of Guilds and Cottage Industry

Another interesting effect may be the growth of a new sort of *guild* network. The idea of a guild network is patterned after the guild economy that existed in the middle ages. That economy was structured around craftsmen's guilds, such as blacksmiths or bards; the modern guild economy might be structured along modern professional lines. For example, there might be software engineering guilds. Indeed, the concept of the *Virtual Guild,* whose members are drawn from all over the world, may arise in parallel with the concept of the Virtual Corporation. Anyone who is on an interactive service can become an information provider—through E-mail, chatting, and file transfers, if nothing else. Of course more formal structures for becoming an information provider exist within services such as First Virtual's InfoHaus as well.

Utilizing the Internet, people will extend their reach as information providers far beyond their homes. The little guy will have the capability to run a business as a cottage industry—meeting customers, qualifying customers, and selling to customers, sight unseen.[4] In particular, the ability to perform microtransactions using digital money, selling facts a penny a piece, or reports $1 a page will enable a renaissance of cottage industry in the information age.

It seems clear that digital money will cause a fundamental transformation of our thinking about corporations and work. Even at the level of accounting procedures and transactions, our thinking must evolve to fit the new era.

E-Commerce Transactions and Accounting Costs

In business, the fundamental principle of a transaction has always been: *The cost of performing a transaction must be low relative to the value of that transaction.* However, low is not an agreed-upon word. Here are some examples of *low* transaction costs:

- Today, the U.S. telephone system's cost of accounting amounts to one-third of their total revenue. By system, we mean people and machines that keep the system going. This is a relatively high accounting cost. Why so high? Because their business model is based on accounting for every single call. The consumer's cost of a call averages 30 cents, and of that amount, 10 cents would go toward accounting for the call!
- In contrast, today's credit card world has a 2-percent cost. By the way, of that 2 percent, a large portion goes to offset losses due to fraud. Merchants carry the burden of that 2 percent cost.
- Banks as a whole charge a roughly 2-percent differential for all their work. That means that they pay depositors x percent, while making loans at $x + 2$ percent.
- Grocery stores operate on a very slim profit margin. They get 1.5-percent profit on their total sales volume.

How will Internet commerce affect our thinking about accounting and transactions?

Redefining Transactions

In the realm of Internet commerce, the very concept of a transaction changes. New kinds of transactions can and must be incorporated into our thinking. In businesses today, we can identify three basic categories of transactions, and three sizes of transactions:

◆ Business to business
◆ Business to person
◆ Person to person

These transactions can be classified according to size. The sizes of transactions would be, conveniently enough:

◆ Large
◆ Medium
◆ Small

Large transactions are primarily business-to-business transactions. As Dan says, "No one delivers an airplane without really getting paid." Medium and small transactions can occur in any of the three categories. We can plot these categories together as a chart. Figure 6.6 shows some examples of transactions that fit in each category and size.

In Internet commerce, something interesting occurs: A whole new category of transaction presents itself. You might think of it as the *microtransaction*. Figure 6.7 illustrates the new scope of

Large	Planes	Autos	College tuition
Medium	Parts	TVs	Birthday gift
Small	Office supplies	Sweater	Town board items/garage sales
	Business-Business	Business-Person	Person-Person

Figure 6.6 Kinds of transactions familiar to us today.

transactions that become possible in Internet commerce, using infinitesimally divisible quantities of digital money.

In fact, in a new world of Internet commerce, billing and payment are logically separate but they can be physically the same. This new model of transactions lays the foundation of a new business architecture that blends just-in-time production with in-the-moment payment. One typical example of just-in-time production could be stock quotes, delayed 15 minutes, offered on the network for 10 cents per quote, paid for in-the-moment using digital money.

It probably will take a while before many businesses would feel comfortable performing large (airplane-size) transactions over the Internet. However, smaller transactions already are becoming popular as more companies set up their own Web sites to distribute software or other information-based products, or as consumers make use of services such as First Virtual's InfoHaus to obtain information.

Microtransactions and Costs

Since the new transaction model allows transactions smaller than we've seen before, microtransactions and even *nanotransactions,*

Large	Planes	Autos	College tuition
Medium	Parts	TVs	Birthday gift
Small	Office supplies	Sweater	Town board items/garage sales
Micro	Real-time payment for delivery of numerous small items/components	Web Page Hits Cartoon of the day	Person becomes a microbusiness
	Business-Business	Business-Person	Person-Person

Figure 6.7 Possibilities for Internet transactions.

it's possible that in some cases the cost of processing the transaction may turn out to be larger than the value of the individual transaction itself.

For instance, if you were searching a database interactively and wanted to issue the command, "give me the top 100 winners/records," and you know that the downloading cost is 1 cent per record.

In this case, the cost (in time and resources) of verifying each cent of digital money is higher than the cost of downloading an individual record itself. For these types of transactions, it's cost effective to operate with the principle that the buyer gets a roll of nickels to spend on transferring records. So, instead of spending a penny per record, the server charges a nickel for every five records.

Essentially, this method of charging creates a conceptual model of batch processing (grouping together) the digital pennies to beat the transaction cost. Instead of checking the validity of each penny, it checks every fifth penny. It's as if a customer went to a bank and turned in a roll of nickels. Of course, there's always the possibility that there are some wooden nickels inside the roll. See Chapter 8, *The New Wooden Nickel,* for more discussion about fraud and counterfeiting in the new era.

Preferential Transactions

Today, we think of preferential transactions in terms of rush services, like overnight mail, or improved quality of service, as when shopping in a boutique. We expect to pay a little more for better service. Because digital money creates the possibility of micro-transactions and even nanotransactions (currency is much more liquid), the fascinating possibility exists for adding just a little bit to every transaction to improve the quality of service obtained. For example, online response time might be improved 20 to 30 percent per second for a couple of extra nanocents.

In old movies, the rich gentleman with *savoir faire* slipped the Maitre D'Hotel a tip when he wanted a better table. Now we can talk meaningfully about *Maitre D' nanoslips.* If you're willing and able to pay, you can buy better service, moment by moment. A new class of service may be available for purchase every millisecond.

For instance, a small company in Los Altos, California, called Agorics, Inc., is developing a technology that uses a marketplace metaphor for parceling out system services. *Agora* was the ancient Greek word for marketplace. In the Agorics system, system resources such as CPU cycles and memory space are bought and sold as commodities on an open market by concurrently executing processes. Each process has a *budget* for getting its task done and must bid for services. If several processes require a lot of CPU time, the price of CPU cycles goes up. If a process can trade off CPU time for memory space, it's likely to get a better deal. If a process is willing and able to pay, it can get a higher quality of service by outbidding its counterparts.[5]

Using technology like that of Agorics, a customer could obtain higher-quality service, say, for downloading a digital video, if he were willing to pay for it. Or a vendor could utilize Agorics's technology to guarantee its customers the highest quality service.

In the case of real-time video, if this agoric facility is used to speed up downloading of pay-per-view movies from cable servers, customers can benefit in another way: Cheaper boxes in homes could work just as well as more expensive ones.

In general for Internet commerce, the marketplace metaphor holds: Prices can change as often as needed to match demand. One particular form of the marketplace metaphor is already working for Jem Computers, a liquidator of excess computer inventories. Prices at Jem drop as goods remain unsold, but bargain hunters may miss out if they wait too long. By the way, Jem sells its inventory through Open Market, Inc. (Open Market is described in Chapter 2, *Dramatis Personae*.)[6]

Pricing an Internet Transaction

The question arises: What is a fair cost, or a recommended percentage cost, for an Internet transaction? In other words, what is a fair profit for an Internet-based company to make from each transaction? Certainly it helps to consider the relative cost of the transaction compared to the absolute cost of creating the product when determining a fair transaction cost.

At some level, a company's profit is just the sum total of the price it charges to conduct each transaction. So how can a company become profitable in the world of Internet value exchange? For lack of a well-understood strategy in this new arena, let's look at a specific example and see what relevant questions emerge.

The Perils of Company X

As an introduction to some potential difficulties facing an Internet-based business that's trying to respond to its customers with excellent advertising, innovative products, and terrific services, let's consider Company X, a software company that's trying to set up its product distribution and customer payment services over the Internet (Figure 6.8).

Suppose that Company X has created a Web site from which customers can download a software product for a 90-day trial period. At the end of that time, the customer is obliged to pay for the software or cease using it. How can Company X collect from these Internet customers? How can it ascertain that customers who do not pay actually cease using the product?

Even if it had a reliable collection mechanism, how can Internet-based Company X keep its books? Certainly Company X's

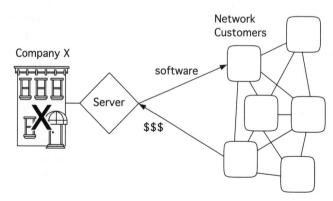

Figure 6.8 Company X.

revenue cannot be recorded based on the number of software downloads, because not all of those customers will pay. Perhaps a historical model needs to be developed that lets the company estimate what percentage of downloaders eventually will pay. And how *do* you reliably bill a customer over the Internet?

Company X's Software Product

Consider Company X's software product that's sold across the Internet. How much should they charge for it? Development costs are the same as for any software development project. But after that, the whole pricing structure changes. With no floppies or CDs to press, cost of goods, cost of manufacturing, and distribution costs are equal to the cost of maintaining a server and a phone line so that customers can connect and download the software. No need for fancy packaging here, either.

What are the costs of producing and distributing a software product on the Internet? Some of the costs remain familiar, but until a business like Company X has gained some experience, others have to be reexamined on a case-by-case basis, or invented from scratch. Among the factors to consider are:

- Cost of goods: Should be much lower if delivered over a network, especially documents.
- Cost of manufacturing: Could be much lower if no *hard* media are manufactured.
- Cost of distribution: Should be much lower if distributed by network.
- Cost of development: Probably won't change much.
- Cost of customer support: Probably won't change much.
- Cost of maintenance and upgrades: Cost of distributing upgrades could be much lower.

What about accounting costs? Accounting (billing, collection, and supporting recordkeeping) may represent a significant portion of internal development costs for the Company's first product or two. Why? Especially for early products, a company may need to develop its own accounting software that keeps track of network-based delivery from an in-house server. Eventually, off-the-shelf software will be available for setting up in-house servers that download information-based or software-based products and collect the fee. In the meantime, for a small fee, First Virtual's Info-Haus or a similar service offers Company X the ability to perform accounting and payment collection on downloads.

In the case of Company X, whose product is software, the cost of accounting for the downloading transaction is probably a small percentage of the cost of developing the software product itself. For instance, if Company X's product costs $59.95, and the cost of development was $50,000, the development cost of the accounting software may amount to $5,000 (10 percent). The cost of accounting for each individual (download) transaction could be brought down to around 5 cents: certainly less than one-tenth of a percent of the cost of the product.

But for CyberCash and others, such as searching services where the customer is charged for the service rather than for the information (which usually is free on the Internet), the transaction *is* the product. How will businesses handle that situation?

Example: CyberCash's Business Transaction Model

Cybercash's model for making money serves as one example for readers interested in exchanging value on the Internet. How does Cybercash make money? Who pays how much, when, and to whom?

Essentially, CyberCash's transaction model is a hybrid: It is more or less a cross between a bank and a postal service. First, CyberCash gets paid on a kind of postal service model, for being the envelope and the stamp whenever a transaction occurs. And second, like a bank, they get paid a little more if they take a risk on the amount of the transaction (a percentage).

For microtransactions, CyberCash charges a percentage of the nickel. Why charge a percentage of each nickel's worth and not simply a percentage of each individual transaction? As we discussed previously, in the section called, "Microtransactions and

Costs," because microtransactions are not checked in real time, and there inevitably will be some loss (risk). To CyberCash, it's not worth the accounting cost to charge a percentage of each transaction in that case.

Because CyberCash enables a style of commerce that has never before existed, instantaneous delivery with instantaneous payment, in another sense, Cybercash becomes an extension of the merchant. In general, the seller pays CyberCash's fees for the transaction service. The major difficulty lies in determining an acceptable percentage for that transaction cost. Is that worth 10 percent, 20 percent, 5 percent? Right now, no one knows what the market will accept.

Rethinking the Basics

CyberCash's model illustrates dramatically that new models for pricing and payment are needed for Internet commerce. Most likely, new business billing and bookkeeping models will be required as well, and they may need to be worked out as we go along. For example, what does *30-day net* mean in an era of on-demand payment? For online credit-card purchases, the credit-card company still carries the monthly balance of your account. But what will happen as we move toward *true* digital money? It's likely that we'll lose at least some of the benefit of the float.

What we *do* know is this: Many products that are being bought and sold using digital money (bits) have a low, potentially zero, manufacturing cost. The product has some value to the buyer, and there is great value to the seller in getting the transaction completed at all. Therefore, in this case, the seller should be happy to pay CyberCash, or some other provider of digital money services, something for enabling that exchange.

Charge for Service vs. Charge for Information

The same can be said for how to charge for online search services: New models are needed. It's of value to the customer to have the information delivered with the assurance that the search was thorough. It must be worth something to the customer to have confidence in the services rendered; therefore, they should pay for the service (the transaction) rather than for the information (the goods), although the customer does receive a package of information at the end of the process. (Usually, there is free information plus pointers to additional copyrighted information that must be paid for separately.)

The *pay for searching transaction* model stands in contrast to the model that First Virtual's InfoHaus (among others) upholds. On the InfoHaus, the user pays expressly for the information that's downloaded, and the searching is strictly do-it-yourself.

As the distinction between services and information becomes blurred, businesses will learn to make fine discriminations about the value they're offering. Some will offer information straight from the producers, some *information resellers* can offer added value to the information by certain searching, sorting, or indexing activities they offer.

chapter seven

Electronic Information Exchange

"Who are you?" said the Caterpillar.

"I—I hardly know, Sir, just at present—at least I know who I was when I got up this morning, but I think I must have been changed several times since then."

—Lewis Carroll, *Alice in Wonderland*

On the Internet, exchanging information is no different than exchanging money, except that money exchange already is massively regulated. As the Internet marketplace develops, other forms of information will develop their own regulatory environments. For instance, personal information, such as medical records, legal records, and school records, will need to be protected by certain regulations about their transfer. And given the size and strength of the entertainment market, standards undoubtedly will develop for buying and selling videotapes, books, and audio recordings, to name a few.

In the new era of Internet commerce, the entire concept of personal identity will change. You'll have an online identity, certified by a local or perhaps a national authority. Your identity will be a *stamp of approval* that accompanies information you send, and gives you access to information you need.

This chapter discusses how these developments in the electronic handling of information will change the way we operate as individuals, and the way we operate as businesses. As consumers, our identities will need to be substantiated in new ways so that we can do business. As corporations, we may find ourselves working with other corporations more closely than ever before, exchanging goods and information much more quickly and efficiently, thereby eliminating some of the overhead required to maintain full-size procurement organizations. We may find our employees working more from home, thus reducing the overhead associated with maintaining full-time office space for every employee.

In the next chapter, *The New Wooden Nickel,* we will discuss online identity as it relates to the possibility for fraud in an electronic world. For the purposes of this chapter, we'll assume that a system has been worked out that prevents the sorts of identity-related fraud we will discuss.

Certification

One of the more interesting aspects of the widespread use of public-key cryptography is the need for a digital certification process for public keys. A digital certificate is a *digital ID card* that notarizes the connection between a particular RSA public key and its owner's identifying information, in the same way that a driver's license notarizes the connection between your photograph, your name, and your birth information. A certificate would be used to verify any sort of information exchange across the Internet, whether between individuals or between corporations.

Without a digital certificate, there is no way to guarantee that a public key actually belongs to the person or company it represents. For instance, without certification, someone might accept an impostor's signature as an authorization for a financial transaction, or transmit secret information to an unfriendly party.

A digital certificate contains the name of the organization that created the certificate (the issuer), the owner's public key, the owner's identifying information, a serial number, and a set of validity dates. Figure 7.1 shows an example: Alice's digital certificate.

Every time Alice sends a message, she attaches her certificate. The recipient of Alice's message first uses her certificate to verify that Alice's public key is authentic, then uses the public key to verify the message itself. Using a certificate system, only the public key of the certifying authority has to be widely publicized—Alice need transmit only her public key and her certificate to properly identify her messages.

Certification is not a part of private-key encryption systems such as DES, because the security of the cipher depends on maintaining the secrecy of the (single) key.

PGP, the encryption algorithm distributed by Mr. Phil Zimmerman, has an interesting certification method: It isn't a hierarchy, but a system of annotations. If someone you trust has annotated a certificate by adding his credentials, you have good reason to trust that certificate. (Of course, if I *don't* happen to know you, how do I even know it's *you* who annotated the message?) PGP is discussed fully in Chapter 3, *Cryptography: Secret Writing*.

Certificates and Certifying Authorities

To use certificates to good advantage, a high degree of trust must be associated with the process of binding a digital certificate to a

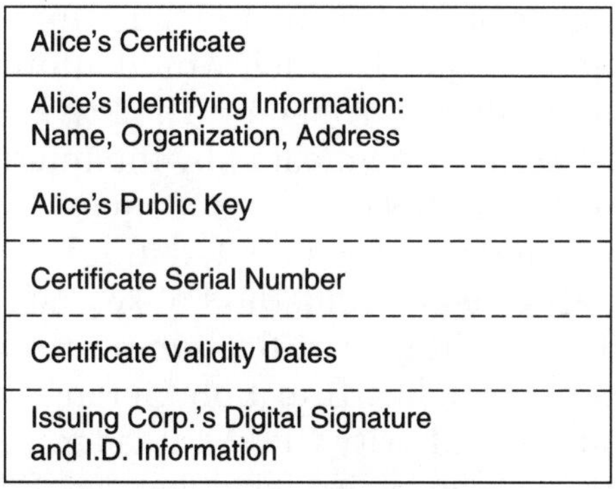

Figure 7.1 Alice's digital certificate.

person or an organization. A town may issue certificates to its citizens, a university may issue certificates to its students, and a company may issue certificates to its employees.

Certificates will be issued to people or corporate entities only after proof of identity has been established, and any of these different certification authorities may have different policies about how identity is established so that certificates may be issued. For instance, some authorities may require a driver's license or birth certificate, some may want the certificate request to be notarized. Still others may require the fingerprints or retinal prints of the requestor.

Issuing a certificate means that the certifying authority (CA) attaches its own digital signature to a document that attests to the relationship between Alice and her public key. Whenever Alice needs to demonstrate the legitimacy of her public key, she can produce her digital certificate, digitally signed by the Certifying Authority.

Certification Hierarchies

The public-key credential of the certifying authority itself must be beyond dispute. To prevent the proliferation of forged certificates, the CA must publicize its public key, provide a certificate from a higher certifying authority, or both. The possibility of *certification hierarchies* arises from this need to certify the certifiers (Figure 7.2).

Based on the global nature of Internet communication, clearly there is a need for a global certificate infrastructure (Gee, maybe ultimately an interstellar one?), which would allow for multiple certification hierarchies to interoperate. The Privacy-Enhanced Mail (PEM) effort that has been created by the Internet Engineering Task Force is a step in this direction. Request for Comments (RFC) 1422, a PEM standards document, defines the protocols that would enable a certificate-based method of key management, such as we have described, within a certification hierarchy.

At the top of the proposed certification hierarchy sits the Internet Policy Registration Authority (IPRA). It is too early to tell whether IPRA will form the basis of a global certificate infrastructure, but it is certain that IPRA will play a major role. If it is adopted, the IPRA will authorize several *policy certification authorities* (PCAs) beneath it. Each PCA will have its own policies

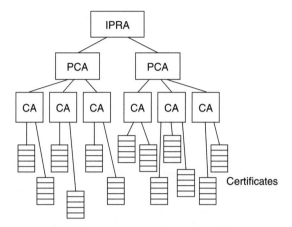

Figure 7.2 Proposed certification hierarchy.

about entering the PCA and operating within it. Each PCA will authorize certification authorities to operate within that PCA. Each CA will issue certificates to users for their own use.

Certification Hierarchies in Practice

Using certificates, it is convenient to establish a chain that corresponds, for instance, to a company's organizational hierarchy. Within a corporation or other organization, certificate issuers can be established to provide certificates to other users within the organization. This internal chain of certification also is called a *certification hierarchy.*

Typically, digital certificates are tracked within a corporation or other organization using products such as RSA Data Security's Certificate Issuing System (CIS). One or a few people within the corporation establish themselves as certificate issuers. For instance, there might be an authorized digital certificate issuer for each division of a business.

To obtain digital certificates for each division of a corporation, each certificate issuer (within the corporation) generates a key and submits it to the certifying agency (outside the corporation) with other appropriate proof of identification. For example, in the case of CIS, the keys and identifying documents would be submitted to RSA Data Security for certification. Once the approved digital certificates for each division are returned from RSA, the corporation's divisional digital certificate issuers are ready to begin issuing certificates to other employees. (Say that three times, as fast as you can.)

Another example of a certificate-issuing protocol is Apple Computer's Open Collaborative Environment (AOCE). Using AOCE, Alice can generate a key pair and then request and receive a certificate for her public key. To satisfy AOCE, her certificate request must be notarized.

The more familiar the sender is to the receiver of the message, the less need there is to enclose and verify certificates. For instance, when Bob sends his first message to Alice, he might enclose a long certificate chain to verify his public key. As she reads Bob's first message, Alice stores Bob's public key, and thereafter she has no need of the certificate chain.

A good rule of thumb in using certificates is to send just long enough of a chain that the highest-level certificate in the chain is well-known to the receiver. For instance, in a business exchange, the sender might enclose his company's certificate. But if his company is unknown to the receiver, the sender might need to enclose two certificates: his company's certificate and the CA's that certified the company.[1]

Exchanging Personal Records

Technology changes us. Our sense of identity expands from a fingerprint, to include a picture: now, in the age of electronic information exchange, to encompass digital certificates. Online identity can become richer than just a photo ID, or it can be leaner—just a name or a number—but it had better be correct, because penalties for abuse are likely to be stiff. Online identity could be considered a privilege: You'll be allowed to register so that you can do business, and that will be the way it's done. A lot of new regulations no doubt will be needed to create a safe environment when personal information is routinely transferred online.

For example, privacy regulations will need to be established about who can see a medical record, or who can modify a medical record. These regulations probably would be enforced based on certification. For instance, if my certificate says I'm So-and-So, Esq., an attorney at So & So, Inc., or if it verifies that I'm an M.D., I may legitimately obtain access to legal records or medical records, respectively. Confidential records that might require certification for access might include:

- Legal records
- Medical records
- School records
- E-mail

In fact, there is a big controversy about the status of E-mail—is an E-mail message a valid record? If so, would E-mail messages have to be archived forever? If E-mail is a way of exchanging information, which it certainly is, it needs to be trackable when it is used as part of a record-keeping system. The E-mail medium is unique, different even than most other electronic media, so it needs a different set of rules—for instance, in a permanent E-mail archive, what do you do about messages like, See you at lunch? (At SRI, we just archived them with all the rest. It would take way too much time and be too intrusive to read everyone's mail file just to save a few reels of magtape.—L.L.)

Electronic Information Exchange and Democracy

Electronic information exchange promises to alter our ideas about democracy and how it works. Computerized voting, free access to government documents, and electronic taxpaying all could make a contribution to a new democracy, a democracy founded much more upon the grassroots opinions of a well-informed people, much less dependent upon representative principles.

Computerized Voting

Computerized voting might someday be implemented if we could establish a system in which:

- Only authorized voters can vote.
- No one can vote more than once (one identity only, please).
- No one can determine for whom anyone else voted.
- No one can change anyone else's vote.
- All voters can make sure that their vote was accounted for in the final tabulation.
- Everyone knows who voted and who didn't.

In essence, we must establish a protocol that prevents cheating while maintaining individual privacy. One way to accomplish computerized voting is using blinding. (Blind digital signatures were introduced in Chapter 4.) The blind voting protocol can dissociate the vote from the voter while maintaining the ability to authenticate the votes. Although there are some other details we've left out related to setting up a central tabulating authority (CTA) that cannot influence the election, here is a basic idea of how it might work for Bob:

1. Bob generates a set of messages that contains a valid vote for each possible outcome; that is, for each question on the ballot, he must generate a *Yes* message and a *No* message. Also within each message, Bob places a large, randomly generated serial number to avoid duplications with other voters' messages. Bob naturally keeps a list of all his serial numbers.

2. Bob blinds all of his messages individually and sends them to the CTA. (See Chapter 4 for a discussion of blind signatures.)

3. The CTA checks a central voter database, making sure that voter Bob has not submitted a previous set of blind votes. If everything checks out, the CTA signs each message in Bob's set individually. Then it sends the signed messages back to Bob and stores Bob's name in the *voted already* database.

4. Bob unblinds the messages that the CTA has signed and returned to him. Notice that Bob's messages are signed

but unencrypted (after the blinding factor is removed), so he can see which is the Yes vote and which is the No vote.

5. Bob finally, actually, *votes*, by choosing one of the messages, encrypting it with the CTA's public key, and sending it in.

6. The CTA decrypts the votes, checks Bob's signatures, checks its database for duplicate serial numbers (no sending the same vote twice!), saves the serial number, and adds the vote to the tabulation. The CTA publishes the full result of the election, including every serial number and its associated vote.

7. Using the serial number, Bob can confirm that his vote was tabulated correctly.

In this system, there are only two ways to cheat, and only the CTA can cheat. First, if it can keep a record of who sent which vote, it can figure out who voted for whom. Second, if it wants, it could also generate a large number of signed, valid votes.

This system is shown only by way of example. Several more complex electronic voting systems have been proposed, and some of them seem quite usable. In most of the systems, however, there is a CTA that must be trustworthy.[2]

What might the implications of such a voting system be? Here are some possible nightmare and dream scenarios, as proposed by *The Economist*, first the nightmare: Suppose a country decides to make its laws by letting anybody who wishes send a proposal onto the information highway. Then, every Saturday night, every adult citizen will be invited to vote on these ideas. Further suppose that on some particular Friday night there's a race riot and six or seven white people are killed. The next evening? Zip, zap, new legislation: out with all the Pakistanis, Algerians, Turks, Hispanics, or whomever.

Now the dream: Congress, having once again failed to balance the Federal budget, decides to put the problem to the people. The various options are presented online, and the voters express their preferences. In a few rounds, all the conflicts are sorted out and zip, zap, a balanced budget that satisfies the majority of the people.

Realistically, neither the nightmare nor the dream would be likely to come true, but the possibilities that this technology enables are fascinating. What we're really talking about here is moving back toward direct democracy, away from powerful lobbyists and special interest groups. The Internet offers the opportunity to make representative democracy a 200-year *interim solution*, potentially creating a bridge between direct voting in classical Greece and direct voting via Internet in twenty-first-century America. Last year in Buenos Aires, Al Gore spoke of "forging a new Athenian age of democracy."[3]

Certainly the Internet offers a new way for politicians to communicate with voters. The Internet has no space limits and it is open to all. For instance, before the 1994 congressional elections, Kim Alexander of the California Voter Association set up an Internet server on which voters had access to over 300 documents, most of them written by the candidates. These documents were consulted 14,000 times.[4]

In many ways, the Internet is destined to change the face of U.S. politics. Look for candidate voting records and campaign finance reports to be published and analyzed online. Web sites will provide transcripts of Q&A sessions that go on behind the scenes, too. Political action committees, special interests, and watchdog groups will be joining in.[5]

The Government and Electronic Information Exchange

Since Al Gore first began to speak about the National Information Infrastructure, the U.S. government has been involved in developing new ways to utilize the Internet. Recently, House Speaker Newt Gingrich unveiled a Congressional Web Site, called THOMAS in honor of Thomas Jefferson. (THOMAS can be found at http://thomas.loc.gov.) THOMAS is administered by the Library of Congress. It carries the proceedings of the House floor with only a 24-hour delay, and Don Jones, creator of the THOMAS server, is working to turn that into a real-time availability. Mr. Jones feels that technology such as THOMAS can create better opportunities for democracy, because it takes the media out as the middlemen between the government and the public. Says Mr. Jones, "It gives the public the right to choose where they get their information."[6]

   Indeed, the United States government has made over 10,000 documents available on the Internet. In pre-Internet days, these documents would have been published on paper. Now it is much easier for environmentalists to search through these documents and locate the nearest factory emitting toxic waste, as registered on the Toxics Release Inventory.[7]

Electronic Taxpaying

The Internal Revenue Service had a great idea a few years ago: Let's let millions of taxpayers phone in their returns. In 1996, that's what some 26 million people who use the 1040EZ form will be able to do. They can call an 800 number and tell a voice-recognition computer their vital statistics: Social Security number, amount of tax withheld, and taxable income. The machine will tell them on the spot how much tax they owe, or how much refund is due. This system promises to save millions of tax dollars for the IRS, and perhaps it will make tax day somewhat less appalling.[8]

Newspaper Internet Alliance

Eight large newspaper companies representing 123 U.S. newspapers have formed an alliance called New Century Network. Their goal is to develop a single nationwide system for offering their news and other information services over World Wide Web sites. The eight founding partners are: Advance Publications, Cox Newspapers, the Gannett Company, the Hearst Corporation, Knight-Ridder, the Times Mirror Company, and the Washington Post Company. It will be up to individual local papers to set costs for subscription and advertising. (*The New York Times,* April 20 1995, C6.)

Yet all of these taxpayers still will have to mail paper copies of their forms in 1996, because Congress requires that all returns must be signed with a pen. When digital signatures are accepted on tax returns, we'll know they're definitely here to stay.

What Can Electronic Information Exchange Do for My Business?

Over the past decade, the banking and financial industries have invested heavily in information automation and networking technologies, made to handle an ever-increasing number of financial transactions. For example, the Clearinghouse for Interbank Payment Systems coordinates nearly $2 trillion worth of transactions a day. The U.S.'s network of more than 75,000 automated teller machines (ATMs) processes over 6 billion transactions per year. One analysis of the New York Stock Exchange suggests that electronic trading saves stock buyers and sellers hundreds of millions of dollars annually.

Here are some examples of how the emergence of reliable electronic commerce in the banking industry has helped some individual financial institutions so far:

- Visa's peak capacity for processing credit-card transactions grew from 30,000 per day in 1978 to over 1.4 million per day in 1991, while its response time for authorizations dropped from 5 minutes in 1973 to 1.1 seconds in 1991.

- Citibank, through the deployment of an ATM network in 1977, increased its market share from 4 percent to 13.4 percent.

- Mellon Bank, by installing a computer-based network to resolve credit-card disputes, reduced its backlog of customer complaints from 5,200 to 2,200, reducing the average resolution time from 45 days to 25 days.[9,10]

The electronic telecommunications networks are pervasive; however, their benefits remain elusive unless we change the way we do business. Says Daniel Shubert, Director of Client/Server Technical Services for Electronic Data Systems Corporation, "The technology is here. The problem is not with the technology, but with the corporate processes. Companies must fundamentally change the way they do business, and that's hard."

In industry after industry, companies are reaping the benefits of electronic information exchange (EIE). For example, BP America, Inc., the U.S. subsidiary of British Petroleum, Inc., is establishing a system that will process electronically at least 40 percent of the 440,000 invoices it receives each year. With this system, BP expects to eliminate duplicate purchases and negotiate bulk rates.

The future could be grim for companies that don't get it. "Whole industries will restructure or disappear," warns Robert M. Curtice, the Director of Arthur D. Little's North American Management Consulting Group. "For some companies, such as banks, if they haven't already started doing [electronic commerce], it may already be too late."

George T. Shaheen, managing partner of Andersen Consulting, concurs: "The ability to do more and more commerce over a network is at the forefront of everybody's thinking. What's going to happen—because we want it to—is that the network is going to take time, distance, and space out of the question."

A networked corporation can do business anytime, anywhere. It can get a jump on corporations that still do business the old way. It no longer matters where your best and brightest talent resides: No two of First Virtual's executive staff have the same zip code. Sweden's L.M. Ericsson Company has 17,000 engineers in 40 research centers, located in 20 countries worldwide, all linked by a network. Their development teams in Australia and England work together to create a design, then zip the blueprint to a factory in China for manufacturing.

Networks are starting to allow companies to vacate expensive office space, because the employees can get their work done from home, on the road, or wherever they may be. In fact, a British Telecom study reported by the Gartner Group indicates that the average telecommuter works 11 percent more hours than his or her office counterpart, and that reduced costs for office space and other overhead items save employers an additional amount equal to 17 percent of annual salary costs.[11]

> ### *Telecommuters: Great Taste, Fewer Calories*
>
> Thirty-seven million U.S. households now have at least one person gainfully employed at home. Of these, the 8.4 million telecommuters comprise the fastest growing segment of the home-based worker market, according to Link Resources. Jack Nilles, author of *Making Telecommuting Happen*, estimates that by working at home one to two days a week, a telecommuting employee saves the company between $6,000 and $12,000 a year, due to increased productivity, reduced needs for office space, and lower turnover. (*Business Week*, 4/17/95, p. 106.)

And the biggest payoff for companies is when they can use EIE to improve the quality of their customer relationships, whether by delivering better service through an E-mail bulletin board, or by lowering costs as the network enables just-in-time inventory control. For example, two years ago, Del Monte began receiving daily electronic inventory reports from grocers. The retailers used to have to keep four weeks of inventory on hand to avoid shortages; now they need keep only 10 days of inventory, because Del Monte automatically issues a restocking order when the inventory falls below a predetermined level.[12]

Example: Saturn Corporation

For its Saturn cars, General Motors developed an infrastructure that lets Saturn and its numerous suppliers operate as one company, using electronic information exchange. Saturn and its suppliers reduced overhead in all organizations, increased cooperation, and broke one of the oldest rules in any corporation's unwritten rule book: Treat vendors as adversaries.

How does it work? Component suppliers do not wait for GM to send a purchase order; they simply consult the production schedule database. After the parts are shipped, the vendor sends an electronic message to Saturn, saying in effect, "These are the parts we have sent you." When the parts arrive, the receiving clerk scans the bar code printed on them. The scanning computer tells the clerk which department needs these parts and initiates payment to the vendor.[13]

The interesting thing about this model is that it may point the way to how we all will be doing business in the new era of Internet commerce. Producers and their suppliers may find it mutually beneficial to work together more closely, to operate more cooperatively. Internet technology can help them exchange information quickly and easily, and with confidence that confidential information will remain confidential.

Negotiations and Disputes Online

It is quite possible that disputes may arise online regarding contracts or information services. Eventually, it probably will become necessary to develop protocols for mediating disagreements within the electronic realm.

One such company, AMIX, the American Information Exchange Corporation, was the first to provide an online information service that allowed for negotiating contract work and enforced a set of dispute-resolution techniques. For instance, a consulting contract could be negotiated within the AMIX system, duly registered, and time-stamped. The contract could be, for example, a technical writing contract, or any contract in which deliverables could be made available strictly online. The AMIX system helped enforce the contract and the relationship between the parties. For example, if the contractor was late in delivering a milestone, and the hiring party wished to prevent delivery of further milestones, he or she could enter a Terminate command, which prevented further deliveries. Or on a more friendly note, the parties could renegotiate the contract online. If both parties agreed, the new terms took effect. If one party did not ratify the new proposal, the old terms continued unchanged. Payment was arranged through preestablished accounts for the buyer and the seller.*

* *AMIX Software Guide,* American Information Exchange Corporation, Mt. View, CA 94043, 1992.

Unfortunately, AMIX apparently was too early for its time (1992). It exists no longer, falling instead into the category of noble experiments. However, it seems certain that the ideas from AMIX will be seen again as online information exchange and contract negotiation become prevalent.

Animated Online Chat

Fujitsu Cultural Technologies and CompuServe Information Service will collaborate on WorldsAway, a totally graphical chat environment where animated *avatars* interact in a virtual cocktail party. Each participant can control his or her avatar, making it walk across the room, sit down, and so on. Conversation is depicted cartoon-style in a balloon over the avatar's head. Characters can move, examine, exchange, and sell objects online using tokens, and can even invite other characters to their own private residences for some one-on-one chat time. The service will be widely available soon. (Information & Interactive Services Report, 3/10/95, p. 3.)

Limits to Legislation

Regarding the electronic exchange of information online, it's important to realize that you always will have a certain amount of freedom. Although some governments and other authorities are trying to prevent public utilization of encryption, or to regulate online identities, there is always a possibility of creating subliminal channels within a nondescript message: They can't physically prevent it, even though they can try to stop it legally. The Electronic Frontier Foundation and other individual liberty groups are working to ensure the public's right to use encryption, in the name of the First Amendment and rights to privacy. The legal ramifications of these issues are explored in Chapter 9, *Legal Questions.* The technology that makes encryption impossible to stop is also discussed, in the section called "Subliminal Channels."

Not Our Idea of Electronic Information Exchange

Here, unfortunately, is a good example of what many people fear may happen over the Internet, especially if encryption is allowed:

British anarchists have used the Internet network to link up with international terrorist groups—including The Sons of Glendower in Wales; Direct Action in France; and the Anti Imperialist Cell (AIC), a German anarcho-terrorist group—and coordinate the disruption of schools, looting of shops, and attacks on multinational firms.

The anarchist campaign was launched at a conference entitled Anarchy in the U.K., held in London last October. It began with a call to arms by Ian Bone of the extremist Class War organization, who said violence was the only way to overthrow the state.

Members of the audience were encouraged to liaise on the Internet by Ian Heavens, a computer programmer. As an editor of *Spunk*, the biggest anarcho-computing directory in Britain, Heavens has distributed files that include advice on how to overthrow the government by robbing banks, disabling police vehicles, stealing documents, and inciting readers to arm themselves.

The technical resources and computer skills of the anarchists have surprised police and experts. "We have been amazed at the level of organization of these extremist groups who have appeared on the Internet in a short amount of time," said Simon Hill, editor of *Computing* magazine, the trade journal. Police have arrested a Scottish man—the first U.K. arrest for allegedly encouraging violence using a computer—and plan to question several others for suspected public order and fraud offenses. "Anarchists now represent a significant threat," said one officer.

The anarchists invited sympathizers from abroad to join in attacks on the British economy. Some anarchists plan regular looting trips to London, asking British contacts for legal advice and addresses of suitable stores. A notice for a future expedition advised: "Shopping is fun when everything is free." *This is not our idea of Internet commerce!*

Said one spokesman, "The findings show the need for international agreements that ban groups preaching violence from the information superhighway. Current laws were framed in the age of print. We need a new framework of rules for the age of electronic communication."[14]

The New Wooden Nickel

"In my youth," said the sage, as he shook his grey locks,
"I kept all my limbs very supple
By the use of this ointment—one schilling the box—
Allow me to sell you a couple?"

—LEWIS CARROLL, *ALICE IN WONDERLAND*

Computer bits are made to be copied—how do you deal with
fraud and counterfeiting in a digital world? In a world of digital
certificates, certifying authorities, and numbers that are money,
there exists a tremendous potential for fraud, the new wooden
nickel in the new era of Internet commerce.

Fraud for Fun and Profit

As a starting point for discovering all of the wonderful new kinds
of fraud that might be perpetrated in the new era of Internet commerce, one can think of many schemes that might be aimed at
obtaining false digital credentials from a certifying authority (CA).
For instance, consider the following attempt:

Suppose Bob wants to impersonate Alice. To carry out his
attack, Bob generates a key pair and sends the public key to a CA
saying, "I'm Alice. Here is my public key. Please send me a certificate." If the CA is fooled and sends Bob a certificate, he can send
a verifiably signed digital message to Alice's bank, saying "I wish
to withdraw $10,000 from my account. Please send me the
money." (The E-mail confirmation used by First Virtual is directed

at a similar type of fraud: purchase requests generated fraudulently in the name of another.)

To prevent this type of fraud, the CA must verify that a certificate of request did indeed come from its purported author. That is, the CA must require sufficient evidence that it actually is Alice who requested the certificate. For example, the CA may require Alice to appear in person and show a birth certificate.

If Bob's first attempt to obtain a false credential fails, perhaps then he will try to bribe Fred, who works for the certifying authority, to issue him a certificate in Alice's name. This type of fraud can be prevented from requiring the cooperation of two or more CA employees to issue a certificate; Bob now has to bribe two employees instead of one.

Unfortunately, there may be other ways to generate a forged certificate by bribing only one employee. For instance, if each certificate request is logged by only one employee, that employee could be bribed to stick a false request into the stack of real requests.

If Bob fails in his attempts to bribe an employee of the CA, there is at least one more attack he can try: Bits don't yellow with age, so Bob can forge an old document. Suppose Bob tries to factor the modulus of the certifying authority. It may take him 15 years, but he finally succeeds. Now Bob has an expired private key of a certifying authority, and he can forge a document dated 15 years ago

---

What Is the Factoring Problem?

Factoring is the act of splitting an integer into a set of smaller integers, called *factors*. When multiplied together, these factors form the original integer. Prime factorization requires splitting an integer into factors that are prime numbers. For example, the prime factors of 15 are 3 and 5. Every integer has a unique prime factorization.

Factoring is the problem upon which several public-key cryptosystems are based, including RSA. Factoring the modulus of a certifying authority would allow an attacker to figure out that CA's private key. The larger the modulus, the more resistant to attack by factoring it becomes.

attesting to the public key of some other person, say, Frank. Now Bob can forge a document, signed by Frank 15 years ago, perhaps a will that leaves everything to Bob. This attempt raises the issue of how to authenticate a digitally signed document dated many years previously.

Certifying Older Documents

Like a credit card, a key normally expires after, say, two years. A document signed with an old key should not be accepted. However, some legal agreements such as long-term leases and real estate contracts are cases in which it is necessary for a digitally signed document to be regarded as valid for much longer than two years.

One proposal for solving this problem is that there should be long-term keys as well as the normal two-year keys. To preserve them from compromise, long-term keys should have much longer modulus lengths than two-year keys, and they should be stored under maximum security. For example, if a given long-term key expires in 50 years, any document signed with that key would remain valid within the specified 50-year time frame.

What happens if a long-term key is compromised? The key must be placed on a *certificate revocation list* (CRL). CRLs are lists maintained by certifying authorities that give information about current keys that have been revoked before their scheduled expiration dates. Unfortunately, a 50-year key might have to remain on a CRL for 50 years, until it expires![1]

Notice that none of Bob's attacks upon the CAs threatens the privacy of communication among other users, as might result from a successful attempt to obtain the key of a secret-key distribution center, or the compromise of a Kerberos authentication server.

Storing Private Keys Securely

To prevent fraud, it is extremely important that individuals and agencies store their private keys securely. If the key of a certifying authority were compromised, for example, it could lead to unde-tectable forgeries: An attacker with the private key of a certifying authority could forge entire certificates (see Chapter 3, *Cryptography: Secret Writing*, for more information about certifying authorities.) To prevent this type of fraud, certifying authorities, such as corporations, can keep their private keys in a special, high-security box, known as a *certificate signing unit*, or CSU (Figure 8.1).

A CSU destroys its contents if opened, and it is shielded from attacks using electromagnetic radiation. Even the employees of the certifying authority should not have access to the key itself, only the ability to use the key in the process of issuing certificates. In some implementations, a CSU is activated by a set of physical keys that are capable of storing data. These *data keys* are imple-mented in such a way that several employees must use their keys together to activate the CSU. Thus, a sole disgruntled employee cannot produce false certificates.

If a CSU is destroyed, say, in a fire, it will not compromise the private key of the CA. All certificates signed by a destroyed CSU are still valid, as long as the verifier still has the corresponding

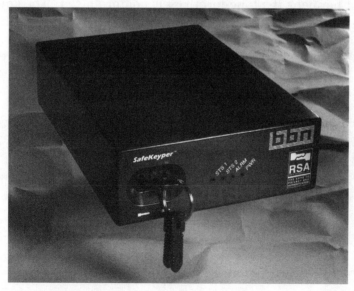

Figure 8.1 A CSU unit, RSA's SafeKeyper. (Photo courtesy of RSA, Inc.)

public key. Some CSUs keep encrypted backup copies of the private key inside the CSU box that can be decrypted and restored, in case of loss. It is likely that some CSUs will be manufactured that enable a lost private key to be restored into a new CSU.

Bolt, Beranek, and Newman (BBN) sells a CSU unit. RSA Data Security has created a full certificate-issuing system based on the BBN CSU unit.

Even if CAs store their keys securely, the keys might become targets for an extensive factoring attack. For this reason, CAs should use very long keys, preferably 1,000 bits or longer, and they should change their keys often. Top-level CAs might be an exception to this rule, since their keys are likely to be incorporated into software used by many verifiers.

Individuals must take care never to store their private key in plaintext form. The simplest storage mechanism for personal keys is just to encrypt the private key under a password and store the result on disk, never revealing the password to anyone or writing it down anywhere. It may also be helpful to store the encrypted key on a disk that is not accessible by network, such as a floppy disk or a local hard disk. Eventually, private keys may be stored on smart cards, in electronic wallets, or other portable hardware.

Key Compromise

If an individual's key is compromised, that is, if Alice suspects that an attacker may have obtained her private key, she must assume that some unwanted eyes can read her encrypted messages and forge her name on documents. A compromised key is treated much like a stolen credit card of today, but the consequences may be worse.

If she believes her key has been compromised, Alice must immediately notify her certifying authority and have her old key placed on a certificate revocation list. Then Alice must generate a new key and have it certified. She probably will want to use her new key to re-sign any important documents that she had signed with the old key. Alice should find a way to store her new key differently than the old key, to prevent another compromise.

If a CA's key is compromised, it must immediately cease issuing certificates under its old key and change to a new key. If there is a suspicion that false certificates have been issued, all certificates must be recalled and reissued using the new key. Notice that the compromise of a CA's key doesn't invalidate the user's personal public keys, just the certificates to which they point for authentication. If the key of a top-level CA is compromised, the event should be considered catastrophic, because that key may be built into the very software that verifies certificates.

Key Revocation

There are a number of reasons why a key might be revoked. Certainly one reason is when a key is compromised. Another case is when an individual posesses a key that includes a corporate title, such as Bob Boring, Vice President of Marketing, Boring Communications, Inc., and Bob is no longer with the company.

Each certifying authority maintains a list of revoked keys that it had certified originally. Since expired keys should not be accepted in any case, a key is removed from the CRL once it expires. Although CAs maintain individual CRLs, there may also be a need for a central CRL repository, such as a network site that contains the latest CRLs from many organizations. Furthermore, a financial institution such as a bank might need an in-house CRL repository to make CRL searches feasible for every transaction.[2]

Key Expiration

All keys must expire to preserve their owners against a long-term factoring attack. The expiration time must be shorter than the expected factoring time. Or conversely, the key's length must be long enough to make the chances of factoring before the expiration date negligible. A key's expiration date will always accompany the public key in any certificate or directory listing.

Key Directories

What does Alice do if she wants to find out Bob's public key? Certifying authorities may provide directory services for certificates they have issued. All directory services must be secure against tampering, so users can be certain that a public key listed in the directory actually belongs to the person listed. Otherwise, encrypted, sensitive information may go to the wrong person.

One or more commercial public key directory services is expected to develop eventually, serving as an online white pages or yellow pages-style directory. These directory services may elect to comply with ITU X.509 standards, which means they would contain certificates as well as public keys for listed individuals. If the certificates are also present, security is no longer an issue; the keys will be accompanied by certificates attesting to their authenticity. (Or is it an issue? See "The Identity Problem," later in this chapter.)

Digital Time Stamps

Another way to prevent fraud, or to prove that a digital document existed at a particular time, is to create a system of digital time-stamping. A digital time-stamping service (DTS) issues time stamps that associate a date and time with a digital document in a cryptographically strong way. Later, that time stamp can be used to prove that the electronic document existed at the time of its time stamp. For example, a physicist with a brilliant idea can write it down with a word processor and have the document time-stamped. Later, he can prove that he deserves a Nobel Prize, even though a rival may have published first, because of the file's time stamp.

Here's how digital time-stamping could work. If Bob signs a document and wants it time-stamped, he computes a message digest of the document (using a secure one-way hash function). Then he sends the message to a time-stamping service, which sends in return a digital time stamp document that includes 1. the message digest, 2. the date and time it was received by the time-stamping service, and 3. the digital signature of the time-stamping service. Since a message digest does not reveal the content of the document, the time-stamping service can't eavesdrop on any of the documents it time stamps.

When Bob presents the document to verify its creation date later, a verifier recomputes the message digest to make sure it matches the digest in the time-stamp document, then it verifies the digital signature of the time-stamping service on the document.

To be reliable, digital time stamps must not be forgeable. The digital time-stamping service must have a very long key if it wants the stamps to be reliable for several decades. Also, the key must be stored with utmost security, such as in a tamperproof box. The date and time must originate from a clock that will be accurate for several years or even for decades, preferably stored inside the same tamperproof box as the key. Finally, it must be made infeasible to produce time stamps without the key and the clock inside the box.

Actually, Bellcore has created a cryptographically strong, software-only time-stamping method that avoids the need for tamperproof hardware. The Bellcore method combines hash values of documents into data structures called *binary trees*, whose *root* values are published periodically in the newspaper. The time stamp associated with the document is the publication date of the newspaper. A time stamp consists of a set of hash values that allow a verifying party to recompute the root of the tree. Since the hash functions are one-way, the set of validating hash values cannot be forged.[4]

Digital time-stamping is extremely important for verifying digital documents that must remain valid over many years, such as leases or long-term contracts. Suppose a landlord and a tenant sign a 20-year lease. The public keys that were used to sign the lease will expire in about two years, and solutions, such as re-verifying the keys or re-signing the lease every two years, require the cooperation of both parties. If one party becomes unhappy with the lease in the meantime, he or she may refuse to re-sign. Registering the lease with a digital time-stamping service is a good solution. Then, both parties receive a copy of the signed document, which can be used years later to enforce the original terms of the lease.

Eventually, digital time stamps are likely to be used for everything from long-term corporate contracts to personal diaries or letters. Because digital documents do not physically yellow or otherwise show their age, the only way to determine their authenticity 100 years from now would be with a digital time stamp.

Digital time stamps also provide a solution to at least one kind of cheating with digital signatures, which is claiming that a key has been compromised in order to reneg on an agreement. Suppose Alice signs a document, then wishes to claim she did not. She could conveniently lose her key (e.g., on a smart card) in some public place, or she could publish the key anonymously. Then she could claim that someone else signed the document, not her. Digital time stamps might prove that Alice signed the document before the key was compromised. Of course, Alice could still cheat by claiming the key was compromised earlier. If the recipient of digitally signed documents routinely has them time-stamped, the effects of this sort of cheating can be limited. In that situation, only documents signed before the key loss are considered valid, similarly to how we treat lost credit cards nowadays.

The Identity Problem

We're accustomed to having identities solidly linked to a corporeal presence. We use physical tokens to identify ourselves: driver's licenses, passports, credit cards. Usually, these identifying documents can be undeniably linked to an individual by a photograph, a thumbprint, or similar means. In cyberspace, it ain't necessarily so.

Multiple Identities Fraud

For instance, Alice could obtain multiple keys, thus multiple identities. It might be fairly easy to obtain different certificates through different certifying authorities if they don't communicate regularly with each other. If Alice wants to commit tax fraud, it could be quite convenient to have multiple identities. Or she could commit an untraceable crime: If she used one of her identities only to commit the crime, never again would she use that identity. Even if the authorities knew the *identity* of the criminal, that *person* would never be heard from again.

To prevent this sort of fraud, there has to be some mechanism whereby checks are made whenever someone registers a public key. Perhaps a public key would be registered at birth. But then what if the parents applied for multiple public keys? In the end, the uniqueness of an individual seems to come down to trust.

Renting Passports

Suppose Alice wants to travel to Argentina, but the government won't give her a visa. Carol, who has a visa, offers to rent her identity to Alice. (Bob offered, too, but there were obvious problems.) Carol sells her private key to Alice, and Alice goes happily off to Argentina, pretending to be Carol.

Meanwhile, Carol has a perfect alibi. Carol commits her crime while Alice is in Argentina.

Alice is free to commit crimes in this scenario as well. She commits her first crime as Carol just before she leaves for Argentina, near Carol's home. The police will come looking for Carol. Carol will claim she rented her identity to Alice, but who would believe such a story. It wouldn't do much for their friendship, would it?

Of course the real problem is that Alice isn't actually proving her identity, she's proving that she knows a piece of secret information. What is being abused is the link between the person (physical) and the identifying information. One way to solve this problem would be to create a police state in which all citizens would have to prove their identity frequently: every morning, at each street corner, and so forth. It all comes down to trust.[5]

Counterfeiting

When we refer to counterfeiting, we refer specifically to fraudulent use of digital money. After all, it seems easy and natural to spend the same *cyberdollars* again and again; they aren't real, they're just numbers. Specifically to discourage counterfeiting, all cyberdollars are registered. After they are spent, cyberdollars are added to a list of used digital money. These lists would need to be centrally maintained, or someone could just try to use the same digital dollars at another bank or store.

Speaking more broadly, there's always an overhead cost associated with detecting counterfeit digital money. Therefore, it's ultimately a financial decision about whether to test for counterfeiting in real time. Testing usually involves searching lists of names, numbers, or both, probably over a network. The relevant question becomes: What is the possibility for loss in this transaction? For higher-value transactions, most merchants will want to test for counterfeiting in real time. For microtransactions and nanotransactions, counterfeiting detection is likely to be done on a *batch* basis, as in once every nickel's worth. Thus, there's probably room for a few wooden nickels in the new era.

Techniques for detecting counterfeiting may change over time, but the principles remain essentially the same. In dealing with the possibility of counterfeiting, a merchant has two basic options:

- ◆ Detect counterfeiting in the moment.
- ◆ Detect it later and make sure the perpetrator is hurt by it through the use of some penalty, perhaps the loss of credit.

Certainly there will be some loss due to counterfeiting, that is, spending the same digital money twice, but that loss is likely to be less than the expense of testing individual microtransactions. Actually, compared to the perils involved in fraud related to secure key management, the possibilities for counterfeiting digital money seem easy to handle.

Accountability in Cyberspace

Although this book has devoted many pages to issues around Internet security, on balance, those are primarily technical concerns. They're certain to be worked out. In fact, the real problem with business in cyberspace isn't providing security, it's creating an atmosphere of accountability. Isn't the very anonymity of an

E-mail identity an incentive for fraud, for scandal? When no one knows who you really are, you can do whatever you want! Essentially, the need for Internet security is just a symptom of the fact that no one has to be accountable in cyberspace—yet.

As the commercialization of the Internet increases, the environment must inevitably change. Suppose we all have smart cards with our identifying information on them, duly certified by all the proper authorities, and we have to plug in our smart cards whenever we want to use the Internet. It will be just like having a credit check each time we log in. Talk about accountability! Problems with harassment of women online will disappear overnight, don't you think?

Once we plug in that smart ID card, businesses and other organizations can verify our identity, our credit record, and anything else they need to know, using channels that businesses and business auditors already use today. They can contact the local utilities companies to find out if we get a utility bill sent to the address we've listed, they can call the phone company and verify phone service, and so forth. All these things already are a matter of public record today. Identity verification using the Internet may be somewhat faster, but it is fundamentally no different than what already happens. Internet privacy legislation must be designed to prevent abuse of this information, but cannot stop it from being gathered in the name of commerce.

To the part of the Internet community that enjoys free exchange of ideas and information, or to the part of the community that uses anonymity as an unfortunate mask to hide behind when they lash out at others, this scenario may sound a bit disappointing. But to gain the convenience that digital money and Internet commerce offer, we will have to strike a mature balance between too much anonymity and too much authority. As in any community, all the good citizens of cyberspace must be able to walk without fear.

What all these technological solutions are aiming to provide is an environment of trust, because trust is the basis upon which all human interactions are founded. One element that encaches the development of trust is a body of legal precedent. The next chapter, *Legal Questions,* examines some of the controversies that surround the development of digital money and Internet commerce.

chapter nine

Legal Questions

*As a means of espionage, writs of assistance
and general warrants are but puny instruments
of tyranny and oppression when compared
with wire-tapping.*

—JUSTICE BRANDEIS, 1928

The new era of electronic commerce has begun to raise many new
legal and social questions and controversies. The topics covered in
this chapter and the next are not strictly about digital money and
Internet commerce, but about the legal and social ramifications of
digital money and Internet commerce. We've included them to
provide a basic indication of issues and opportunities that are
likely to arise as the new era evolves.

Issues such as privacy and the control of encryption technology
by governments have been alluded to throughout this book. This
chapter offers a more thorough examination of a few salient questions in these areas. Over time, answers to our questions in this
volatile area must be worked out so that digital money and electronic commerce can become fully integrated into our lives and
our laws.

By reading this chapter, you might avoid some possible legal
pitfalls in establishing an online business venture. Among the
specific legal questions this chapter covers are privacy, the legal
status of digital signatures, copyrights for online materials, and
existing legislation in the United States that regulates the export
of cryptographic technology. It also discusses the proposed Communications Decency Act that has passed the U.S. Senate, and
addresses issues about online privacy.

Are Digital Signatures Real Signatures?

Will digital signatures stand up in court? Preliminary legal research indicates that digital signatures in fact meet the requirements of legally binding signatures for most purposes, including commercial use as defined in the Uniform Commercial Code (UCC). At the request of NIST, the General Accounting Office (GAO) has presented a formal opinion that digital signatures will meet the standards of handwritten signatures.[1]

Even so, the validity of digital signatures has not yet been challenged in a courtroom. To carry the weight of handwritten signatures, a digital signature must actually be used to sign a binding document, then it must be challenged in court by one party. The court will take the opportunity to consider the security of the digital signature scheme and issue a ruling. Over time, a body of precedent will arise about situations in which a digital signature may or may not be binding (such as cases of alleged fraud, and so forth).

These court rulings will undoubtedly engender guidelines regarding acceptable digital signature methods, key sizes, and other security precautions required for a digital signature to be legally binding. Until this body of precedent is established, it is highly advisable that two parties who wish to use digital signatures should sign a paper contract stating that in the future they wish to be legally bound by any documents signed by them according to a specified digital signature scheme and a specified key size.[2]

Digital signatures actually have the potential to carry greater legal authority than handwritten signatures. For instance, if a ten-page contract is signed by hand on the tenth page, there is no guarantee that the first nine pages have not been altered in any way. If the contract is signed using digital signatures, a third party can verify that not one byte of the contract has been altered.

Are My Copyrights Valid on the Internet?

Another issue to be sorted out before Internet commerce can truly take off is the problem of protecting copyrighted material online. Because it is so easy to redistribute and reuse information through

E-mail or by downloading it, the electronic world threatens to take away the control that publishers heretofore have had over the printed word. And the subject matter for potential infringement expands daily, as sound, video, and graphics—all of which are protected by copyright—appear online.

Some publishers are reluctant to employ online services because data flows so freely, and there has been a general philosophy among Internet users that online information should be free. Carol Risher, Vice President for Copyright and New Technologies at the Association for American Publishers, in Washington, feels that a protectionist approach is warranted. "In the future," Ms. Risher says, "companies will protect their copyrights by means of tracking devices—which determine how the information has been used—built into online services. Intelligent agents could be used for tracking and pricing transactions."

Others disagree. Publishers who have been involved with online publishing thus far seem satisfied with measures they're currently taking to protect their copyrights. Craig Kerwien, an executive editor for Ziff-Davis Interactive, in Cambridge, Massachusetts, states that "a written licensing agreement signed by the subscriber, coupled with the necessity of stepping through copyright-notice screens before the user can access information, seems adequate. As far as we know, there hasn't been much abuse." Mr. Kerwien also acknowledged that companies would not necessarily know what infringements might be occurring.

Basically, there are two sides to the copyright coin: protectionism versus open access to information. Says one professor who specializes in law and technology issues at an east coast law school: "The companies that choose to go the protectionist route will suffer because there are a thousand other sources of information in the online world."[3]

In general, copyright protection applies to all original works of authorship fixed in a tangible medium of expression. All works that were created in the United States after January 1, 1978 are protected automatically under federal law the moment they are created.

Before computers became popular, it seemed clear that copyrightable *works* consisted of things that could be experienced by the naked eye or ear, such as plays, paintings, or music. Questions began to arise when these works began to appear online. However, computers actually add little to our existing copyright precedent.

For instance, copyrighted music and videos were recorded on magnetic tape, which was the forerunner of magnetic floppy disks. For decades before that, copyrighted films were recorded on celluloid, which must be run through a projector to achieve the illusion of moving pictures.

Materials that are specifically protected by copyright online are:

- Messages posted to Usenet, mailing lists, and bulletin boards, including individual messages and entire threads
- Electronic mail messages
- Computer software, including entire applications, patches, add-ons, and utilities
- Data files of all kinds, including:
   Text, hypertext, and formatted documents
   Multimedia works
   Databases
   Visual images, clip-art files, textures, and other image files
   Sound and music samples, MIDI files
   Animation loops

Congress enacted the copyright law to encourage authors to invest their time and effort in creating valuable works, by promising they will be able to charge others for copies. In the case of performed works, the copyright applies for attending a performance; in the case of displayed works, for viewing the work.

Software copyrights are pivotally important to the computer industry, and ever-newer kinds of copyrightable works, such as multimedia and virtual reality, will continue to raise questions.[4]

What Is the Legal Status of an Online Service: Carrier or Publisher?

A $200 million lawsuit was filed recently against Prodigy that points out many issues in online publishing, not to mention online freedom of speech. Stratton Oakmont, the investment banking firm, filed suit against Prodigy for comments posted in a Prodigy bulletin board called Money Talk. New York Court Judge Stuart Ain, hearing the case, granted a partial summary judgement against Prodigy. In his decision, Judge Ain found Prodigy to be a publisher of the statements in question, and he said the system operator of Money Talk, Charles Epstein, acted as Prodigy's agent for the purposes of acts and omissions in this case.

Online services and small bulletin boards (BBSs) around the world customarily allow users to post messages that air their personal thoughts on a wide range of events, issues, trends, business activities, government actions, personal topics, and so forth. In fact, this freedom has been a defining parameter across the Internet, commercial online service providers, and small BBSs.

Brian Ek, director of communication at Prodigy said, "Because we have a sysop [system operator] and guidelines, and [because of] the fact that we do not allow obscenity, the judge said that we are a publisher and as such we can be sued for libel. We disagree with this entirely and, of course, we will file an appeal."

"On a larger scale," Ek continued, "this affects the entire industry and places us all between a rock and a hard place. As an industry, we are often criticized for not controlling what members place online. The climate in Washington is wanting to see more control and, at Prodigy, we have attempted to walk that line of freedom of speech while applying guidelines."

"With this decision, we are now presented with either letting everything and anything be posted without any guidelines or we become a publisher and all of our bulletin boards are merely editorial content."

"It is important to realize that the online industry is a new form of communication and [it] needs legal definition. As it stands now, we have older laws which apply to print standards being applied to the electronic world community."[5]

Prodigy quickly appealed the decision. In fact, the case was settled out of court, leaving future cases to set legal precedent.

One result of cases like the Prodigy case is that forum hosts may come to be viewed as extremely important to the operation of an online service. Hosts may even be elevated to the status of company officials, since the company obviously is betting its reputa-

> ### *Regulate the Net?*
>
> Martha Siegel, part of the legal duo that caused an uproar last April by sending E-mail messages advertising their green-card services to 6,000 Usenet groups, thinks the Internet is prime for regulation: "[T]here's no great difference between communications through the computer and other media. That's why we believe the FCC should officially take control of the Internet, just as it has all other communications media. The Internet is too big and powerful to go without official regulation. The public needs to be protected, and we have no doubt it will be. In a very short time, the dust will settle, and the mainstreaming of the Internet will be complete." (Inc. Technology, Summer 1995, p.44.)

tion and a lot of money on what messages the hosts decide to allow in their forums.

What Is the Governmental Perspective on Encryption?

Already, the laws of many countries attempt to regulate the uses and availability of encryption technology. For instance:

- ◆ The U.S. regards strong encryption as a military weapon, and forbids export of strong encryption devices.
- ◆ France regards any encryption as illegal for its citizens, but it permits export of encryption devices.

Two government agencies control the export of encryption software from the United States: the Bureau of Export Administration (BXA) and the Office of Defense Trade Controls (DTC) in the State Department, an office which is authorized by Defense Trade Regulations. In general, DTC requires that it see all applications first, then it usually transfers control of the approval process to the BXA. DTC takes its orders from the NSA, while BXA works for COCOM. Historically, the DTC has been reluctant to grant export licenses for encryption products stronger than a certain level, but it is not widely publicized what that level is exactly.[6]

In March 1992, the Computer Security and Advisory Board, an official advisory board to NIST, voted to recommend a national policy review of cryptographic issues, including export policies. Currently, export policy still is defined by agencies concerned with national security, rather than by agencies dedicated to encouraging commerce.[7]

> TIP: Expect United States export policies with regard to encryption to change frequently over the next few years.

Legislation: Old and New

On April 17, 1995, the White House released the President's long-awaited Executive Order on the classification of national security information. The order still permits classification of information relating to cryptology, but some changes were made. The new order requires the automatic declassification of most secret information 25 years or older. However, the order exempts information from automatic declassification if it falls into a narrow exemption category, including information that would "reveal . . . a cryptographic system or activity."

Efforts to revise the current Executive Order (issued by President Reagan in 1981) began soon after the Clinton Administration assumed office. EPIC actively monitored the revision process and urged a relaxation of classification standards generally and of those governing cryptographic information specifically. In comments submitted in July 1993, EPIC staff urged removal of cryptology from the categories of information presumed to be classifiable. EPIC noted that the "designation of a routine privacy-enhancing technology as presumptively a national security matter is inconsistent with the end of the Cold War and the dramatic growth of commercial and civilian telecommunications networks. . . . [Cryptographic] technology today plays an essential role in assuring the security and privacy of a wide range of communications affecting finance, education, research, and personal correspondence."

Under the Reagan order, cryptology was singled out as a separate and independent category. The new Clinton order refers instead to "intelligence activities (including special activities), intelligence sources or methods, or cryptology." This formulation suggests a recognition that information concerning encryption technology should be classified only if it relates to intelligence uses of the technology, as opposed to the increasing use of encryption in civilian applications. The language, however, remains ambiguous and does not comport with the growing opinion that cryptography should not be presumptively tied to national security classification.

The classification of cryptographic information has already hampered the public's ability to monitor the government's activities in the area of civilian communications security. Information relating to the Digital Signature Standard (intended for the authentication of unclassified electronic transmissions) was withheld from disclosure under the Reagan executive order. Likewise, key information concerning the Clipper encryption initiative (including the underlying Skipjack algorithm) was classified and placed beyond public review.[8]

Books Legal, Disks Not

Mr. Phil Karn, since 1993, has been attempting to seek export approval of a diskette of cryptographic sourcecode created as a supplement to Bruce Schneier's *Applied Cryptography* book. Though the book is legally exportable, and the diskette contains nothing but an exact duplication of code already in the book, Karn's Commodity Jurisdiction Request has repeatedly been denied. The Administration maintains that the source code is somehow not the same as the printed version, but that its translation to *machine-readable format* on the diskette imbues it with *value-added* qualities. One surmises that the Department of State may not have heard of scanners and manual typing, which render any text machine-readable.

Below is the text of a letter written by Mr. Karn's attorney to the Department of State. It expresses extremely well the feeling people have that the government is utilizing delaying tactics and generally mishandling situations related to export of cryptographic materials.

April 28, 1995

Mr. Thomas E. McNamara
Assistant Secretary
Bureau of Political-Military Affairs
Room 7325A
Department of State
Washington, DC 20520

Dear Mr. McNamara:

On December 5, 1994, we wrote on behalf of our client, Mr. Philip R. Karn, Jr. of San Diego, California, to appeal the adverse determination of Deputy Assistant Secretary Martha C. Harris, with regard to Mr. Karn's appeal of a determination by the State Department's Office of Defense Trade Controls (ODTC) in CJ case 081-94. On February 28, 1995, we met with you and representatives of the Department of Justice and the National Security Agency, to provide additional information and explain our position. We have not heard anything more about this appeal since that meeting.

All relevant facts are known to the Department and to the interested agencies. While all of us recognize the importance of the issues raised in this case, the issues are neither complex nor analytically difficult. As you know, it has appeared to us and to other observers that the licensing delays that Mr. Karn and others who seek licenses relating to cryptographic materials have experienced fit a pattern of procrastination by federal agencies, which appears to be based on the publicly stated policy of the National Security Agency to attempt to deter the further spread of strong cryptography as much as

Continued

they can, notwithstanding the fact that the technology at stake is already widely available, as documented in our appeal. In short, it continues to appear that NSA is using the tactics of delay and decision-avoidance in an effort to continue to chill the First Amendment activities of Mr. Karn and others interested in cryptography.

Mr. Karn has patiently attempted to comply with established procedures throughout this matter. His initial request for a commodity jurisdiction determination was filed on March 9, 1994, and was denied by ODTC on May 12, 1994. That adverse decision was appealed to Dr. Harris on June 7, 1994. Dr. Harris affirmed the adverse decision on October 7, 1994. The issues involved had been pending before your department since Mr. Karn filed his 1993 request for a commodity jurisdiction determination on the book, *Applied Cryptography.* In short, the Executive Branch has had the issue in this case before it for over a year. We have repeatedly been assured that the matter is receiving "high-level attention" and has generated significant interagency discussion.

The continued delay in rendering a decision in this matter is inexplicable except on the assumption that the Executive Branch intends, by its inaction, to chill the activities of Mr. Karn and others. As you know from our earlier submission, the chilling effects of this system of prior restraints lies at the heart of the constitutional difficulties of the ITAR regime that have been previously identified by the Department of Justice.

Please be advised that while we would prefer to obtain a decision on our appeal from your office, we will not continue to wait for an event that apparently will not occur. Mr. Karn has requested that we seek judicial review of this matter not later than June 15, 1995, whether or not your decision has been issued. We will take such action, unless, of course, you render a favorable decision before that time.

Cordially,

Kenneth C. Bass, III
Thomas J. Cooper

More documents from the Karn case can be found at:

http://www.eff.org/pub/Privacy/ITAR_export/Karn_Schneier_export_case/
gopher.eff.org: 1/EFF/Privacy/ITAR_export/Karn_Schneier_export_case
ftp.eff.org: /pub/Privacy/ITAR_export/Karn_Schneier_export_case/

Cybercash, Inc. has received the U.S. Commerce Department's approval to export its electronic payment software, despite a robust encryption algorithm. Only small amounts of data can be entered, and the software won't run if altered.
(*Wall Street Journal*, 5/8/95, B10.)

Specific U.S. Legislation on Encryption

In the United States, cryptography still is covered under the same legislation as an F-16 fighter plane or a TOW missile; it is a munition. If you plan to export any cryptographic algorithms, your best plan is to obtain a copy of the applicable legislation and a good lawyer.

The legislation that governs the export of cryptography is called the Defense Trade Regulations. It is interesting to note that this legislation formerly was called the International Traffic in Arms Regulation (ITAR), and the DTC was formerly known as the Office of Munitions Controls. Perhaps these new names are designed to reflect the fact that cryptography is becoming an increasingly important part of U.S. defense? In any case, we have included some relevant portions of the U.S. Defense Trade Regulations in Appendix B.

Does the Government Regulate the Internet?

The United States government has begun to draft legislation attempting to regulate the content of messages sent over the Internet. On June 15, 1995, the United States Senate passed the Communications Decency Act, which restricts the kinds of information flowing across the Internet, in an effort to protect children from gaining access to inappropriate materials. Since a slightly different version of the legislation was passed in the House, the bill has gone into committee for consideration at this writing. Many U.S. citizens feel that the Communications Decency Act restricts their freedom of speech under the First Amendment to the U.S. Constitution. The legislation is popularly believed to be unconstitutional, and it may be challenged in court if it becomes law.

Sponsored by Sen. Jim Exon (D-Nebraska), the amendment originated as an independent bill titled Communications Decency Act of 1995 (CDA), but subsequently was attached to the Senate's omnibus telecommunications deregulation bill. We will continue to refer to it here as the CDA. It is intended, according to its sponsor, both to prohibit "the [computer] equivalent of obscene telephone calls" and to prohibit the distribution to children of materials with sexual content. One mother comments in an Internet forum:

> *I truly believe that [this type of] content is not "dangerous." Interpretation of content is what is actually dangerous. The answer to the dilemma of pornography and children is for parents to teach their children how to responsibly interpret and deal with pornography, not to pretend that it doesn't exist or censor the real world.*
>
> *I believe that in the end, whether it is governmental or parental, censorship does more harm than good for children. Children WILL be exposed to sex and violence, they always have and they always will. Sex and violence are both natural things. By not addressing it in the family, parents fail to prepare their children for the real world. Puritainism-based censorship only mystifies sex and violence thus making children "more" interested and "less" prepared.*

Specific Provisions of the CDA

The Communications Decency Act would change the language of Title 47, United States Code, Section 223, a section that primarily does two things:

◆ It prohibits *obscene or harassing* phone calls and other similar, abusive uses of the telephone.

◆ It imposes regulation (promulgated and administered by the Federal Communications Commission) on telephone services that provide so-called *indecent* content, and prohibits those services from providing legally obscene content.

The amending language drafted by Sen. Exon and passed by the Senate substantially restructures and alters the provisions of this section in an effort to bring computer communications under the statute. If the Senate-approved language becomes law, provisions in the amended statute will:

1. Expand the scope of the statute from telephones to *telecommunications devices* (such as computers, modems, and the data servers and conferencing systems used by Internet sites and by commercial providers, such as America Online and CompuServe).

2. Define as a criminal offense any communication that is legally obscene or indecent if that communication is sent over a telecommunications device "with intent to annoy, abuse, threaten, or harass another person".

3. Penalize any person or entity who, by use of a telecommunication device, "knowingly . . . makes or makes available" any content or material that is legally obscene.

4. Penalize any person or entity who "knowingly . . . makes or makes available" to a person under the age of 18 any content or material that is indecent.

The CDA outlines affirmative defenses for persons or entities who might otherwise be liable under the statute's criminal provisions.

In spite of the efforts of Sen. Exon to address in this revision of his legislation those criticisms and constitutional issues raised by earlier drafts of it, the language of the CDA as passed by the Senate threatens the First Amendment rights both of online service providers and of individual citizens.

Criminalizing Constitutionally Protected Speech

None of the CDA's prohibitions of obscene communications raise any constitutional issues; it is well-settled law that obscene content is not protected under the Constitution. In contrast, CDA's restrictions on indecent speech are deeply problematic.

What is indecent speech and what is its significance? In general, indecent speech is nonobscene material that deals explicitly with sex or that uses profane language. The Supreme Court has repeatedly stated that such indecency is constitutionally protected. Further, the Court has stated that indecent speech cannot be banned altogether—not even in broadcasting, the single communications medium in which the federal government traditionally has held broad powers of content control.

The section of the CDA dealing with obscene or harassing communications penalizes not only the sending of obscene communications, but also those that are indecent. This prohibition of indecent content, even though limited somewhat in application by the section's intent requirement, is unconstitutional on its face.

Under the CDA, jurisdiction over computer communications is given to the FCC. Heretofore, the FCC has had content control over only two specific types of communications media:

- Broadcasting media, such as TV and radio (and broadcasting-related technologies, such as cable TV)
- The narrow class of telephone-based commercial services that requires the assistance and support of government-regulated common carriers.

In no other communications medium does the government have the constitutional authority to impose broad regulation of indecent content.

The justification for the federal government's special role in regulation of broadcasting is twofold. The first rationale for such a broad regulatory role was the *scarcity of frequencies* argument, which appears in the Supreme Court's decision in *Red Lion Broadcasting Co. v. FCC (1969).* In that case, the Court held that there is a finite number of workable broadcasting frequencies, and that the scarcity of this important public resource entails that the airwaves be allocated and supervised by the federal government in order to best serve the public interest. The second rationale for a special government role in broadcasting appears in *FCC v. Pacifica Foundation* (the Seven Dirty Words case discussed earlier). In this case the Court argued that broadcasting is an especially pervasive medium that intrudes into the privacy of the home, creating a constant risk that adults will be exposed to offensive material, and children to indecent material, without warning.

The justification for regulation of the telephone-based services is grounded in the government's special role in supervising common carriers. Since the telephone systems of this country, many of which amount to monopolies, are common carriers, they are appropriately under the jurisdiction of the FCC. It makes sense for phone-sex services, which rely on the cooperation of common carriers, to fall under FCC jurisdiction as well. Neither the broadcasting rationales nor the common-carrier rationale support government content control over computer communications. Why not?

First of all, the new medium of computer-based communications—which may occur over everything from large-scale Internet access providers and commercial conferencing systems to the PC-based bulletin-board system running in a hobbyist's basement—isn't afflicted with *scarcity.* Computing hardware itself is increasingly inexpensive, and one of the basic facts of modern computer communication is that whenever you add a computer to the Internet, you increase the Internet's size and capabilities.

Second, computer-based communications aren't *pervasive,* as that term is used in the Pacifica case. In the world of broadcasting, content is *pushed* at audiences by TV and radio stations and broadcasting networks—audiences are primarily passive recipients of programming. In computer communications, in contrast, content is pulled by users from various locations and resources around the globe through the Internet, or from the huge data servers maintained by such services as Prodigy and America Online. Exposure to content is primarily driven by user choice.

For users with even minimal experience, there is little risk of unwitting exposure to offensive or indecent material.

Finally, online service providers aren't common carriers and don't want to be—it is the nature of this kind of service that providers must reserve the right to make certain basic choices about content. In contrast, a common carrier, such as AT&T or BellSouth, has to take all comers. (If online service providers were treated as common carriers, we might imagine a day when the FCC requires that an NAACP-sponsored BBS carry hateful messages from members of the Ku Klux Klan.)

In sum, the narrow constitutional justifications for content regulation of two specific types of media do not extend to traditional print media, films, or oral conversations. Clearly, there is no constitutional rationale for extending intrusive content-regulatory control to online communications. This means that the CDA's shoehorning of online communications into the jurisdiction of the FCC is itself unconstitutional.

It is clear that Congress could not constitutionally grant the FCC the power to tell *The New Yorker* not to print profane language—even though children might come across a copy of *The New Yorker.* Surely it is equally clear that Congress cannot grant the FCC the authority to dictate how providers like Netcom and CompuServe handle content that contains such language.

The Moral: Computer communications pose different problems and require different solutions than other media.

Suppose that the federal government had the constitutional authority to regulate indecency in computer communications. Still, it would be required by the First Amendment to employ only the "least restrictive means" in doing so. In the Sable case, the Court noted that there are means less restrictive than a total ban for protecting children from indecent content on phone-sex services. These means include such measures as requiring procedures that verify customers' ages, and denying services to minors.

The Exon language creates an affirmative defense for online service providers who implement the same types of procedures that the FCC now requires of phone-sex services. But what works for phone-sex services clearly would not work for computer-communications services. In this fundamentally different medium, those FCC-enforced procedures are not a "least restrictive means"—in fact, they are potentially among the most restrictive.

The language that penalizes anyone who "makes or makes available" indecent content to a minor would require an access provider such as Netcom to cease carrying the entire **alt.sex.*** hierarchy, the great majority of which is First-Amendment-protected speech. Suppose Netcom tried to avail itself of legal immunity for transmitting indecency by, say, limiting subscriber access to the "indecent" Usenet newsgroups to Netcom subscribers age 18 or over. Since Netcom, like all Internet access providers, is also a Usenet distribution node, *the company would still be liable;* since, by passing "indecent" Usenet traffic through, it would "make available" that indecent content to minors elsewhere on the Net who aren't Netcom customers.

This analysis is not intended to imply that no government regulation of computer communications would meet the "least restrictive means" qualification. As a practical matter, the Internet is uniquely suited to measures that protect sensitive users and children from offensive content, while allowing the full range of constitutionally protected speech. The computers that users employ when accessing the Internet and those that providers use to administer an online service are highly intelligent and programmable devices. Using them, it is relatively easy to design tools with which individuals can filter offensive content and parents can screen content for their children. The government's promotion of the development and implementation of such tools, if done in a way consistent with First Amendment guarantees, most likely would qualify as a "least restrictive means."[10]

How will this conflict of laws, needs, and interests get sorted out? There must be legal, technological, and organizational components to a good solution. Clearly, the legal precedent does not exist for upholding civil liberties in the electronic realm, so individuals may be forced to rely on technological solutions in the meantime.

Digital Pseudonyms

One technological solution that could assist individuals in their efforts to uphold their civil liberties online is by approved use of *digital pseudonyms.* The technology of digital pseudonyms is another application of digital signature technology.

Currently, many Western countries require their citizens to carry identification documents. In the United States, driver's licenses are being upgraded to perform that function. In general, efforts toward creating machine-readable national identity documents are expanding internationally. Already, organizations are using data such as name, birthdate, and birthplace to link their records with those of other organizations.

Using digital pseudonyms, an individual has a different *name* with each organization, something like a different E-mail name. No other identifying information need be given, since the sender of a message (or a pile of digital money) can be sufficiently identified based on cryptographic keys. For a casual purchase at a shop, a one-time pseudonym could be used. In an ongoing business relationship, such as a banking relationship, the same pseudonym would be used repeatedly. Organizations can protect themselves by limiting individuals to a single, known pseudonym, and by finding ways to ensure that individuals are held accountable for abuses perpetrated under any of their pseudonyms.

Because individuals have input into creating their pseudonyms, they can rest assured that their pseudonyms cannot be linked and cannot be used by anyone else. Although the codes could be broken in principle by guessing enough keys, in fact the guessing is infeasible because of the enormous number of possible keys.

If an individual uses a smart card as an identity card (smart cards are discussed in Chapter 4, *Digital Money: The Cuneiform of a New Age*), simple mathematical proofs can demonstrate that the pseudonyms cannot be linked, even under the extremely unlikely (perhaps even paranoid?) scenario of all organizations colluding and all communication lines being tapped.[11]

The Facts of Life: Encryption Cannot Be Stopped

A fundamental reality about encryption is that it cannot be stopped by technical means. Why not? Cryptographic material can be disguised within other material. For instance, it's not possible to tell whether you're looking at an encrypted message when it's hidden in a picture.

To explain: Suppose you have a digitized picture of the Mona Lisa, in 24-bit color. If you utilize the low-order bit to contain your encrypted message, the picture still just looks like the picture. Why? That bit is noise at the visual level. Furthermore, if the cost of transmission is low enough, it's worthwhile to transmit such pictures. And without the key, it's impossible to unlock the *noise.* (Is it or isn't it a secret message? Only the keyholder knows for sure.) This ability to hide information within another message is referred to as *creating a subliminal channel.* Subliminal channels, for better or worse, can provide some basic freedoms.

Civil Liberties in Europe

Overlaying all of these questions and observations is case law in various countries or other dominions. For example, Europeans have a much more stringent set of rules regarding personal data about individuals. Did you know that it's against the law in Germany to send someone unsolicited sales material? A business must get potential customers to request sales materials. It must find a way to get them attracted—a factor that certainly changes the tenor of advertising! Also, it's absolutely against the law to say anything that's not verifiably true in an advertisement in Germany. And it's against the law to export personal financial information from county to country in Europe. But how do you stop it?

What Constitutes Privacy in an Electronic Age?

Of all the issues we have discussed in this chapter, privacy is probably the most important concern among citizens. In a seminal law review article in 1890, Samuel Warren and Louis Brandeis defined the right of privacy as "the right to be left alone."[12]

More recently, privacy was defined by one academic as "the claim of individuals, groups, or institutions to determine for themselves when, how, and to what extent information about them is communicated to others."[13]

Today, there is a thriving U.S. industry dealing in personal information. Over 10,000 lists are available for rent containing personal information about individuals. According to a 1990 estimate, the business of selling personal information was a $3-billion-per-year industry. More than ever, personal computers provide access to services that provide personal information about individuals. Most Americans have no idea about what information is being collected, or how it is being used.

For example, Mead Data Central, Inc., which operates the legal database called Lexis, also operates a database called Lexis Finder, which is a nationwide white-pages directory that includes the addresses, telephone numbers, and other information about 111 million individuals. Typical entries provide the names of individuals that reside at a particular residence, their month and year of birth, their telephone number, when that number was first listed in the telephone directory, their dwelling type (single family, multifamily, and so forth), whether they own the residence, and the median value of homes in the surrounding census tract. Prodigy and CompuServe also provide access to databases containing personal information about individuals.

With all this going on, it's no wonder that some people feel computerization is robbing individuals of their ability to monitor and control the ways in which information about them is used. Public and private sector organizations acquire extensive amounts of personal information, and the individuals involved do not know whether this information obtained about them is inaccurate, outdated, or otherwise inappropriate. Automated payment systems and other electronic consumer transactions are expanding the possibilities for surveillance and perhaps even intrusion into personal affairs.

On the other hand, organizations enjoy the efficiency and cost-cutting opportunities created by automated information-gathering. Also, it's obviously good for organizations to computerize in ways that reduce the possibilities for fraud, such as the abuse of social services, by creating more pervasive and massively interlinked identity records. Of course, the resulting potential for misuse of such data is alarming.

A seemingly inevitable conflict is growing, between the needs of organizations for lower costs and better protection from crimes such as fraud, and the needs of individuals for privacy.

Here is an excerpt from the testimony of FBI Director Louis Freeh before the House Committee on Judiciary, Subcommittee on Crime, May 3, 1995:

> . . . With respect to the authorities that we have, as we testified in the Senate last week, the FBI is very comfortable with the Attorney General guidelines. I feel very confident that, interpreted broadly, and certainly within the Constitution, those guidelines give me and my agents the authority we need to investigate and prevent, in many cases, what would be clear violations of criminal law and clear terrorist activity within the United States. . . .
>
> We need the authority to trace money, explosives, nuclear materials, and terrorists. Pen registers and trap-and-trace devices are necessary in counterterrorism as well as counterintelligence cases. The threshold ought to be the same in a criminal case as in a terrorism case. It's critical that investigators have increased access, short of a full-blown grand jury investigation, to hotel, motel, and common-carrier records.
>
> . . . Encryption capabilities available to criminals and terrorists, both now and in days to come, must be dealt with promptly. We will not have an effective counterterrorism strategy if we do not solve the problem of encryption. It's not a problem unique, by the way, to terrorists. It's one which addresses itself to drug dealers and cartels and criminals at large. There are now no legally available means in some dangerously few cases to exclude and remove alien terrorists from the United States. Again, that's an issue that this committee has already taken up.
>
> These are tools. These are not new authorities. These are tools with which to use our current statutory authority, all, in my view, well within the Constitution. And the addition of

those resources, which are people and technologies, will give us the ability to deal with these cases as well as prepare for and prevent other incidents, such as the one we've seen recently.[14]

The central law protecting the privacy of electronic communications today is the Electronic Communications Privacy Act (ECPA). Originally enacted in 1968, the early ECPA legislation was directed at overzealous government agents in the aftermath of the Watergate scandal. In 1986, the ECPA was broadened to become the ECPA as we know it. The law was intended to aid the blossoming cellular-phone industry by prohibiting private and governmental interceptions of cellular communication.

The general rules of the ECPA are fairly clear:

◆ It is illegal to intercept messages while those messages are in transit, except in narrowly defined circumstances of extreme necessity.

◆ It is illegal to gain access to communications less than 180 days old, except under warrant.

The first major test of the ECPA was decided in Texas in 1992. The case was *Steve Jackson Games v. United States.* Secret Service agents mistakenly seized a company's entire electronic bulletin board contents, including many private E-mail messages between employees. The company sued the government for violating the ECPA, among other laws, claiming that the government had violated the privacy rights of each user by failing to obtain the proper authority for the seizure, as required by the ECPA. Unfortunately, the court awarded each user only $1,000 for the government's misbehavior. Incidentally, the court also ruled that E-mail messages that had not yet been received were not counted as intercepted for the purposes of the ECPA, clearly a misunderstanding of the nature of E-mail.

Although the ECPA provides some protection, it allows some important gaps. First, the ECPA does not prohibit interception by the actual providers of electronic communications services, such as the telephone companies, system administrators, or network administrators. However, the ECPA does prevent these service providers from disclosing the information to others, except in cases of extreme threat or emergency.

Furthermore, the ECPA does not apply to in-house, corporate networks, which are not considered to be public communications channels. To make matters worse for employees, the employer usually is considered to be the provider, and can therefore intercept messages at will.

Finally, the ECPA does not prohibit governmental agents from obtaining E-mail using undercover identities. If a false identity of the agent is the proper addressee of the message, it can be utilized legally. Undercover agents log on to many, if not most, systems.[15]

Other Forms of Privacy Protection Online

Common Law Privacy Rights: It is illegal to disclose someone's personal affairs in public. Personal privacy rights most often are asserted when a disclosure is made to a large audience. Celebrities or other public figures naturally give up a certain amount of protection under common law privacy rights, the bounds of which may vary from state to state.

Personal Data Privacy Rights: No single law protects individuals from having personal data used or disclosed. Certain sensitive types of information, such as banking and medical records, are protected by statute. Also, video stores may not remarket their customers' names. This area of privacy protection is likely to see a lot of activity as Internet participation increases.

Freedom of Assembly: The Constitution protects our right to free assembly, especially in any situation where disclosure of members' identities may lead to an effort to damage or destroy an organization. This law actually has not yet been tested in the context of the Internet, but it would apply to the right of mailing lists, bulletin boards, or online services not to disclose their members' names.

Business Confidentiality: Businesses expect privacy on the Internet, and the law protects their rights, especially where trade secrets are involved.

Privacy Protection Act: Federal law protects materials collected and prepared for publication. This law actually came about as a means of protecting the First Amendment rights of journalists.

Privacy Summary

Here is a summary of the forms of privacy protection granted online:

- ◆ Privacy of Electronic Messages: The Electronic Communications Privacy Act
- ◆ Privacy of Personal Affairs from Public View: Common law privacy rights
- ◆ Privacy of Personal Data from Use in Databases: Personal data privacy laws
- ◆ Privacy of membership in Groups: Constitutional right of freedom of assembly
- ◆ Privacy of Company Information: Business confidentiality and trade-secret rights
- ◆ Privacy of Materials in Preparation for Publication: Privacy Protection Act[16]

What's the Business Angle?

In the culture of the Internet today, people may be reluctant to give your company information if they are not certain how or by whom it will be used. As we discussed in Chapter 6, *The Evolving Cyber Economy,* if you provide a service or something else that's of value to your customers, they may willingly provide you with personal information that assists you in better serving their needs. It would be good business to respect your customers' online privacy rights and other civil liberties online, thereby creating an environment of trust and mutual benefit. Naturally, it is also a good idea to make sure that employees understand the privacy rights that a corporation has online.

chapter ten

Technology in Service to Humanity

Global economics does not speak to the public need for meaningful work, affordable housing, fulfilling education, adequate medical care, a clean environment, honest and accountable government, social and cultural renewal, or simple justice.

—John Taylor Gatto, New York State Teacher of the Year, 1992

Is electronic commerce, a worldwide electronic community, a viable alternative? How will we integrate this new technology into our lives without becoming slaves to computer technology, which certainly contains within it the seeds for becoming alienated from common human reality? How will we prevent the disturbing trend toward a society of information haves and have-nots so that everyone can benefit from the new era of Internet commerce?

This chapter examines a few of the pertinent social and humanitarian questions that are raised by the coming transformation that is the topic of this book. The first, most basic, and perhaps most surprising question we encountered was this: Do we really need digital money?

Do We Really Need Digital Money?

In the process of interviewing people for this book, we were struck by the question some people asked: Do we really need digital money? Why can't we just stick with the systems we have in place now? Who do you think is behind the phenomenon of digital money? Even though we're obviously in support of digital money and Internet commerce as important keys to the future of this planet, it seems worthwhile to examine these questions more seriously.

Another way to ask this question might be: How is Internet commerce and digital money improving what we already have? One answer: Let's look at the commercialization of the Internet as just one more example of the inexorable process of technology transfer from the academic community into the domain of mainstream commerce.

Think back to the 1960s, when it was the space program that gave America the sense that technology was coming down into the commercial arena out of taxpayer-funded government research. Today, in the 1990s, it is the Internet that echoes that same phenomenon: What was originally a taxpayer-funded project is now providing business opportunities in the mainstream.

Traditionally, large corporations provide funding for blue-sky research and development efforts, hoping to obtain just this result: new technology they can apply to making better, more competitive products. In this case, government-funded research has produced a technology that is enabling better ways of doing business (Figure 10.1)!

In this case, what the Internet provides is a way of communicating more efficiently. Let's face it, essentially every business

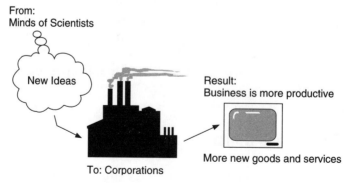

Figure 10.1   The flow of ideas from research to commercial use.

transaction discussed in this book as Internet commerce could be done over the telephone, in a pinch. But the Internet provides broadened communications bandwidth—it's more fun than the phone, it has colored pictures, movies, music! It's exciting! It's cool!

For instance, if I'm a Texas commodities broker selling some cow bellies, I can sell them over the telephone or over the Internet. We all understand how that would be done over the phone: in words, backed up with a written contract. On the Internet, well, we could have pictures of the cow bellies, dancing cows, singing cows, whatever. In either case, I still have to negotiate an agreeable price, get a contract signed, verify the credentials of the purchaser, and find out where to ship them.

Indeed, in the realm of Internet commerce, business as usual in the course of time will become business as usual. We're just automating and speeding up some routine business functions, such as phone and postal services, which long ago were not so routine themselves. The Pony Express was pretty exciting in its day, too.

Basically, merchants and corporations are excited about digital money and Internet commerce because it makes their business communications easier and cheaper—lower advertising costs and lower transaction costs. Also, the consumer has less time to think things over if it's so easy to make purchases online with digital money. Consumers like digital money and Internet commerce because they enjoy the convenience and time-saving nature of online shopping. As better technical solutions are advanced for problems that arise in online contract negotiations and ajudication, even dispute resolution is likely to become less expensive online.[1]

Life in the New Era

How will life look in the new age of digital money and a global information infrastructure that forms the basis of a global economy? In 1995, the global population will exceed 5.7 billion people. By 2050, it is estimated that 10 billion people will share this planet. Population growth in industrialized nations slowed to replacement levels in the last 50 years, while less developed regions experienced increased population growth. The reasons for this growth are many, including the contributions of organizations, such as the World Health Organization and United Nations' Children's Emercengy Fund (UNICEF), that have reduced infant mortality rates and increased lifespans. How will all of these people find employment so they can rise above a subsistence lifestyle?

For all its ills, capitalism has managed to put a lot of people to work worldwide. It has decreased the number of people living below the poverty line in many areas. In Chile, for instance, unemployment dropped from 18 percent in 1981 to about 6 percent today. In India, increased employment between 1972 and 1988 helped reduce the poverty rate from 51.5 percent to 29.9 percent. At the same time, literacy rates increased from 34 percent to 50 percent. If we continue this trend of increasing the access to information and innovation, advancing technology promises to improve the chances of employment and the standard of living for the next generation.

The development agendas advanced by organizations, such as the World Bank and the International Monetary Fund, advise these less-developed regions to create export-oriented economies. But unlike the nations that grew before them, these regions may have a difficult time developing without assistance from a global communications infrastructure, since they must compete with a host of nations that are already developed.[2]

New Work: Technology in Service to Humanity

In *The End of Work,* Jeremy Rifkin states that information technologies will continue to replace jobs such as telephone operators who look up phone numbers, postal workers who read addresses, and bank tellers who dispense cash. Not to fear. We, the authors, believe that advancing technology will eventually rehumanize work and distribute the world's wealth more equitably, creating a global economy that's ultimately satisfying and sustainable.

Images abound of dark futures, but ignore them. The International Labor Organization (ILO) in its first report on global employment stated that 30 percent of the world's workforce is either unemployed or underemployed, the highest level since the 1930s. The ILO also estimates that in the next 25 years over 1 billion people will be added to the global work force, mostly in developing regions. What the ILO report fails to mention is the growth of informal or alternative economies, and the employment they'll generate. This type of employment consists, for example, of street vendors, recyclers, mobile car wash services, and any other job that people can create for themselves.

According to the ILO, these alternative kinds of workers are the underemployed. Their report does not mention the vital role that these workers play in sustaining local economies. Many of these particular entrepreneurs define their niches by the waste created from other employers, yet each enterprise plays an important role, no matter how small or transitory it may be.

Many people are worried about the state of the U.S. economy. Jobs are leaving the United States. For instance, software vendors such as Microsoft now employ computer programmers in diverse regions of the world for a fraction of what they pay workers in advanced, industrialized nations. U.S. software engineers are in a state of outrage.

Yet these same technologies and job migrations that are putting bank tellers and software engineers out of work will make people available to supply the increased demand for jobs that require social interaction, such as home health-care providers, child care workers, and specialized educators.

Economically speaking, it's time to stop thinking locally or even nationally and start thinking globally. Shifting these software jobs raises the incomes of workers in places like India and Russia to many times what they earned previously, and it distributes capital into new, developing communities. In the long term, we all will benefit. Software jobs affect only a minor segment of the world's population. But improved communications technologies can improve the business prospects of families all over the globe.

Imagine a family that lives in India or Peru. Imagine that they make rugs for a living. To expand their market possibilities and improve their profits today, they must sell their rugs to a middleman, either a retailer or an exporter, if they wish to sell their rugs outside their immediate locale. What happens? The price of that rug increases first at the transaction with the middleman, then again and again as it is sold to others along the economic food chain, until the consumer, at the top of the food chain, pays the highest price of all for it. And the family in Peru or India sees little of that money (Figure 10.2).

Internet commerce offers an alternative solution. As communities begin to connect to the global communications network, they can join the new frontier. With a computer and an adapted imaging system, small producers in remote areas can put images of their products onto a global electronic economy network (GEEN). They gain the opportunity to sell their product to distant, quite possibly more wealthy, consumers. Everyone benefits, except perhaps the middlemen, who are now free to become social workers. (For more discussion of collapsing value chains, see Chapter 6, *The Evolving Cyber Economy*.)

By excising middlemen and reducing marketing costs, producers will receive more of a premium for their products. They also may find ways to sell their products remotely into a niche market that values their products. Thus, the local economy benefits because the producer receives a better profit, and the consumers benefit because they receive more choices at lower cost. The competitive nature of the traditional retail economy, combined with the directness of the GEEN will keep prices as low as possible.

What the GEEN will need to develop and maintain, technologically, is the capability for quick searches and the adaptability to respond to an individual's tastes. Intelligent agents may play a role in creating these capabilities.[3]

Everyone needs productive work. Our personal vision is that the Internet be the alternative, the revolutionary force that will

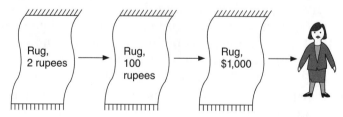

Figure 10.2   Resale of a rug.

restore balance to our world. By itself, it is just a piece of technology, but in the hands of caring human beings, it can serve as a catalyst for creating the kind of world we've always said we wanted to create.

Four Basic Needs

It has been said that a person has four basic needs: food, clothing, shelter, and fun. Internet commerce probably can't give us food, clothing, or shelter directly (although it can give them to us indirectly, with new purchasing power and convenience). But it certainly can and will give us fun.

Dan says: "In the worlds of bits, everything is really cheap as hell to produce. Once you've overcome the engineering costs, the distribution costs are minor. We can just be giving each other more and more happiness, to the extent that we can get happiness out of bits: info, movies, audio, vr, and so on."

Of course some kinds of fun are inherently physical, such as lying on a beach, but that's after you've overcome the basic needs. Sometimes, your body has to physically be somewhere to collect the happiness. But we may have more time for physical fun as well. Fun will come to us in the form of more leisure time, less commuting in traffic, more movies on demand, less expensive software products because distribution costs will be lower, and so forth. All of this fun might pay off in other ways, too.

The Internet and U.S. Education

The current U.S. government administration has a goal of interconnecting all classrooms by the year 2000. Various corporations and industry programs also promise support for improving education through the use of computers and networking technology.

At least in theory, the U.S. Department of Education would be the best entity to bring together all the considerations about accessibility, content, and general support for K through 12 education. If we are to meet the goal of connecting all U.S. classrooms to the

Internet by the year 2000, it will require a well-organized effort to create needed software, secure state government and community approval of materials and of the instructional environment, and to provide hands-on training and assistance to teachers as they move into this new teaching medium. Interestingly enough, the problem of providing support for network-based resources in education is even larger than the problem of providing support for research networking, so there also is a need for ongoing research into better designs and implementations of technology that can be applied in the realm of education. If networking is to add to the educational process, mainstream educational services must be reliably available over the network.[4]

If mainstream education services indeed are made available on the Internet, perhaps new options for schooling at home will be realized in parallel to new options for working at home.

From Family Unit to Global Community

Frederick Hayek, an Austrian economist, gave a fabulous talk on PBS when he was in his late 80s. The talk was based on the idea that society hasn't caught up with itself, that the growth of technology has taken it beyond its historical roots.

Society began with the family unit. Within the family unit, people knew how to take care of everyone. For example, if Aunt Martha was an invalid, people took care of her—the family met her needs. Or if one of your boys was a recalcitrant knucklehead, you found ways to contain him. Basically, people know how to mete out justice when everyone in the community is personally known.

As villages formed, commerce began, and economic specialization occurred. Still, people knew who the village drunk was, and the village community found a way to take care of (most likely) him (or possibly her). Eventually, maybe the town had to build a jail for those who belonged to no family. Still, within the village someone always had sufficient knowledge about the truth of each individual's situation to be able to mete out justice. So, over the centuries, society has basically worked up rules about taking care of people.

Here's the problem today, the problem that will translate quite neatly into cyberspace: In a group larger than a village, no one knows anybody. Society does not know how to deal with large collections of people because of the factor of anonymity. How do people know how to dispense justice when they don't know the individuals involved?

For instance, people haven't figured out how to handle the less fortunate. Or, to put it another way, how do you know how to care for your neighbor when you don't know who your neighbor really is and therefore don't know what your neighbor really needs? In a global community, how do you love thy neighbor as thyself when thy neighbor is so far away?

The Need for Communities in Cyberspace

Will Internet commerce give us better tools and rules to care for each other? It could if we retain our sense of community online. How can we do that? Getting input, giving feedback, creating buy-in are even more important skills in an online community, because there's a lack of moment-to-moment feedback. Most likely, technology can and will be created to assist us in the process; we will learn how better to relate to one another in cyberspace. Indeed, we will have to. As individuals move into the realm of global internetworking, we may learn more about the customs and taboos of other nations and other cultures than we ever cared to know. At first, we may feel quite uncomfortable sorting out the definition of pornography, say in Saudia Arabia, from its definition in Amsterdam. And there is jurisdictional precedent to suggest that individuals in the United States could be prosecuted for offenses that they did not know were crimes in other countries.[5] Our mutual understanding, our tolerance, and our legal systems must evolve to allow for a global community. And slowly but surely, they will.

Hayek points out that evolution means survival of the fittest, where fitness is a measure of success in a given landscape. If you change the landscape, people's fitness characteristics change, but the exciting thing is this: eventually you'll find your tribe. For example, could it be that watching television and playing video games is preparing your children to meet their generation, the online generation?

In the early days of families, as Hayek noted, no doubt it was hard for people to find rules that worked. We're still on the path to Damascus. It may take time to figure out the answers that work for *us*. We're in the stage of early experiments with building a sense of community online. For instance, there will be official online directory services. But what's really the best way to find out about Bill? Ask someone who knows him. Let's make sure that every online Bill is part of a community.

Personal Accountability

Dan got removed from a jury once. It was a case in which the accused had entered a plea of insanity. Our dear coauthor rebelled, saying:

> *No, I don't think anybody's insane. I was insane once and I remember it, the moment when I felt nuts in a personal crisis. I just said to myself, Boy, Dan, you're not coping, you're crazy, you don't know what to do next. But you* do *know that you're doing the best you can and that what you do will be measured by others. So when you're feeling lost and crazy, you're still you. Pleading insanity is looking for absolution of responsibility from one's own actions. But you can't ever get rid of that, really.*

Insanity aside, there's certainly more than one way to solve the problems of life! People throughout the world have constructed different sets of rules that enable them to get along. Some rules, like left-side or right-side driving, don't work across boundaries, however. In a one-village world, if we take away all the rules that don't work across boundaries, the common rule set no doubt is very small. For instance, is the golden rule "Do unto others . . ." a good, perhaps singular, common rule? It seems to be a good start, because it implies personal accountability.

Social Redemption?

How can we paint a good future? Arno Penzias (of Bell Labs) gave an interesting talk at Uniforum about five years ago. (He won the Nobel prize in physics for discovering background radiation in the universe.) He talked about the new world of the network as a mechanism for returning to the village of old, because "If everyone can see what you're doing, you're going to behave better." He spoke of the networked world as a way to remoralize society. Not so much Big Brother, as it were, but Big Mother.

Today, there are people who actually steal. We wonder: How can people think that's right? They feel they must steal to survive. How will we handle these people in a global community? We could try something new. In New Guinea, there's a system of paying for crimes: You pay the person you injured, and every crime has a price. It's a village society with the wisdom in it to understand that you've got to redeem perpetrators, reintegrate them, otherwise the village breaks down.

Preventing the Virtual Ghetto

In the information age, knowledge is wealth. As we discussed in Chapter 6, *The Evolving Cyber Economy,* information-based wealth can be shared and no one ends up with less. Such wealth keeps growing. At present, however, access to the source of this wealth—information technology and the skill to use it—is restricted to the world's information haves. What they have are the computers, the modems, and the knowhow to pan gold from the cyberspace datastream. The gold that consists of information and learning within that datastream may, indeed, be endlessly minable, but not by the world's information have-nots—those who lack the technology and training of the technologically privileged.

Millions of technologically-disenfranchised have-nots who cannot afford the cost of that technology and training are walled off from potentially life-changing tools and knowledge, isolated in the virtual ghetto. Meanwhile, a growing information economy and its opportunities surround them. Escaping from this virtual ghetto means being able to afford the cost of the technology and training needed to prepare themselves to share in the production of information-based wealth.

Unlike long-entrenched ghettos, the new virtual ghetto is preventable. But what is the cost of prevention? At the local level, surprisingly little in dollars. Startup costs are under $10,000, and annual operating costs can be kept to a dollar or two per community member.

Cooperating computer-literate volunteers from businesses, libraries, schools, churches, and municipal agencies can do most of what needs to be done. Together, they are the means of prevention. All that is needed is the will, the cooperation, and the skill to apply practical strategies at the grassroots level, where the virtual ghetto is growing. There is increasing evidence that this can be done in any community where people want to do it.

This work is already happening in a few locally developed telecomputing networks. Information haves are working with have-nots to prevent proliferation of the ghetto mentality in their midst. These community-based, community-building efforts enable the technologically disenfranchised to learn and earn the technology and training needed to transform the virtual ghetto into an economically viable zone of opportunity.

To help communities understand what they can do to achieve electronic equity, a coalition of socially concerned not-for-profit organizations in the U.S., called the Learning and Information Network for Community Telecomputing (LINCT; see Chapter 2), has developed a low-cost model that communities can adopt and adapt to enable the technologically disenfranchised to learn and earn the computers and skills needed to mine the cyberspace datastream.[6]

Dr. Curtiss Priest, PhD, Director of LINCT, postulates the need for a public hand, analogous to Adam Smith's invisible hand, that equitably regulates and balances the access to information technology in our society for the sake of the public good. To quote Adam Smith:

> . . . he intends only his own gain, and he is in this, as in many other cases, led by an invisible hand to promote an end which

was no part of his intention. Nor is it always the worse for society that it was no part of it. By pursuing his own interest, he frequently promotes that of society more effectually than when he really intends to promote it.[7]

Dr. Priest seems to hold the complementary viewpoint: that by promoting the good of others, through the Public Hand, we will ultimately promote our own good. To quote Dr. Priest:

Let us look at the role of the public hand by examining some examples:

1. Public Good—In our society we believe that basic civil knowledge is critical to the functioning of our society. It is for this reason that we educate everyone in history and civics. In an information society we would wish to continue to assure that everyone can access and use information related to the public good. In fact, the level of knowledge and access might be expected to increase as it becomes easier and cheaper to provide for the public good. As the result of our concern for public good, we will wish to examine the continuing role of public institutions such as libraries and schools. We will wish to ensure that these institutions can function well in the new information infrastructure (or cyberspace).

2. Equity—As described early, we are at risk of creating virtual ghettos. Why is this offensive? Not only do virtual ghettos work against our interest in the public good, in the first example, but virtual ghettos offend our sense of fairness and justice. We wish, as a society, to ensure that no matter what station a person has, that station will be assured a minimal standard of access to information.

3. Freedom—Ithiel Poole wrote a famous book called *Technologies of Freedom*. He rightly identified that communication technologies are technologies of freedom. These technologies intrinsicly increase the "choice space" and increase freedom. In our society, we have strong sanctions to preserve freedoms and, thus, in cyberspace we

will wish to continue those sanctions and make sure that no person or corporation infringes on those liberties.

4. Privacy—Privacy is a strange beast. To those who know us well, we need be less private; yet to others, who may threaten our liberties, we need to maintain secrets. Information is central to privacy. From medical records to criminal records we are continually at risk of someone knowing something about us and using it against us. This argues for legislative and public policy to guard privacy. (Yet nowhere in the Constitution or the Bill of Rights is there a "right to privacy.")

By considering the characteristics of information that follow, you may be able to work out your own examples of where the Public Hand is needed, either in our current society or in our future society.

Characteristics of Information

In a market-driven, information-centered economy, it is helpful to identify those areas in which markets naturally will tend to undersupply information, or in which economic and other forces may cause information technology to disturb the moral or ethical bases of society.

To help pinpoint these areas, it is useful to identify the features that distinguish information from other forms of property. The following discussion, adapted from a paper by Dr. Priest, describes 15 characteristics of information as it is found in commerce and business transactions. These characteristics are useful for any general inquiry into the nature and purpose of information in society.

These characteristics are divided into three categories:

◆ Qualities of information as a commodity; that is, the distinguishing features of information that influence how it is consumed

◆ Qualities of information that potentially make it difficult to produce and consume information as a commodity

◆ Qualities of information that are not related to its consumable nature, but to human rights and concerns

Information as a Commodity

1. Intrinsic Co-production: It is the nature of information to be instrumental in achieving other goods and outcomes. This characteristic makes information inherently more valuable than goods that are not instrumental in nature.

2. Time-Constrained Consumption: It is the character of information consumption to occupy more consumer time per dollar expenditure than other commodities. This characteristic, combined with its relatively low reproduction cost (Characteristic 3) has long-run implications for employment.

3. High Development to Reproduction Cost Ratios: The cost of developing new information is high in comparison to the cost of reproducing existing information. The implications of this characteristic: Information development has inherent economies of scale and scope, and the resulting market structure would tend to include large corporations as information providers.

4. Relevance, More Variable across Consumers: It is the character of information that a particular piece usually is acquired only once. In other words, each consumer has a unique *information consumption profile.* This characteristic tends to work in the opposite direction of low reproduction costs, because it implies that information will tend to become increasingly customized and particularized. (See Chapter 5, *New Business Concepts.*)

Characteristics Related to the Difficulty of Producing and Consuming Information

5. Public Good: Information can be considered a public good, that is, the same information can be used concur-

rently by many consumers without mutual interference. Things that have substantial public-good characteristics, such as national defense, recreational parks, and safety facilities such as lighthouses, usually are supplied by the government to reduce the free-rider problem associated with inappropriability.

Inappropriability

Inappropriability is the difficulty of receiving full market compensation for the creation of information due to the problem of exclusion, which is the problem of keeping people who have not paid for the information from obtaining it. The result usually is underproduction and undercompensation.

Nondepletability

Information does not dissipate with use. New producers must compete with past producers (but society benefits with an overall accumulation of knowledge).

6. Externalities: Externalities are the effects of information, usually positive, that are not accounted for in its price. For example, information obtained as education has considerable positive externalities, because it tends to reduce unemployment and increase the general social welfare. You might think of externalities as *intangible effects*.

7. Indivisibilities (of Supply): Information must be purchased in lumps; these lumps may be vastly greater in size than the amount of information actually sought. This characteristic, along with the tendency of consumers to select unique sets of information for consumption (variable relevance), will contribute to the development and utilization of information technology that reduces indivisibilities and permits customization. (See Chapter 5, the "Mass Customization" section.)

8. Economies of Scale and Scope: Information has two natural economies of scale: 1. decreasing unit costs as the

scale of operation is increased, and 2. decreasing costs associated with joint production. Historically, information distribution in media, such as the telegraph, telephone, radio, and television, has exhibited sufficient economy of scale and scope that government regulation was required to reduce the problems associated with natural monopolies.

9. Uncertainty and Risk in Production: Firms generally are reluctant or unable to produce information when risks and uncertainties are present. A problem, in particular, is the generation of basic knowledge when that task requires substantial investment in research.

10. Information/Knowledge: Information about information is less likely to be available if there are problems related to searching (appropriability). This lack of availability leads to underconsumption.

11. Nonmonetizability: Some of the value of information is not expressible in monetary terms. For instance, information provides the basis for education, communication, and other activities that are difficult to value monetarily: The contribution of these activities to the welfare of society is largely intangible.

12. Transaction Costs: Transaction costs are the additional costs incurred by the producer related to utilizing the value of information. (N.B.—Transaction costs, in the economic sense, are those costs associated with negotiation, contracting, and enforcement, and traditionally do not refer to the general costs related to distributing or transmitting information.) Transaction costs make a major contribution to indivisibilities in the supply of information, because contracting and enforcement costs are difficult to reduce below a certain minimum.

13. Equity/Distribution Considerations: At anytime a society may decide that the distribution of goods is inequitable. This decision is made according to various principles regarding equity and fairness.

An example may better help to clarify this last concept: John Rawls argues that one can think in terms of a social contract made from a *primal position.* The primal position is a situation in which no individual knows his or her personal *station* in society, but agrees to a contract that divides goods based on abstract *fair* principles. For instance, one argument related to capitalistic society is that everyone might agree to have some people better-off than others if that situation also made others better-off than they would otherwise be. This argument is Rawls's justification of high salaries for the heads of industry.[8]

In terms of information, we can think in terms of minimal information standards that we would all wish to maintain. That is, no matter your station in society, you could be assured that you would have access to a certain minimum information base. In today's society, that minimum standard probably is provided by television and newspapers.

As a society becomes increasingly information-centered, the minimum information base might be raised: Information is central to a person's ability to be comfortable and capable in such a society.

Characteristics not Related to the Market for Information

14. Intrinsic Relationship to Human Welfare: Human welfare arises when individuals and groups achieve their desired outcomes. Information is related to human welfare intrinsically, because it inherently facilitates the achievement of desired outcomes.

15. Intrinsic Relationship to Freedom and Privacy: Freedom—Information affects the range of choices available to the individual. With more information, the range of choices usually increases; therefore, one could define freedom as a lack of restriction on choices. Thus, information leads to greater freedom.

    Privacy—Incomplete information may result in defamation of character. Therefore, to reduce the probability of defamation, information must selectively be made private.

By focusing on the nine characteristics related to market failure and the characteristics related to freedom and privacy, we can better understand the need for a public hand. The market may fail to produce adequate information and make it available to all, and it could come to pass that individuals or organizations that wished to gain power by restricting individual freedom or privacy would attempt to control access to information. The public hand works to counteract these effects, intentional or unintentional though they may be.[9]

Digital Money: Use or Misuse?

As this book has attempted to illustrate, Internet commerce and digital money create the potential for a better world by providing, among other things, convenient shopping methods and opportunities for distributed work. In fact, the opportunity for Internet commerce presents us with one of the most powerful possibilities for upliftment that the world has seen. Unfortunately, where technology is concerned, if the power for good exists in it, there also exists the possibility for its misunderstanding, misdirection, and misuse.

The scientists and businesspeople who have created the technology that's making Internet commerce available to us are pioneers who have opened up to us a new world, and we as individuals must not let their creation be perverted. By promoting better communication and simplifying the logistics of life, the new era of Internet commerce offers us more time for relaxation, for enjoyment, and for helping our fellow human beings.

Alternatively, by enabling invasion of the previously confidential information about us, the Internet could allow for the ultimate enslavement of humanity. The choice is ours. We as individuals have the ironic moral responsibility of guarding this technology with our lives, so that we are not enslaved by it. We must make wise choices in its use. Our duty is to see that this technology is accessible to all and oppressive to none. Our duty is to see that the best possible future for everyone arrives as soon as possible.

For instance, Mr. Philip Zimmerman may serve as an example to us—though he may pay dearly for it, he has enabled many people to obtain privacy from the prying eyes of potentially oppressionist regimes. May we all have the courage to challenge the law if the time should come that "the needs of the many outweigh the needs of the few."[10]

In a recent interview with Internet World magazine, Mr. Zimmerman stated: "Here is the most important point I can make: We are building a technological infrastructure that, if inherited by a future government, could allow them to monitor every movement and every communication of their political opposition. If the government ever changes, if it ever takes a bad turn, this could be very bad for democracy.

"That is really the most important thing. It is not that I believe the current government is an evil government. I don't believe we have an evil government, even though a lot of Libertarians believe that we do. But someday we might have an evil government. It happens. Sometimes bad people, even criminals, can be elected. Building good crypto into a democracy's communications infrastructure is like child-proofing your house. . . . John Perry Barlow has painted an anarchist picture in the preface to my book, but I don't agree that crypto will lead us towards anarchy. Our society is more resilient than that."[11]

Practopia

Life with Internet commerce is most likely to become, as Alvin Toffler writes in the *Third Wave:*

> *A* practopia—*neither the best nor the worst of all possible worlds, but one that is both practical and preferable to the one we had. Unlike a utopia, a practopia is not free of disease, political nastiness, and bad manners. . . . In short, a practopia offers a positive, even a revolutionary alternative, yet [it] lies within a range of the realistically attainable.*
>
> *One can glimpse in it a civilization that makes allowance for individual difference, and embraces (rather than suppresses)*

racial, regional, religious, and subcultural variety. A civiliza-
tion built in considerable measure around the home. A civiliza-
tion that . . . is pulsing with innovation, yet which is also
capable of providing relative enclaves of stability for those who
need or want them. . . . A civilization facing unprecedented
historical choices—about genetics and evolution, to choose a
single example—and inventing new ethical and moral stan-
dards to deal with such complex issues. A civilization that is at
least potentially democratic and humane. . . .[12]

Human exchanges and human well-being are based on a foundation of trust. If we create an environment of openness and trust, the Internet can indeed help us create a civilization that is democratic and humane.

Classic Cryptography

If you need detailed technical information about cryptography, such as if you're planning to set up a secure Internet site, we recommend that you read Bruce Schneier's excellent book, *Applied Cryptography*. It contains algorithms and source code examples. *Applied Cryptography* is the most complete, authoritative source we have found. This appendix provides a brief historical summary and overview based on portions of Mr. Schneier's book, with many thanks to Mr. Schneier.

The Evolution of Secret Writing

What is commonly thought of as cryptography usually is a system based on substituting one letter or number for another. Before computers, cryptography was based strictly on character substitution or on character transposition. In fact, the better cryptosystems performed both operations, many times each.

The primary change from historical cryptography to computer cryptography is that algorithms today work on bits instead of characters. With few exceptions, good cryptographic algorithms still tend to combine elements of substitution and transposition. The change from character to bits is just a reduction in the size of the alphabet from 26 elements to 2 elements!

There are actually three kinds of cryptography: code books, substitution ciphers, and transposition ciphers.

Code Books

Code books are rudimentary cryptographic tools. In a code book, typically one entire word is substituted for another word, such as a substitution of *dolphin* for *submarine.* The drawback of using a codebook is that, if a word you want to use isn't in the book, you can't say it in the message. Code books might also be particularly subject to interception or prying eyes if left unguarded. And everyone has to have a copy of the code book.

Substitution Ciphers

Any cryptosystem that's based on substitution is called a *substitution cipher.* In a substitution cipher, each character in the plaintext is substituted for another character in the ciphertext.

Classical cryptography gives four basic substitution ciphers:

- ◆ Simple substitution ciphers
- ◆ Homophonic substitution ciphers
- ◆ Polyalphabetic substitution ciphers
- ◆ Polygram substitution ciphers

Simple substitution ciphers are ciphers in which each character of plaintext is replaced by a corresponding character of ciphertext. A common example of a simple substitution cipher today is a cryptogram in a newspaper.

One famous substitution cipher is called the Caesar Cipher, which of course was allegedly used by Julius Caesar. In the Caesar Cipher, each plaintext character is replaced by the character *three to the right mod 26.* That is, *A* would be replaced by *D, B* would be replaced by *E, W* by *Z, X* by *A, Y* by *B,* and *Z* by *C* (Table A.1)

Another simple substitution cipher, which is commonly found on UNIX systems, is called ROT13. It rotates every letter 13 places. Thus, the letter *a* is replaced by *n, b* by *o,* and so forth. Conveniently enough, encrypting a file twice with ROT13 restores the original text. ROT13 is used in E-mail messages to hide potentially offensive text or to avoid giving away the solution to a puzzle. It isn't intended to provide data security (Table A.2).

TABLE A.1 The Caesar Cipher (or ROT3)

A → D	G → J	M → P	S → V	Y → B
B → E	H → K	N → Q	T → W	Z → C
C → F	I → L	O → R	U → X	
D → G	J → M	P → S	V → Y	
E → H	K → N	Q → T	W → Z	
F → I	L → O	R → U	X → A	

TABLE A.2 Operation of the ROT13 Substitution Cipher

A → n	G → t	M → z	S → f	Y → l
B → o	H → u	N → a	T → g	Z → m
C → p	I → v	O → b	U → h	
D → q	J → w	P → c	V → i	
E → r	K → x	Q → d	W → j	
F → s	L → y	R → e	X → k	

Simple substitution ciphers are good for children's games. They can be broken easily because they do not hide the frequency with which the underlying plaintext characters occur. Thus the need arises for more complicated ciphers.

Homophonic substitution ciphers are ciphers in which a single character of plaintext can map to any of several characters of ciphertext. For example, the letter *a* in plaintext might correspond to 4, 16, 22, or 53 in the ciphertext. These ciphers were used by the Duchy of Mantua as early as 1401. They are much more complicated to break than a simple substitution cipher, but they still cannot completely obscure the statistical properties of the underlying plaintext message. Table A.3 illustrates a homophonic substitution cipher.

Polyalphabetic substitution ciphers contain multiple simple substitution ciphers. For instance, a polyalphabetic substitution

TABLE A.3 Sample of a Homophonic Substitution Cipher

Homophonic Substitution Cipher				
A →	4	16	22	53
B →	5	17	23	54
C →	6	18	24	55

cipher might use five different simple substitution ciphers, which change according to the position of the character in the plaintext to be encoded.

Polyalphabetic substitution ciphers were invented by Leon Battista in 1568. They were used by the Union army in the American Civil War. Many commercial computer products still use ciphers of this form, although they can be broken easily.

In a polyalphabetic substitution cipher, a set of one-letter keys is used. Each key encrypts one letter of the message. The first key encrypts the first letter, the second key encrypts the second letter, and so forth, until all the keys are used. If there are 20 one-letter keys, every twentieth letter is encrypted using the same key. This repetition is called the *period* of the cipher (Table A.4).

In the days of classical cryptography, ciphers with longer periods were significantly more difficult to break than ciphers with short periods. However, with modern computers, the period of the cipher doesn't make much difference. A special kind of polyalphabetic cipher is a running-key cipher, in which one text is used to encrypt another text. In a running key cipher, the period of the cipher is the same as the length of the text.

Polygram substitution ciphers encrypt blocks of characters in groups. For instance, the sequence *aba* in the plaintext might correspond to *eff* in the ciphertext.

The Playfair cipher is a polygram substitution cipher that was invented in 1854. It was used by the British during World War I. It encrypts pairs of letters together.

Transposition Ciphers

The other important kind of cipher from classical cryptography is the *transposition cipher*. In a transposition cipher, the characters

TABLE A.4 Grossly Simplified Polyalphabetic Substitution Cipher

Polyalphabetic Cipher with Period of 2
A → use ROT3 → C
B → use ROT13 → O
C → use ROT3 again → F
D → use ROT13 again → Q

in the plaintext remain unchanged, but their order is shuffled around. Many modern cryptosystems use transposition, although it does pose some difficulties because it requires a lot of memory and may require messages to be of a certain length.

In a simple transposition cipher, the plaintext is written onto graph paper horizontally in rows, but it is read off vertically, in columns. To decrypt the message, one writes the ciphertext vertically in columns and reads it off horizontally in rows, as in Figure A.1.

The German ADFGVX cipher, used during World War I, is a transposition cipher (that also uses simple substitution). For its day, it was a very complex cipher, but it eventually was broken by a French cryptanalyst, Georges Painvin.

Cryptographic Machines

In the 1920s, several mechanical devices were invented to automate the process of encryption. All of these machines were based on the concept of a *rotor,* which was a mechanical wheel. The rotor wheel was wired to perform a general cryptographic substitution, such as *F* for *A*. In fact, these machines were called rotor machines.

Each rotor machine has a keyboard and several rotors. Each rotor has 26 positions and performs a simple substitution, a Caesar Cipher, in fact, for every character that is typed. Besides making a simple substitution, the rotors all move, and each moves at a different rate. The combination of all the rotors makes the machine secure, primarily because a machine with *n* rotors has a period of 26 raised to the *n*th power.

The most famous rotor machine was called The Enigma. It was used by the Germans during World War II. The Enigma had a plugboard to permute the plaintext, and a reflecting rotor that forced each rotor to operate on each character twice. As compli-

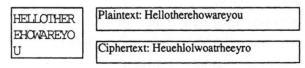

HELLOTHER
EHOWAREYO
U

Plaintext: Hellotherehowareyou

Ciphertext: Heuehlolwoatrheeyro

Figure A.1   Transposition cipher.

cated as The Enigma was, it nevertheless was broken during World War II.[1]

Development of DES

In the early 1970s, most people knew that the military used special equipment to disguise their communications, but few understood the science of cryptography. Although several small companies sold cryptographic equipment, primarily to overseas governments, each device was different. No two devices could communicate. No one could even (openly) certify whether any of these devices was secure.

In 1972, the National Bureau of Standards (NBS), now known as the National Institute of Standards and Technology (NIST), started a program to protect computer and communications data. One part of that program dictated that they test and certify a single, standard cryptographic algorithm to protect digital data during transmission and for storage. These design criteria for the algorithm were published in May 1973 in the *Federal Register:*

- The algorithm must provide a high level of security.
- The algorithm must be completely specified and easy to understand.
- The security of the algorithm must reside in the key; the security must not depend on the secrecy of the algorithm.
- The algorithm must be available to all users.
- The algorithm must be adaptable for use in diverse applications.
- The algorithm must be electronically implementable in electronic devices.
- The algorithm must be efficient to use.
- The algorithm must be able to be validated.
- The algorithm must be exportable.

In response, a few mathematicians submitted some crude outlines of algorithms, none of which met the design criteria: There was little public expertise, although there was considerable interest. The NBS published a second request in 1974. This time, they received one promising candidate from IBM, called LUCIFER. The NBS requested help from the NSA in evaluating the algorithm's security and its acceptability as a federal standard.

In fact, the NSA suggested some modifications to the proposed algorithm, but the final result was published by the NBS in March 1975 along with a statement from IBM granting a nonexclusive, royalty-free license to make, use, and sell an apparatus that implemented the algorithm. At first, many cryptographers were leery of the NSA's *invisible hand* in developing the DES algorithm. They were afraid the NSA had installed a trapdoor, perhaps something like the trapdoor in the proposed Clipper chip. Nevertheless, after some controversy, DES was adopted as a federal standard by the NBS in November of 1976, authorized for use on all unclassified government communications. DES has twice been readopted as the federal standard, the most recently in 1992. The consensus among government agencies, at least as reflected in one statement made by the Office of Technology Assessment, seems to be that DES will reach the end of its useful lifetime by 1997 or 1998. Yet DES lives on in a large installed base of systems.[3]

An interesting note: In retrospect, some cryptographers decided that the NSA's work on developing DES made it more resistant to penetration rather than less. At the time DES was developed, the science of differential cryptanalysis, which compares and analyzes pairs of ciphertexts, was almost unknown outside the NSA. Differential cryptanalysis is one of the strongest attacks, yet DES is highly resistant to attacks by differential cryptanalysis. Recently, however, the developers of the original algorithm at IBM revealed that they also knew about differential cryptanalysis at the time. So exactly what was the result of the NSA's involvement?

For years, it was debated whether DES encryption is an algebraic group. That is, is encrypting a certain plaintext under one DES key, then encrypting that result again under another DES key always equivalent to encrypting under a single DES key? It was decided recently, after years of speculation and circumstantial evidence, that DES is not a group. Therefore, it would follow that techniques such as triple encryption, which was adopted in the X9.17 and ISO 8732 standards, actually do increase the security of DES. Triple encryption is believed to be the equivalent of doubling the key size to 112 bits.[4]

Regulations Governing Cryptography Export

Part 120—Purpose, Background, and Definitions
§120.1 General.
(a) Purpose. Section 38 of the Arms Export Control Act (22 U.S.C. 2778) authorizes the President to control the export and import of defense articles and defense services. It is the purpose of this subchapter to implement this authority. The statutory authority of the President to promulgate regulations with respect to exports of defense articles and defense services was delegated to the Secretary of State by Executive Order 11958, as amended (42 FR 4311). By virtue of delegations of authority by the Secretary of State, these regulations are primarily administered by the Director of the Office of Defense Trade Controls, Bureau of Politico-Military Affairs, Department of State (35 FR 5422).

§120.10 Export—Permanent and Temporary.
Export means:
(1) Sending or taking defense articles out of the United States in any manner, except by mere travel outside of the United States by a person whose personal knowledge includes technical data; or
(2) transferring registration, control or ownership to a foreign person of an aircraft, vessel, or satellite covered by the U.S. Munitions List, whether in the United States or abroad; or
(3) Disclosing or transferring in the United States any defense articles to an embassy, any agency or subdivision of a foreign government (e.g., diplomatic missions); or

(4) Disclosing or transferring technical data to a foreign person, whether in the United States or abroad; or
(5) Performing a defense service on behalf of, or for the benefit of, a foreign person, whether in the United States or abroad.
A launch vehicle or payload shall not, by the launching of such vehicle, be considered export for the purposes of this subchapter. Most of the requirements of the subchapter relate only to exports, as defined above. However, for certain limited purposes, the controls of this subchapter apply to sales and other transfers of defense articles and defense services (see, e.g., Section 126.1) of this subchapter.

§120.11 Foreign person.
Foreign person means any natural person who is not a "citizen or intending citizen" of the United States within the meaning of 8 U.S.C 1324b(a)3. It also means any foreign corporation, business association, partnership, society, trust, or any other entity or group that is not incorporated or organized to do business in the United States, as well as *international* organizations, foreign governments and any agency or subdivision of foreign governments (e.g., diplomatic missions). The term *intending citizen* means a person who has been lawfully admitted to the United States for permanent residence (and maintains such residence) under the Immigration and Naturalization Act (8 U.S.C. 101(a), 1101(a), 60 Stat 163).

§120.17 Person.
Person means a natural person as well as a corporation, business association, partnership, society, trust, or any other entity, organization or group, including governmental entities. If a provision in this subchapter does not refer exclusively to a foreign person (Section 120.11) or a U.S. person (Section 120.27), then it refers to both.

§120.19 Public domain.
Public domain means information which is published and which is generally accessible or available to the *public:*
(1) Through sales at newsstands and bookstores;

(2) Through subscriptions which are available without restriction to any individual who desires to obtain or purchase the published information;
(3) Through second-class mailing privileges granted by the U.S. Government;
(4) At libraries open to the *public* or from which the *public* can obtain documents;
(5) Through patents available at any patent office;
(6) Through unlimited distribution at a conference, meeting, seminar, trade show or exhibition, generally accessible to the *public,* in the United States;
(7) Through *public* release (i.e., unlimited distribution) in any form (e.g., not necessarily in published form) after approval by the cognizant U.S. government department or agency (see also Sec. 125.4(b)(13)).

§120.23 Technical data.
Technical data means, for purposes of this subchapter:
(a) Classified information related to defense articles and defense services;
(b) Information covered by an invention secrecy order;
(c) *Software* as defined in Sec. 121.8(f) directly related to defense articles;
(d) Information, other than *software* as defined in 120.23(c), which is required for the design, development, production, processing, manufacture, assembly, operation, repair, maintenance, or modification of defense articles. This includes, for example, information in the form of blueprints, drawings, photographs, plans, instructions, and documentation. This also includes information that advances the state of the art of articles on the U.S. Munitions List. This definition does not include information concerning general scientific, mathematical or engineering principles commonly taught in schools, colleges, and universities. It also does not include basic marketing information on function or purpose, or general system descriptions of defense articles.

§120.27 U.S person.
U.S. person means a person (as defined in Sec. 120.17 of this part)

who is a citizen or a national of the United States, or has been lawfully admitted to the United States for permanent residence (and maintains such residence) under the Immigration and Naturalization Act (8 U.S.C. 101(a), 1101(a), 60 Stat 163). It also means any corporation, business association, partnership, society, trust, or any other entity or group that is incorporated or organized to do business in the United States. It also includes any governmental (federal, state, or local) entity. it does not include any foreign person as defined in Sec. 120.11 of this part.

Part 121—The United States Munitions List

§121.1 General. The United States Munitions List

Category XIII—Auxiliary Military Equipment
(b) Speech scramblers, privacy devices, cryptographic devices and software (encoding and decoding), and components specifically designed to be modified therefore, ancillary equipment, and protective apparatus specifically designed or modified for such devices, components, and equipment.

§121.8 End-items, components, accessories, attachment parts, firmware, software, and systems.
(e) *Software* includes but is not limited to the system functional design, operating systems, and support software for design, implementation, test operation, diagnosis, and repair.

Part 125—Licenses for Export of Technical Data and Classified Defense Articles
§125.1 Exports subject to this part.
(a) The export controls of this part apply to the export of technical data and the export of classified defense articles. Information which is in the *public domain* (see Sections 120.19 and 125.4(b)(13)) is not subject to the controls of this subchapter.

§125.2 Exports of unclassified technical data.
(a) General.
A license (DSP-5) issued by the Office of Defense Trade Controls

is required for the export (and return to the U.S. if applicable) of unclassified technical data unless the export is exempt from the licensing requirements of this subchapter. If the unclassified technical data is related to a classified defense article, and classified technical data or defense articles that may subsequently be required to be exported must be described, along with the address and telephone number of the U.S. government office that classified the information. In the case of a plant visit, details of the proposed discussions must be transmitted to the Office of Defense Trade Controls for an appraisal of the technical data. Seven copies of the technical data or the details of the discussions must be provided. Only one copy must be provided if a renewal of the license is requested.

(b) Patents.
A license issued by the Office of Defense Trade Controls is required for the export of technical data whenever the data exceeds that which is used to support the domestic filing of a patent application or to support the foreign filing of a patent application whenever no domestic application has been filed. Requests for the filing of patent applications in a foreign country, and requests for the filing of amendments, modifications, or supplements to such patents, should follow the regulations of the U.S. Patent and Trademark Office in accordance with 37 CFR Part 5. The export of technical data to support the filing and processing of patent applications in foreign countries is subject to regulations issued by the U.S. Patent and Trademark Office pursuant to 35 U.S.C. 184.

(c) Disclosures.
Unless otherwise expressly exempted in this subchapter, a license is required for the oral, visual, or documentary disclosure of technical data by U.S. persons to foreign persons. A license is required regardless of the manner in which the technical data is transmitted (e.g., in person, by telephone, correspondence, electronic means, etc.). A license is required for such disclosures by U.S. persons in connection with foreign visits to diplomatic missions and consular offices.

Notes

Foreword

1. Grateful acknowledgment to James L. Pelkey. "The Emergence of Economic Life: Computer Communications 1968–1988," in Manuscript.

Chapter 1

Figure 1.1: Information obtained from Commerce Department, Killen & Associates, quoted in *Business Week,* June 12, 1995, p. 70.

1. Paul E. Hoffman, *Internet Instant Reference,* Sybex books, San Franscisco, 1994.
2. Paul E. Hoffman, *Internet Instant Reference,* Sybex books, San Franscisco, 1994.
3. Vinton Cerf, "Computer Networking: Global Infrastructure for the 21st Century," http://www.isoc.org.
4. Clinton Wilder, "A New Safety Net," *Information Week,* April 24, 1995, pp. 14–15.
5. "IP Next Generation Overview," ConneXions: The Interoperability Report, vol. 9, no. 3, March 1995, pp. 2–18.

Chapter 2

1. Mitch Wagner, "On-line Cash and Credit Move Closer to Reality," *Open Systems Today,* February 20, 1995, p. 169.
2. Gary Welz, "New Deals," *Internet World,* June 1995, p. 40.

3. Steve Higgins, "Headquarters Is Cyberspace for New Financial Company," *Investor's Business Daily,* December 28, 1994.

4. Jeffrey Kutler, "Information Highway Looking More and More Like a Business Route," *American Banker,* November 18, 1994.

5. Wendy Bounds and Jared Sandberg, *Wall Street Journal,* February 15, 1995.

6. Jeffrey Kutler, "Information Highway Looking More and More Like a Business Route," *American Banker,* November 18, 1994.

7. Jeff Ubois, "Shop 'Til Your Modem Drops," *Internet World,* June 1995, p. 48.

8. Philip Elmer-Dewit, "Mine, All Mine," *Time,* June 5, 1995, pp. 46–54.

9. Gail Bronson, "A Coup for Microsoft," *Interactive Age,* May 22, 1995, p. 1.

10. Philip Elmer-Dewit, "Mine, All Mine," *Time,* June 5, 1995, pp. 46–54.

11. John Evan Frook, *Interactive Age,* May 22, 1995, p. 44.

12. Fara Warner, "Online Services Try to Define Their Identities," *Wall Street Journal,* July 12, 1995, B1.

13. "Electronic Commerce and the NII," Putting the Information Infrastructure to Work: Report of the Information Infrastructure Task Force Committee on Applications and Technology, National Institute of Standards and Technology (NIST), U.S. Department of Commerce, May 1994, p. 34.

14. Cathy J. Medich, Executive Director, CommerceNet, personal communication, May 1995.

15. Anthony M. Rutkowski, Executive Director, Internet Society, "Today's Cooperative Competitive Standards Environment for Open Information and Telecommunication Networks and the Internet Standards Making Model," speech given at the Standards Development and

Information Infrastructure Workshop, June 1994,
http://www.isoc.org.

16. James Massey, "An Introduction to Contemporary Cryptology," Proceedings of the IEEE, vol. 76, no. 5, May 1988, pp. 533–549.

17. Bruce Schneier, *Applied Cryptography*, John Wiley & Sons, New York, 1994, p. 441.

18. Gary Weiss, "Online Investing," cover story, *Business Week,* June 5, 1995.

Chapter 3

1. *Wall Street Journal,* April 28, 1995.

2. RSA, Inc.

3. Schneier, op. cit.

4. "Frequently Asked Questions About Today's Cryptography," RSA Laboratories White Paper, October 1993.

5. Schneier, op. cit., p. 231.

6. Schneier, op. cit., pp. 273–274.

7. Euclid's algorithm from: Dickson, Leonard Eugene, *Introduction to the Theory of Numbers,* Dover Publications, New York, 1957, pp. 1–2.

8. Whitfield Diffie, "The First Ten Years of Public-Key Cryptography," Proceedings of the IEEE, vol. 76, no. 5, May 1988, pp. 560–577, quoted in Schneier, op. cit., p. 177.

9. "Frequently Asked Questions about Today's Cryptography," RSA Laboratories White Paper, October 1993, p. 11.

10. Schneier, op. cit., p. 285.

11. Schneier, op. cit., p. 260.

12. "RSA Certificate Services," an RSA White Paper, January 31, 1994.

13. Schneier, op. cit., p. 436.

14. *Wall Street Journal,* April 28, 1995.

15. Bruce Schneier, *E-Mail Security,* John Wiley & Sons, New York, 1995.

16. Schneier, *Applied Cryptography,* op. cit., p. 322.

17. "Frequently Asked Questions about Today's Cryptography," RSA Laboratories White Paper, October 1993, p. 36.

18. Schneier, op. cit., pp. 437–438.

19. E.F. Bricknell, D.E. Denning, S.T. Kent, D.P. Maher, and W. Tuchman, *SKIP JACK Review—Interim Report,* July 28, 1993, quoted in Schneier, op. cit., p. 269.

20. "Frequently Asked Questions about Today's Cryptography," RSA Laboratories White Paper, October 1993, p. 31.

Chapter 4

1. Kevin Dowd, *The State and the Monetary System,* St. Martin's Press, New York, 1989, p. 93.

2. "Electronic Money," *The Economist,* Nov 26–Dec 2, 1994.

3. Dowd, op. cit.

4. H. Meulen, *Free Banking: An Outline of a Policy of Individualism,* Macmillan, 1934, Quoted in Dowd, op. cit., p. 123.

5. White, L.H., *Free Banking in Britain: Theory, Experience, and Debate, 1800–45*, Cambridge University Press, 1984, p. 41, Quoted in Dowd, op. cit., p. 123.

6. Jeffrey Kutler, "Information Highway Looking More and More Like a Business Route," *American Banker,* November 18, 1994.

7. Tatsuaki Okamoto and Kazuo Ohta, "Universal Electronic Cash," Advances in Cryptology—CRYPTO '91 Proceedings, Berlin: Springer-Verlag, 1992, pp. 324–327.

7A. Based on Tatsuaki Okamoto and Kazuo Ohta, "Universal Electronic Cash," Advances in Cryptology—CRYPTO '91 Proceedings, Berlin: Springer-Verlag, 1992, pp. 324–327, quoted in Schneier, op. cit.

8. David Chaum, "Achieving Electronic Privacy," *Scientific American,* August 1992, p. 96–101.

9. Adapted from material on DigiCash's home page. *http://www/digicash.com/index.html*

10. Adapted from material on DigiCash's home page. *http://www/digicash.com/index.html*

11. Adapted from material on DigiCash's home page. *http://www/digicash.com/index.html*

12. "Electronic Money," *The Economist,* Nov 26–Dec 2, 1994.

Chapter 5

1. "The Great American Time Squeeze," Economic Policy Institute, March 1992.

2. Tara Parker-Pope, "Interactive Offerings Have Less Appeal in Europe Than in U.S., Survey Says," *Wall Street Journal,* June 20, 1995.

3. Audrey Choi, "German Minister for the Future Maps the Nation's Itinerary on the Infobahn," *Wall Street Journal,* June 20, 1995.

4. Silvia Ascarelli, "In Europe, Video Games Rated Suitable by Some Censors Draw Others' Scorn," *Wall Street Journal,* June 20, 1995.

5. "Commerce and Society in CyberSpace," an Electric Communities White Paper, Los Altos, California, 1995.

6. Rosalind Resnik, "Business Is Good, NOT," *Internet World,* June 1995, p. 73.

7. Gary Welz, "New Deals," *Internet World,* June 1995, p.37ff.

8. Rosalind Resnik, "Business Is Good, NOT," *Internet World,* June 1995, p. 71.

8A. I wouldn't have known about International Brokers except that I coincidentally met Mr. Jay Baumbard, who is one, as I was writing this book. His business is called Vision Merchandising. More information is available by E-mail on CompuServe at 75753,337. [LL]

9. *CyberMedia 2001,* vol. 1, no. 1, January 1995, p. 10.

Chapter 6

1. Many of the ideas in the first part of this chapter are derived with thanks from concepts presented in *Cyber-Media 2001,* a monthly publication of The CyberMedia Group. Kenneth Lim, Chief Futurist of the CyberMedia Group, was formerly Manager of Corporate Technology Development and Chief Futurist at Apple Computer, where he was responsible for strategic planning and corporate technology assessment. Mr. Lim also spent five years at Dataquest, Inc. during the early 1980s, where he was one of the most widely quoted industry analysts. The CyberMedia Group can be reached at CybrMdaGrp on America Online; 71544,3133 on CompuServe; or (408) 255-5007 by phone.

2. *CyberMedia 2001,* The CyberMedia Group, vol. 1, no. 2, March 1995.

3. *CyberMedia 2001,* vol. 1, no. 2, March 1995.

4. *CyberMedia 2001,* vol. 1, no. 1, January 1995.

5. Agorics, Inc. Company Profile, Los Altos, CA, 1995.

6. Clinton Wilder, "An Electronic Bridge to Customers," *Information Week,* January 16, 1995.

Chapter 7

1. "Frequently Asked Questions about Today's Cryptography," RSA Laboratories White Paper, October 1992, p. 17.

2. Schneier, op. cit.

3. "The Future of Democracy," *The Economist,* June 17, 1995, p. 13.

4. "Democracy and Technology," *The Economist,* June 17, 1995, p. 23.

5. Julie Holder, "Cyber Soapbox," *Internet World,* August 1995, p. 52.

6. "Newt's Net," *Internet World,* August 1995, p. 48.

7. "Democracy and Technology," *The Economist,* June 17, 1995, p. 23.

8. "Annual Report on Information Technology," *Information Week,* July 3, 1995.

9. *National Research Council, Information Technology and the Service Society: A Twenty-First Century Lever,* National Academy Press, Washington, DC, 1994.

10. Thomas H. Davenport, *Process Innovation—Reengineering Work through Information Technology,* Ernst & Young, Boston, MA, 1993.

11. *Fortune,* May 1, 1995, p. 123

12. Catherine Arnst, "Networked Corporations," *Business Week,* June 26, 1995, p. 86.

13. "Electronic Commerce and the NII," Putting the Information Infrastructure to Work: Report of the Information Infrastructure Task Force Committee on Applications and Technology, National Institute of Standards and Technology (NIST), U.S. Department of Commerce, May 1994, p. 29.

14. Adrian Levy and Ian Burrell, Iain Martin and Peter Warren, "Anarchists Use Computer Superhighway for Subversion," EFF Action Alerts-Cyberspace, April 19, 1995.

Chapter 8

1. "Frequently Asked Questions about Today's Cryptography," RSA Laboratories White Paper, October 1992, p. 19.

2. "Frequently Asked Questions about Today's Cryptography," RSA Laboratories White Paper, October 1992, p. 20.

3. "Frequently Asked Questions about Today's Cryptography," RSA Laboratories White Paper, October 1992.

4. D. Bayer, S. Haber, and W.S. Stornetta, "Improving the reliability and efficiency of digital time-stamping," in R.M. Capocelli, editor, *Sequences 1991: Methods in Communication, Security, and Computer Science*, Springer-Verlag, Berlin, 1992.

5. Schneier, op. cit.

Chapter 9

1. The document in question is Comptroller General of the United States, "Matter of National Institute of Technology—Use of Electronic Data Interchange Technology to Create Valid Obligations," File B-245714, Dec. 13, 1991.

2. Schneier, op. cit., p. 454.

3. Lauren Gibbons Paul, "Copyright Law: What's Legal, What's Not," *PC Week,* March 28, 1994, p. 82.

4. Lance Rose, "Copyright on the Networks," Internet Issues and Controversies, p. 1076.

5. Newsbytes@clarinet.com, 26May95, Newsgroups: clari.nb.online, clari.nb.top

6. Schneier, op. cit., p. 449.

7. Schneier, op. cit., p. 454.

8. Electronic Privacy Information Center (EPIC), Washington, DC, info@epic.org, WWW http://epic.org

9. Selena Sol, Women's Wire: EFF: Discussion Folder, "Children on the Web," May 1, 1995. (Another new frontier: What is a proper citation format for an E-mail message?)

10. Selena Sol, Women's Wire: EFF; Action Alerts: "EFF's Analysis of the CDA," Electronic Frontier Foundation, http://www.eff.org, June 18, 1995.

11. Adapted from material on DigiCash's home page. *http://www.digicash.com/index.html*

12. Samuel D. Warren, and Louis D. Brandeis, "The Right of Privacy," *Harvard Law Review* 193, 205 (1890).

13. Alan F. Westin, *Privacy and Freedom*, Bodley Head, London, 1970.

14. Electronic Privacy Information Center (EPIC), Washington, DC, info@epic.org, WWW http://epic.org

15. Lance Rose, "Electronic Privacy," Internet Issues and Controversies, p. 1066.

16. Lance Rose, "Electronic Privacy," Internet Issues and Controversies, p. 1066.

Chapter 10

1. Randall Farmer and Chip Morningstar, "Commerce and Society in Cyberspace," An Electric Communities White Paper, April 1995.

2. Zachary Lynch, "Is Increasing Unemployment an Inevitable Consequence of Advancing Technology?" *Manuscript,* The Departments of Biology and Geography, UCLA, Los Angeles, CA, 1995.

3. Zachary Lynch, "Is Increasing Unemployment an Inevitable Consequence of Advancing Technology?" *Manuscript,* The Departments of Biology and Geography, UCLA, Los Angeles, CA, 1995.

4. Computer Science and Communications Board, National Research Council, *Realizing the Information Future: The Internet and Beyond,* National Academy Press, 1994.

5. Douglas Barnes, "The Coming Jurisdictional Swamp of Global Internetworking," presented November 16, 1994, Austin Cypherpunks, http://www.communities.com/papers/.

6. Ken Komoski, "The LINCT Coalition," presented at the National Association Science Technology and Society, 1995 National Meeting, Arlington, VA, March 4, 1995.

7. Adam Smith, *The Wealth of Nations,* Cannan Edition, Random House, New York, 1937.

8. John Rawls, *A Theory of Justice,* The Belknap Press of Harvard University Press, Cambridge, MA, 1971.

9. Excerpted and adapted from the Character of Information Report to the U.S. Congress, Office of Technology

Assessment 1986, 1994, by W. Curtiss Priest, Center for Information, Technology & Society.

10. Mr. Spock, in *Star Trek IV*.

11. "Hero or Villain?", *Internet World,* August 1995, p. 79.

12. Alvin Toffler, *The Third Wave,* Bantam Books, New York, 1981, pp. 357–358.

Appendix A

1. Bruce Schneier, *Applied Cryptography,* John Wiley & Sons, Inc., New York, 1994. p. 8ff.

2. Schneier, op. cit.

3. Schneier, op. cit., p. 231.

4. Schneier, op. cit., pp. 273–274.

Additional Readings

For readers who want more hands-on information about setting up a business on the Internet, the authors recommend the following books:

HTML

Bebak, Arthur, and Smith, Bud, *Creating Web Pages for Dummies*, IDG Books, Foster City, California, 1996.

Graham, Ian, *HTML Sourcebook,* John Wiley & Sons, Inc., New York, 1995.

Lemay, Laura, *Teach Yourself Web Publishing with HTML in a Week,* Sams Publishing, San Francisco, 1995.

Lemay, Laura, *More Teach Yourself Web Publishing with HTML in a Week*, Sams Publishing, San Francisco, 1996.

Cryptography

Schneier, Bruce, *Applied Cryptography: Protocols, Alorithms, and Source Code in C,* 2nd edition, John Wiley & Sons, Inc., New York, 1996.

Schneier, Bruce, *E-Mail Security,* John Wiley & Sons, Inc., New York, 1995.

Internet Business

Ellsworth, Jill H. and Matthew V., *Marketing on the Internet,* John Wiley & Sons, Inc., New York, 1995.

Angell, David and Heslop, Brent, *The Internet Business Companion*, Addison-Wesley, Reading MA, 1995.

Gilster, Paul, *The Internet Navigator*, 2nd. edition, John Wiley & Sons, Inc., New York, 1994. (Foreword by Vinton Cerf, President of the Internet Society.)

Glossary

Algorithm: A set of steps for carrying out a calculation, a procedure or process usually carried out on a computer.

AOL: American Online, a large online service provider.

Batch Processing: A technique whereby several computer processes are grouped together so they can run more efficiently. Batch processing was originally developed for mainframe computer systems, where each user turned in a deck of punchcards to the computer operator, who then scheduled the jobs for maximum efficiency, running similar jobs in a *batch,* often overnight.

Ciphertext: Encrypted text.

Client/Server Architecture: A model for software wherein two software modules work together to perform a task: There's a server, which provides a specific function or service such as information storage and retrieval; and a client, which requests services from the server.

CompuServe: A major online service provider.

CPSR: Computer Professionals for Social Responsibility.

Decryption: The process of recovering the plaintext of an encrypted message by applying a key.

DES: Data Encryption Standard. DES is the encryption standard for the U.S. government.

EFF: Electronic Frontier Foundation.

E-Mail: Electronic mail, usually mailed over a network.

Encryption: The process of encoding text to maintain its secrecy.

FAQ: Stands for Frequently Asked Questions. Usually, it refers to a list of answers to frequently asked questions about a particular topic.

FTP: File Transfer Protocol. One of the oldest and most basic ways of transferring information over the Internet; no fancy interface like the World Wide Web.

Hacker: A programmer who delights in breaking through codes and security barriers on computer systems, often for destructive or illegal purposes.

HTML: HyperText Markup Language, a subset of Standard Graphical Markup Language (SGML). HTML is used to format documents for publication on the World Wide Web.

HTTP: HyperText Transfer Protocol, the data exchange protocol used for the World Wide Web. HTTP allows transfer of multimedia and hyperlinked data.

Key: A key is a string of digits or letters, and some associated process by which that string can be used to generate ciphertext from plaintext.

Mailing List: An online list to which a person can subscribe and receive, by E-mail, information on a topic of particular interest.

Message Digest: The result of sending a plaintext message through a hashing function. Usually, the message digest is what is actually encrypted, not the raw message.

Modem: A device designed to allow computers access to other computers and to the Internet by dialing in over telephone lines. The word *modem* is an abbreviation of modulator/demodulator.

Netiquette: A system of etiquette that's generally acceptable for online interactions.

PGP: Stands for Pretty Good Protection, a controversial public-key encryption system.

Plaintext: Unencrypted text; readable text in no sort of code.

Private Key: In public-key cryptography, such as RSA, the half of a public-key/private-key pair that is known only to the encoder.

Pseudonym: An online identity that may or may not be related to a person's actual identity.

Public Key: In public-key cryptography, such as RSA, the half of a public-key/private-key pair that is known to the public and can be used to decrypt messages that were encoded by the corresponding private key.

News Groups: Ongoing public conversations online, covering topics of mutual interest. Many online services provide access to newsgroups.

NIST: National Institute of Standards and Technology, formerly NBS, the National Bureau of Standards.

NSA: National Security Agency, a secretive branch of the U.S. government, involved in many aspects of cryptography.

Remailers: Online sites that forward incoming and outgoing mail anonymously.

RFC: Request for Comments. A document posted on the Internet, on an RFC server, to gather public comments on proposed legislation, or more commonly, on technical proposals relating to the development of the Internet itself.

RSA: Stands for Rivest, Shamir, and Adelman, the inventors of public-key cryptography, currently licensable from RSA Data Security, Inc. The term RSA often is used to refer to public-key cryptography in general.

SEC: Securities and Exchange Commission, a regulatory body of the U.S. Justice Department.

Secret Key: An encryption key that must not be divulged, else the security of an encryption cipher is revealed. The U.S. government-standard DES encryption system relies on a secret key.

Spam: A broadcast of unwelcome messages received in an electronic medium, similar to junk mail.

URL: Stands for Universal Resource Locator, which is an address on the World Wide Web.

Usenet: A worldwide, distributed electronic bulletin board.

Website: A *place* on the World Wide Web. A Website consists of a closely related set of HTML documents; for instance, describing a company's products or services, linked together by hypertext pointers. A Website also usually contains pointers to other Websites.

World Wide Web: A huge hypertext document that's a *subnet* within the Internet. The Web, as it is called, is becoming a popular place for businesses to set up an electronic storefront.

WTO: World Trade Organization, an international body devoted to promoting trade.

Index

CATCH THE
Technology Wave